菲迪克(FIDIC)文献译丛

设计采购施工(EPC)/交钥匙工程合同条件

Conditions of Contract
for EPC/Turnkey Projects

国际咨询工程师联合会
中国工程咨询协会 编译

王川 翻译 徐礼章 校译
王川 徐礼章 唐萍 审订

(1999年第1版)
(中英文对照本)

(译者对译文的准确度承担全部责任,
正式使用发生争端时,以英文原版为准)

机械工业出版社

本《设计采购施工(EPC)/交钥匙工程合同条件》(中英文对照本)是按国际咨询工程师联合会(FIDIC即菲迪克)编写的最新英文版本，由FIDIC在中国的成员协会——中国工程咨询协会组织专家编译定稿。

本书不是在菲迪克以往合同基础上修改，而是进行了重新编写，首次推出的。它继承了菲迪克原有合同条件的优点，并根据多年来在实践中取得的经验，以及专家、学者和相关各方的意见和建议，作了重大调整。

本书内容包括设计采购施工(EPC)/交钥匙工程合同的通用条件，附争端裁决协议书一般条件、专用条件编写指南附各担保函格式、以及投标函、合同协议书和争端裁决协议书格式。

本书推荐用于以交钥匙方式提供加工或动力设备、工厂或类似设施、基础设施项目或其他类型发展项目，这种方式(i)项目的最终价格和要求的工期具有更大程度的确定性，(ii)由承包商承担项目的设计和实施的全部职责，雇主介入很少。交钥匙工程的通常情况是，由承包商进行全部设计、采购和施工(EPC)，提供一个配备完善的设施，("转动钥匙")即可运行。

读者对象：工程咨询单位，从事投资、金融和工程项目管理的部门和组织、各类项目业主、建筑施工监理企业、工程承包企业、环保企业、会计/律师事务所、保险公司以及有关高等院校等单位和人员。

图书在版编目(CIP)数据

设计采购施工(EPC)/交钥匙工程合同条件/中国工程咨询协会编译．—北京：机械工业出版社，2002.5(2019.3重印)
(菲迪克(FIDIC)文献译丛)
书名原文：Conditions of Contract for EPC/Turnkey Projects
ISBN 978-7-111-10242-7

Ⅰ.设…　Ⅱ.中…　Ⅲ.建筑工程—工程施工—合同—基本知识　Ⅳ.TU723.1

中国版本图书馆CIP数据核字(2002)第028533号

机械工业出版社(北京市百万庄大街22号　邮政编码100037)
责任编辑：何文军　　责任校对：贾立萍
封面设计：姚　毅　　责任印制：张　博

北京铭成印刷有限公司印刷

2019年3月第1版·第17次印刷
210mm×297mm·15.25印张·486千字
标准书号：ISBN 978-7-111-10242-7
本书定价：105.00元(全套360元)

凡购本书，如有缺页、倒页、脱页，由本社发行部调换

电话服务	网络服务
服务咨询热线：010-88361066	机工官网：www.cmpbook.com
读者购书热线：010-68326294	机工官博：weibo.com/cmp1952
010-88379203	金书网：www.golden-book.com
封面无防伪标均为盗版	教育服务网：www.cmpedu.com

菲迪克(FIDIC)授权书

I herewith authorize CNAEC to translate FIDIC' s publications (but not the publications as edited by other organizations) into Chinese and publish them.

I agree with your statement, as part of the agreement, that you will:

a) provide FIDIC with 10 copies of the translation per document, and

b) make a statement on the inside cover of the translation that the translator takes full responsibility for the accuracy of the translation and that in case of dispute, the original version in English shall prevail.

Peter van der TOGT
Publications manager

[译文]

在此，我授权中国工程咨询协会把 FIDIC 出版物译成中文并出版(但是,不包括其他组织编写的出版物)。

我同意你们的意见，作为协议的一部分，你们应：

a) 向 FIDIC 提供每份文件中译本 10 本；

b) 在译文的扉页上注明译者对译文的准确度承担全部责任，如果发生争端，以英文原版为准。

出版经理：Peter van der TOGT

FIDIC is the French acronym for the International Federation of Consulting Engineers.

FIDIC was founded in 1913 by three national associations of consulting engineers within Europe. The objectives of forming the federation were to promote in common the professional interests of the member associations and to disseminate information of interest to members of its component national associations.

Today FIDIC membership numbers more than 60 countries from all parts of the globe and the federation represents most of the private practice consulting engineers in the world.

FIDIC arranges seminars, conferences and other events in the furtherance of its goals: maintenance of high ethical and professional standards; exchange of views and information; discussion of problems of mutual concern among member associations and representatives of the international financial institutions; and development of the consulting engineering industry in developing countries.

FIDIC publications include proceedings of various conferences and seminars, information for consulting engineers, project owners and international development agencies, standard pre-qualification forms, contract documents and client/consultant agreements. They are available from the secretariat in Switzerland.

FIDIC（中译“菲迪克”）是国际咨询工程师联合会的法文首字母缩写。

菲迪克(FIDIC)是由欧洲三个国家的咨询工程师协会于 1913 年成立的。组建联合会的目的是共同促进成员协会的职业利益，以及向其成员协会会员传播有益信息。

今天，菲迪克(FIDIC)已有来自全球各地 60 多个国家的成员协会，代表着世界上大多数私人执业的咨询工程师。

菲迪克(FIDIC)举办各类研讨会、会议及其他活动，以促进其目标：维护高的道德和职业标准；交流观点和信息；讨论成员协会和国际金融机构代表共同关心的问题；以及发展中国家工程咨询业的发展。

菲迪克(FIDIC)的出版物包括：各类会议和研讨会的文件，为咨询工程师、项目业主和国际开发机构提供的信息，资格预审标准格式，合同文件、以及客户与工程咨询单位协议书。这些资料可以从设在瑞士的菲迪克(FIDIC)秘书处得到。

“菲迪克(FIDIC)文献译丛”出版前言

世界工程咨询业已有上百年的发展历史，成为各国投资建设领域重要的智力服务行业。国际咨询工程师联合会(按其法文缩写 FIDIC,通称菲迪克)成立已有 80 多年，是国际工程咨询业的权威性行业组织，与世界银行等国际金融组织有着密切的联系。菲迪克的各种文献出版物，包括各种合同、协议标准范本、各项工作指南、以及工作惯例建议等，得到世界各有关组织的广泛承认和实施，是工程咨询行业的重要指导性文献。

我国工程咨询业是改革开放以来，在原有工程设计和建设管理队伍基础上发展起来的，承担着为各级投资决策部门和各类建设项目提供战略规划、项目决策、工程设计、以及项目实施管理等投资建设全过程的咨询服务。今后随着我国建设事业的发展，项目的决策与实施要求提供咨询服务的工作量将会大量增长，咨询服务质量要求也将越来越高。特别是我国已加入世界贸易组织(WTO)，投资建设领域既有新的机遇，也有新的挑战。借鉴国外工程咨询的成功经验，努力提高我国工程咨询服务水平，已成为当务之急。

中国工程咨询协会于 1996 年正式加入菲迪克组织，并取得在我国翻译出版菲迪克文献的授权。为了系统介绍菲迪克有关出版物，协会成立了菲迪克文献编译委员会，将以“菲迪克文献译丛”形式，陆续翻译出版菲迪克有关文献。

我们相信“译丛”的出版，将为我国广大工程咨询单位和人员、从事投资、金融和工程项目管理的部门和组织、各类项目业主、建筑施工监理企业、工程承包企业、环保企业、会计/律师事务所、保险公司以及有关高等院校学习国际经验，提供重要帮助。

中国工程咨询协会

编者的话

本书由国际咨询工程师联合会(FIDIC 即菲迪克)编写，于 1999 年出版的新合同标准格式第一版。新版《设计采购施工(EPC)/交钥匙工程合同条件》继承了菲迪克以往合同条件的优点，并根据多年来在实践中取得的经验以及专家、学者和相关各方的意见和建议，作出了重大的调整。在结构、布局和措辞等方面做了重大的修改：统一了条款、定义和措辞；条款数目统一为二十条。此次出版的《设计采购施工(EPC)/交钥匙工程合同条件》，不是在原有合同基础上修改，而是进行了重新编写，首次推出的。1998 年菲迪克在成员协会中推出了试用本，在全世界范围内收集建议和意见，并在一些国家进行试点使用，在经过 1 年多的试用后，于 1999 年才正式首次出版了《设计采购施工(EPC)/交钥匙工程合同条件》。

希望此译本的出版，对我国从事工程咨询、投资、金融和项目管理的部门和组织、各类项目业主、建筑施工监理企业、工程承包企业、环保企业、会计/律师事务所、保险公司以及有关高等院校等人员在学习和运用菲迪克合同条件，有效地解决在国际、国内工程咨询和工程承包活动中的合同管理问题，更好地开拓国内外工程咨询和工程承包市场，促进我国工程咨询业与国际惯例接轨，推动我国工程咨询事业的发展会有所帮助。

翻译过程中，我们虽然尽力想使译文准确通顺，但限于专业知识与语言水平，译文中可能出现不妥乃至错误之处，敬请读者指正。

本书由王川翻译，徐礼章校译，王川、徐礼章、唐萍审校，刘菡、邓冰茹、莫伟平、李莉萍、申晓丹、刘毅、张平、胡仲翔、张甲英、张芳芳、时小军、邓月英、杨海昆、郑海燕、陈雄、曾家平、王新之、唐璐璐、郑海萍等参加了部分章节的编译工作。

中国工程咨询协会 FIDIC 文献编译委员会

INTRODUCTORY NOTE TO FIRST EDITION

FIDIC's Red and Yellow Books (i.e. standard forms of contract for works of civil engineering construction and for electrical and mechanical works) have been in widespread use for several decades, and have been recognised - among other things - for their principles of balanced risk sharing between the Employer and the Contractor. These risk sharing principles have been beneficial for both parties, the Employer signing a contract at a lower price and only having further costs when particular unusual risks actually eventuate, and the Contractor avoiding pricing such risks which are not easy to evaluate. The principles of balanced risk sharing are continued in the new "Construction" and "Plant and Design-Build" Books.

During recent years it has been noticed that much of the construction market requires a form of contract where certainty of final price, and often of completion date, are of extreme importance. Employers on such turnkey projects are willing to pay more - sometimes considerably more - for their project if they can be more certain that the agreed final price will not be exceeded. Among such projects can be found many projects financed by private funds, where the lenders require greater certainty about a project's costs to the Employer than is allowed for under the allocation of risks provided for by FIDIC's traditional forms of contracts. Often the construction project (the EPC - Engineer, Procure, Construct - Contract) is only one part of a complicated commercial venture, and financial or other failure of this construction project will jeopardize the whole venture.

For such projects it is necessary for the Contractor to assume responsibility for a wider range of risks than under the traditional Red and Yellow Books. To obtain increased certainty of the final price, the Contractor is often asked to cover such risks as the occurrence of poor or unexpected ground conditions, and that what is set out in the requirements prepared by the Employer actually will result in the desired objective. If the Contractor is to carry such risks, the Employer obviously must give him the time and opportunity to obtain and consider all relevant information before the Contractor is asked to sign on a fixed contract price. The Employer must also realize that asking responsible contractors to price such risks will increase the construction cost and result in some projects not being commercially viable.

Even under such contracts the Employer does carry certain risks such as the risks of war, terrorism and the like and the other risks of Force Majeure, and it is always possible, and sometimes advisable, for the Parties to discuss other risk sharing arrangements before entering into the Contract. In the case of BOT (Build-Operate-Transfer) type projects, which are normally negotiated as a package, the allocation of risk provided for in the turnkey construction Contract negotiated initially between the Sponsors and the EPC Contractor may need to be adjusted in order to take into account the final allocation of all risks between the various contracts forming the total package.

Apart from the more recent and rapid development of privately financed projects demanding contract terms ensuring increased certainty of price, time and performance, it has long been apparent that many employers, particularly in the public sector, in a wide range of countries have demanded similar contract terms, at least for turnkey contracts. They have often irreverently taken the FIDIC Red or Yellow Books and altered the terms so that risks placed on the Employer in the FIDIC Books have been transferred to the Contractor, thus effectively removing FIDIC's traditional principles of balanced risk sharing. This need of many employers has not gone unnoticed, and FIDIC has considered it better for all parties for this need to be openly recognised and regularised. By providing a standard FIDIC form for use in such contracts, the Employer's requirements for more risk to be taken by the Contractor are clearly stated. Thus the Employer does not have to attempt to alter a standard form intended for another risk arrangement, and the Contractor is fully aware of

第一版 序言

国际咨询工程师联合会(**菲迪克 FIDIC**)的**红皮书**和**黄皮书**(即《土木工程施工合同》和《机电工程合同标准格式》)已广泛推行应用几十年。它们的内容，包括**雇主**和**承包商**间平衡分配风险的原则，受到普遍认可。这些风险分配原则已使双方获益，**雇主**按较低价格签订合同，仅在最终实际发生特殊的非正常风险情况下，才增加进一步费用；而**承包商**避免了对此类难以估计的风险进行估价。此项风险平衡分配原则在新版**"施工"书**以及**"生产设备和设计-施工"书**中继续沿用。

近几年，已注意到很多建设市场需要一种固定最终价格、经常还有固定竣工日期的合同格式。**雇主**对此类交钥匙项目，往往愿意支付更多、有时相当多的费用，只要能确保商定的最终价格不被超过。在此类项目中，有许多项目是靠私人资金融资的，贷款人要求**雇主**的项目成本，比根据**菲迪克**(**FIDIC**)传统合同格式提供的风险分担产生的成本有更大的确定性。经常此类建设项目(即**设计采购施工**(**EPC**)**合同**)只是复杂商业投资事业的一部分，其资金或其他方面出问题将危及整个投资事业。

对于这类项目，**承包商**需要比根据传统的**红皮书**和**黄皮书**，承担更广范围的风险责任。为了取得最终价格的更大确定性，**承包商**往往被要求承担诸如出现不良或未预计到的场地条件等风险，**雇主**编制的雇主要求实际上将导致希望实现的目标。如果**承包商**要承担此类风险，显然**雇主**必须在要求**承包商**签署固定合同价格前，给他时间和机会，使他能得到和研究所有有关资料。**雇主**还需了解，要求负责任的承包商对此类风险做出估价，将会增加建设成本，导致有些项目可能在商业上变得不可行。

即使根据此类合同，**雇主**肯定要承担一定风险，如战争、恐怖主义和类似风险，以及其他不可抗力风险等，但对合同双方来说，在签定**合同**前，讨论一些其他风险分担方案常常是可能的，有时是明智的。在BOT(**建造-运行-移交**)项目的情况下，通常是一揽子的谈判，最初由项目发起人与EPC(设计采购施工)**承包商**协商的交钥匙施工合同规定的风险分配方案，可能需要进行调整，以便对组成整个项目的各类合同间对所有风险的最终分配，进行通盘考虑。

除了要求合同条款确保价格、时间和功能具有更大确定性的私人融资项目最近有了更快的发展以外，长期以来已明显看到，许多国家中的雇主，特别是公共部门，已要求类似的条款，尤其对交钥匙合同是这样。他们经常不遵照**菲迪克**(**FIDIC**)的**红皮书**或**黄皮书**，而将条款做了修改，把**菲迪克**标准合同中分给**雇主**承担的风险转移给**承包商**，实际上去掉了**菲迪克**平衡分配风险的传统原则。**菲迪克**对许多雇主的这一要求并没有忽视，但认为对合同各方的这一要求公开给予承认，使之合法化、规范化会更好。通过制订一个**菲迪克**标准格式，供此类合同使用，把要**承包商**承担更大风险的**雇主**要求写清楚，雇主就不必为了采取其他风险分配方案而修改标准格式了，而**承包商**可以充分了解他必须承担的附加风险。很

the increased risks he must bear. Clearly the Contractor will rightly increase his tender price to account for such extra risks.

This form for EPC/Turnkey Projects is thus intended to be suitable, not only for EPC Contracts within a BOT or similar type venture, but also for all the many projects, both large and smaller, particularly E & M (Electrical and Mechanical) and other process plant projects, being carried out around the world by all types of employers, often in a civil law environment, where the government departments or private developers wish to implement their project on a fixed-price turnkey basis and with a strictly two party approach.

Employers using this form must realise that the "Employer's Requirements" which they prepare should describe the principle and basic design of the plant on a functional basis. The Tenderer should then be permitted and required to verify all relevant information and data and make any necessary investigations. He shall also carry out any necessary design and detailing of the specific equipment and plant he is offering, allowing him to offer solutions best suited to his equipment and experience. Therefore the tendering procedure has to permit discussions between the Tenderer and the Employer about technical matters and commercial conditions. All such matters, when agreed, shall then form part of the signed Contract.

Thereafter the Contractor should be given freedom to carry out the work in his chosen manner, provided the end result meets the performance criteria specified by the Employer. Consequently, the Employer should only exercise limited control over and should in general not interfere with the Contractor's work. Clearly the Employer will wish to know and follow progress of the work and be assured that the time programme is being followed. He will also wish to know that the work quality is as specified, that third parties are not being disturbed, that performance tests are met, and otherwise that the "Employer's Requirements" are being complied with.

A feature of this type of contract is that the Contractor has to prove the reliability and performance of his plant and equipment. Therefore special attention is given to the "Tests on Completion", which often take place over a considerable time period, and Taking Over shall take place only after successful completion of these tests.

FIDIC recognizes that privately-financed projects are usually subject to more negotiation than publicly-financed ones and that therefore changes are likely to have to be made in any standard form of contract proposed for projects within a BOT or similar type venture. Among other things, such form may need to be adapted to take account of the special, if not unique, characteristics of each project, as well as the requirements of lenders and others providing financing. Nevertheless, such changes do not do away with the need for a standard form.

These Conditions of Contract for EPC/Turnkey Projects are not suitable for use in the following circumstances:

- If there is insufficient time or information for tenderers to scrutinise and check the Employer's Requirements or for them to carry out their designs, risk assessment studies and estimating (taking particular account of Sub-Clauses 4.12 and 5.1).
- If construction will involve substantial work underground or work in other areas which tenderers cannot inspect.
- If the Employer intends to supervise closely or control the Contractor's work, or to review most of the construction drawings.
- If the amount of each interim payment is to be determined by an official or other intermediary.

FIDIC recommends that the Conditions of Contract for Plant and Design-Build be used in the above circumstances for Works designed by (or on behalf of) the Contractor.

明显**承包商**为了考虑此类额外风险，将正当地增加投标价格。

为**《设计采购施工(EPC)/交钥匙工程》**拟订的这一合同格式，目的不仅要适用于BOT项目或类似投资模式下的设计采购施工(EPC)合同，还可适用于所有大小各类项目，特别是由世界上各类雇主实施的电气和机械、以及其他加工设备项目，这些项目经常处在民法环境下，政府部门或私人开发商都希望项目能在固定价格交钥匙的基础上，严格地由双方磋商。

采用这种格式时，雇主必须理解，他们编写的“**雇主要求**”在描述设计原则和生产设备基础设计的要求时，应以功能作为基础。应允许并要求投标人对所有相关资料和数据进行核实，并做好任何必要的调查研究。他还应进行任何必要的设计和他将提供的专用设备和生产设备的详细说明，应允许他提出最适合于他的设备和经验的解决方案。因此，招标程序需允许在**投标人**和**雇主**间，就技术问题和商务条件进行讨论。所有这些事项达成协议后，将成为签订**合同**的组成部分。

随后，应给予**承包商**按他选择的方式进行工作的自由，只要最终结果能够满足**雇主**规定的功能标准。因而**雇主**对**承包商**的工作只应进行有限的控制，一般不应进行干预。无疑**雇主**希望知道和跟踪工程进展，并确保进度计划能够实现。他还希望了解工程质量达到规定要求，第三方不受干扰，性能试验满足要求，以及“**雇主要求**”的其他内容都能照办。

这种类型合同的一个特点是，**承包商**必须证明他的生产设备和装备的可靠性和性能。因此，对“**竣工试验**”给予特别注意。这些试验经常在相当长的期间内进行，而只有在这些试验成功完成后，工程才能**接收**。

菲迪克认识到，私人融资项目往往比公共部门融资项目需要更多的协商。因此，对建议用于BOT或类似投资型式项目的任何标准合同格式，可能必须做出修改。尤其是这类格式可能需要适应每个项目特有，若非专有的特点，以及贷款人或其他融资单位的要求。但是这些修改并不排除对标准格式的需要。

本**《设计采购施工(EPC)/交钥匙工程合同》**条件不适用于下列情况：

- 如果投标人没有足够时间或资料，以仔细研究和核查**雇主要求**，或进行他们的设计、风险评估和估算(特别是考虑第**4.12**和**5.1**款)；
- 如果建设内容涉及相当数量的地下工程，或投标人未能调查的区域内的工程；
- 如果**雇主**要严密监督或控制**承包商**的工作，或要审核大部分施工图纸；
- 如果每次期中付款的款额要经职员或其他中间人确定。

菲迪克建议，上述情况下由**承包商**(或以其名义)设计的工程，可以采用**生产设备和设计-施工合同条件**。

ACKNOWLEDGEMENTS

Fédération Internationale des Ingénieurs-Conseils (FIDIC) extends special thanks to the following members of its Update Task Group: Christopher Wade (Group Leader), SWECO-VBB, Sweden; Peter L Booen (Principal Drafter), GIBB Ltd, UK; Hermann Bayerlein, Fichtner, Germany; Christopher R Seppala (Legal Adviser), White & Case, France; and José F Speziale, IATASA, Argentina.

The preparation was carried out under the general direction of the FIDIC Contracts Committee which comprised John B Bowcock, Consulting Engineer, UK (Chairman); Michael Mortimer-Hawkins, SwedPower, Sweden; and Axel-Volkmar Jaeger, Schmidt Reuter Partner, Germany; together with K B (Tony) Norris as Special Adviser.

Drafts were reviewed by many persons and organisations, including those listed below. Their comments were duly studied by the Update Task Group and, where considered appropriate, have influenced the wording of the clauses. Mushtaq Ahmad, NESPAK, Pakistan; Peter Batty, Post Buckley International, USA; Roeland Bertrams, Clifford Chance, Netherlands; Charles G Borthwick, SwedPower, Sweden; Manfred Breege, Lahmeyer International, Germany; Pablo Bueno, TYPSA, Spain; Nael G Bunni, Consulting Engineer, Ireland; Ian Fraser, Beca Carter Hollings & Ferner, New Zealand; Roy Goode, Oxford University, UK; Dan W Graham, Bristows Cooke & Carpmael, UK; Mark Griffiths, Griffiths & Armour, UK; Geoffrey F Hawker, Consulting Engineer, UK; Hesse & Steinberger, VDMA, Germany; Poul E Hvilsted, Elsamprojekt, Denmark; Lennart Iwar, Lindahl, Sweden; Gordon L Jaynes, Whitman Breed Abbott & Morgan, UK; Tonny Jensen (Chairman of FIDIC Quality Management Committee), COWI, Denmark; Martin Klapper, Hopgood and Ganim, Australia; Philip Loots & Associates, South Africa; Neil McCole, Merz and McLellan, UK; Matthew Needham-Laing, Victoria Russell & Paul J Taylor, Berrymans Lace Mawer, UK; J Gordon Rees, Binnie Black & Veatch, UK; Tim Reynolds, Constant & Constant, UK; David R Wightman & Gerlando Butera, Nabarro Nathanson, UK; the Association of Japanese Consulting Engineers; the Construction Industry Authority of the Philippines; the Dutch Vereniging voor Bouwrecht; the European International Contractors (EIC); ORGAnisme de Liaison Industries Métalliques Européennes (ORGALIME); the International Association of Dredging Contractors; the International Bar Association; the Asian Development Bank; and the World Bank. Acknowledgement of reviewers does not mean that such persons or organizations approve of the wording of all clauses. In particular, EIC and ORGALIME have expressed reservations about some clauses of this EPC Contract.

FIDIC wishes to record its appreciation of the time and effort devoted by all the above.

The ultimate decision on the form and content of the document rests with FIDIC.

致谢

国际咨询工程师联合会(FIDIC即菲迪克)对其新版工作组下列成员特致感谢：瑞典SWECO-VBB的 Christopher Wade(组长)，英国 GIBB 有限公司的 Peter L Booen(主要起草人)，德国 Fichtner 的 Hermann Bayerlein，法国 White & Case 的 Christopher R Seppala(法律顾问)，以及阿根廷 IATASA 的 José F Speziale。

本书是在 FIDIC 合同委员会全面指导下进行编写的，该委员会成员包括：英国咨询工程师 John B Bowcock(主席)，瑞典 Swed Power 的 Michael Mortimer-Hawkins，德国 Schmidt Reuter Partner 的 Axel-Volkmar Jaeger，还有特别顾问 K B (Tony) Norris。

书稿曾经下列许多人员和组织审阅，他们的意见已由新版工作组充分研究，认为适宜的意见已反映在条款措辞中。这些人员和组织包括：巴基斯坦 NESPAK 的 Mushtaq Ahmad，美国 Post Buckley International 的 Peter Batty，荷兰 Clifford Chance 的 Roeland Bertrams，瑞典 Swed Power 的 Charles G Borthwick，德国 Lahmeyer International 的 Manfred Breege，西班牙 TYPSA 的 Pablo Bueno，爱尔兰咨询工程师 Nael G Bunni，新西兰 Beca Carter Hollings & Ferner 的 Ian Fraser，英国牛津大学的 Roy Goode，英国 Bristows Cooke & Carpmael 的 Dan W Graham，英国 Griffiths & Armour 的 Mark Griffiths，英国咨询工程师 Geoffrey F Hawker，德国 VDMA 的 Hesse & Steinberger，丹麦 Elsamprojekt 的 Poul E Hvilsted，瑞典 Lindahl 的 Lennart Iwar，英国 Whitman Breed Abbott & Morgan 的 Gordon L Jaynes，丹麦 COWI 的 Tonny Jensen(FIDIC 质量管理委员会主席)，澳大利亚 Hopgood and Ganim 的 Martin Klapper，南非的 Philip Loots & Associates，英国 Merz and Mclellan 的 Neil Mccole，英国 Victoria Russell & Paul J Taylor，Berrymans Lace Mawer 的 Matthew Needham-Laing，英国 Binnie Black & Veatch 的 J Gordon Rees，英国 Constant & Constant 的 Tim Reynolds，英国的 David R Wightwan & Gerlando Butera，Nabarro Nathanson，日本咨询工程师协会，菲律宾建设工业局，荷兰 Vereniging Voor Bouwrecht，欧洲国际承包商(EIC)，欧洲金属工业联络组织(ORGALIME)，国际疏浚(挖掘)承包商协会，国际律师协会，亚洲开发银行和世界银行。向审阅人的致谢并不表示这些人员和组织对所有条款措辞的赞同。特别是 EIC 和 ORGALIME 曾对此 EPC(设计采购施工)合同的某些条款表示保留。

菲迪克(FIDIC)对所有上述人员和组织付出的时间和精力表示感谢。

对文件的格式和内容的最终决定由**菲迪克**(FIDIC)负责。

FOREWORD

The Fédération Internationale des Ingénieurs-Conseils (FIDIC) published, in 1999, First Editions of four new standard forms of contract:

Conditions of Contract for Construction,

which are recommended for building or engineering works designed by the Employer or by his representative, the Engineer. Under the usual arrangements for this type of contract, the Contractor constructs the works in accordance with a design provided by the Employer. However, the works may include some elements of Contractor-designed civil, mechanical, electrical and/or construction works.

Conditions of Contract for Plant and Design-Build,

which are recommended for the provision of electrical and/or mechanical plant, and for the design and execution of building or engineering works. Under the usual arrangements for this type of contract, the Contractor designs and provides, in accordance with the Employer's requirements, plant and/or other works; which may include any combination of civil, mechanical, electrical and/or construction works.

Conditions of Contract for EPC/Turnkey Projects,

which may be suitable for the provision on a turnkey basis of a process or power plant, of a factory or similar facility, or of an infrastructure project or other type of development, where (i) a higher degree of certainty of final price and time is required, and (ii) the Contractor takes total responsibility for the design and execution of the project, with little involvement of the Employer. Under the usual arrangements for turnkey projects, the Contractor carries out all the Engineering, Procurement and Construction (EPC): providing a fully-equipped facility, ready for operation (at the "turn of the key").

Short Form of Contract,

which is recommended for building or engineering works of relatively small capital value. Depending on the type of work and the circumstances, this form may also be suitable for contracts of greater value, particularly for relatively simple or repetitive work or work of short duration. Under the usual arrangements for this type of contract, the Contractor constructs the works in accordance with a design provided by the Employer or by his representative (if any), but this form may also be suitable for a contract which includes, or wholly comprises, Contractor-designed civil, mechanical, electrical and/or construction works.

The forms are recommended for general use where tenders are invited on an international basis. Modifications may be required in some jurisdictions, particularly if the Conditions are to be used on domestic contracts. FIDIC considers the official and authentic texts to be the versions in the English language.

In the preparation of these Conditions of Contract for EPC/Turnkey Projects, it was recognised that, while there are many sub-clauses which will be generally applicable, there are some sub-clauses which must necessarily vary to take account of the

前言

国际咨询工程师联合会(FIDIC即菲迪克)1999年出版了**4**本新的合同标准格式第一版:

《施工合同条件》,

推荐用于由**雇主**或其代表**工程师**设计的建筑或工程项目。这种合同的通常情况是,由**承包商**按照**雇主**提供的设计进行工程施工。但该工程可以包括由**承包商**设计的土木、机械、电气和(或)构筑物的某些部分。

《生产设备和设计-施工合同条件》,

推荐用于电气和(或)机械生产设备供货和建筑或工程的设计与施工。这种合同的通常情况是,由**承包商**按照**雇主**要求,设计和提供生产设备和(或)其他工程,可以包括土木、机械、电气和(或)构筑物的任何组合。

《设计采购施工(EPC)/交钥匙工程合同条件》,

可适用于以交钥匙方式提供加工或动力设备、工厂或类似设施、或基础设施工程或其他类型开发项目。这种方式,(ⅰ)项目的最终价格和要求的工期具有更大程度的确定性,(ⅱ)由**承包商**承担项目的设计和实施的全部职责,**雇主**介入很少。交钥匙工程的通常情况是,由**承包商**进行全部**设计**、**采购**和**施工**(EPC),提供一个配备完善的设施,("转动钥匙"时)即可运行。

《简明合同格式》,

推荐用于资本金额较小的建筑或工程项目。根据工程的类型和具体情况,这种格式也可用于较大资本金额的合同,特别是适用于简单或重复性的工程或工期较短的工程。这种合同的通常情况是,由**承包商**按照**雇主**或其代表(如果有)提供的设计进行工程施工,但这种格式也可适用于包括或全部是由**承包商**设计的土木、机械、电气和(或)构筑物的合同。

这些合同格式是推荐在国际招标中通用的。在某些司法管辖范围,特别是要用于国内合同的**条件**,可能需要做些修改。菲迪克认为,正式、权威性的文本应为英文版。

在编写本**《设计采购施工(EPC)/交钥匙工程合同条件》**中感到,虽有许多条款可以通用,但有些条款必须考虑特定合同的有关情况做出必要的修改。我们认为可以

circumstances relevant to the particular contract. The sub-clauses which were considered to be applicable to many (but not all) contracts have been included in the General Conditions, in order to facilitate their incorporation into each contract.

The General Conditions and the Particular Conditions will together comprise the Conditions of Contract governing the rights and obligations of the parties. It will be necessary to prepare the Particular Conditions for each individual contract, and to take account of those sub-clauses in the General Conditions which mention the Particular Conditions.

For this publication, the General Conditions were prepared on the following basis:

(i) interim payments, in respect of the lump sum Contract Price, will be made as work proceeds, and will typically be based on instalments specified in a schedule;

(ii) if the wording in the General Conditions necessitates further data which would typically be prescribed by the Employer, then the sub-clause makes reference to this data being contained in the Particular Conditions or in the Employer's Requirements;

(iii) where a sub-clause in the General Conditions deals with a matter on which different contract terms are likely to be applicable for different contracts, the principles applied in writing the sub-clause were:

  (a) users would find it more convenient if any provisions which they did not wish to apply could simply be deleted or not invoked, than if additional text had to be written (in the Particular Conditions) because the General Conditions did not cover their requirements; or

  (b) in other cases, where the application of (a) was thought to be inappropriate, the sub-clause contains the provisions which were considered applicable to most contracts.

For example, Sub-Clause 14.2 [*Advance Payment*] is included for convenience, not because of any FIDIC policy in respect of advance payments. This Sub-Clause becomes inapplicable (even if it is not deleted) if it is disregarded by not specifying the amount of the advance. It should therefore be noted that some of the provisions contained in the General Conditions may not be appropriate for an apparently-typical contract.

Further information on these aspects, example wording for other arrangements, and other explanatory material and a check-list and example wording to assist in the preparation of the Particular Conditions and the other tender documents, are included within this publication as Guidance for the Preparation of the Particular Conditions. Before incorporating any example wording, it must be checked to ensure that it is wholly suitable for the particular circumstances; if not, it must be amended.

Where example wording is amended, and in all cases where other amendments or additions are made, care must be taken to ensure that no ambiguity is created, either with the General Conditions or between the clauses in the Particular Conditions. It is essential that all these drafting tasks, and the entire preparation of the tender

用于多数(但非全部)合同的条款，已包括进**通用条件**中，以便纳入每项合同。

通用条件和**专用条件**共同组成管理各方权利和义务的**合同条件**。对每个具体合同，都需要编制其**专用条件**，并要考虑**通用条件**一些条款中提到**专用条件**的内容。

本文本中**通用条件**根据以下原则编写：

(ⅰ) 关于总额**合同价格**的期中付款，将随工程进展，一般根据规定的分期付款的计划表支付；

(ⅱ) 如果**通用条件**中的措辞需要**雇主**专门规定的进一步资料，这时，条款指明该资料将包含在**专用条件**或**雇主要求**中；

(ⅲ) 在**通用条件**中处理某一事项的条款，可能与不同的合同对该事项采用的合同条款不同时，编写此类条款应用的原则是：

(a) 使用户感到能够简单地删除或不动用任何他们不想采用的规定，要比因为**通用条件**中没有包括他们的要求，而必须(在**专用条件**中)编写附加条款要方便得多；

(b) 在采用(**a**)项办法被认为不适宜的其他情况下，使该条款包含经考虑认为对大多数合同都能适用的规定。

例如，列入**第 14.2 款**［**预付款**］是为了方便，而不是因为**菲迪克**(FIDIC)关于预付款的任何政策。如果该条款由于没有做出预付款额的规定而未被理会，则该款(即使未被删除)也将变为无用。因此，应注意到**通用条件**中包含的一些规定对明显典型的合同可能不适宜。

这些方面的进一步资料、其他规定的范例措辞、以及其他说明性材料和有助于编写**专用条件**和其他招标文件的核查表和范例措辞，都包括在本文本**专用条件编写指南**中。在引用任何范例措辞前，必须认真核对，确保其完全适合特定的情况，否则必须进行修改。

当对范例措辞进行修改，以及所有其他修改或补充的情况下，必须注意确保其与**通用条件**之间，或在**专用条件**各条款间避免产生歧义。重要的是，所有这些起草工作，以及整个招标文件的编写，要委托具有相关专门知识的人员，包括合同、

documents, are entrusted to personnel with the relevant expertise, including the contractual, technical and procurement aspects.

This publication concludes with example forms for the Letter of Tender, the Contract Agreement, and alternatives for the Dispute Adjudication Agreement. This Dispute Adjudication Agreement provides text for the agreement between the Employer, the Contractor and the person appointed to act either as sole adjudicator or as a member of a three-person dispute adjudication board; and incorporates (by reference) the terms in the Appendix to the General Conditions.

FIDIC intends to publish a guide to the use of its Conditions of Contract for Construction, for Plant and Design-Build, and for EPC/Turnkey Projects.

In order to clarify the sequence of Contract activities, reference may be made to the charts on the next two pages and to the Sub-Clauses listed below (some Sub-Clause numbers are also stated in the charts). The charts are illustrative and must not be taken into consideration in the interpretation of the Conditions of Contract.

1.1.3.1	&	13.7	Base Date
1.1.3.2	&	8.1	Commencement Date
1.1.6.6	&	4.2	Performance Security
1.1.3.3	&	8.2	Time for Completion (as extended under 8.4)
1.1.3.4	&	9.1	Tests on Completion
1.1.3.5	&	10.1	Taking-Over Certificate
1.1.3.6	&	12.1	Tests after Completion (if any)
1.1.3.7	&	11.1	Defects Notification Period (as extended under 11.3)
1.1.3.8	&	11.9	Performance Certificate

技术和采购方面的专家进行。

本文本最后附有**投标函**、**合同协议书**和备选的**争端裁决协议书**的范例格式。该**争端裁决协议书**提供了**雇主**、**承包商**和被任命为唯一裁决人或三人争端裁决委员会中的一名成员之间的协议书文本，并(通过引用)体现了**通用条件附录**的条款。

菲迪克(FIDIC)准备出版一本《**施工合同条件**》、《**生产设备和设计施工合同条件**》、以及《**设计采购施工(EPC)/交钥匙工程合同条件**》的应用指南。

为了弄清各项合同活动的顺序，可参考下面两页中的图和下列各条款(有些条款序号也在图中标出)。这些图只是说明性的，不应作为**合同条件**的解释。

1.1.3.1 和 13.7	**基准日期**
1.1.3.2 和 8.1	**开工日期**
1.1.6.6 和 4.2	**履约担保**
1.1.3.3 和 8.2	**竣工时间**(及根据第**8.4** 款的延长)
1.1.3.4 和 9.1	**竣工试验**
1.1.3.5 和 10.1	**接收证书**
1.1.3.6 和 12.1	**竣工后试验**(如果有)
1.1.3.7 和 11.1	**缺陷通知期限**(及根据**11.3** 款的延长)
1.1.3.8 和 11.9	**履约证书**

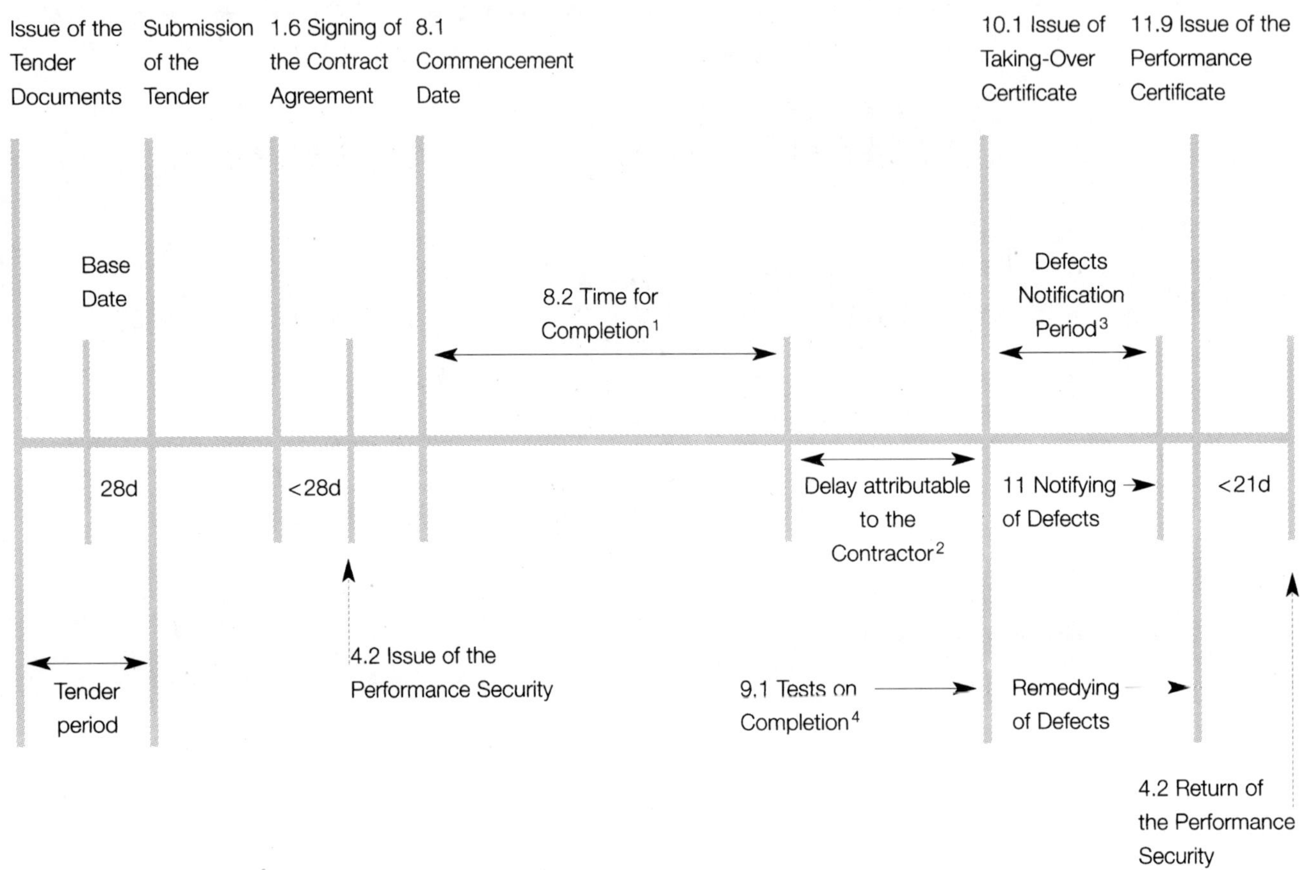

Typical sequence of Principal Events during Contracts for EC/Turnkey Projects

1. The Time for Completion is to be stated (in the Particular Conditions) as a number of days, to which is added any extensions of time under Sub-Clause 8.4.
2. In order to indicate the sequence of events, the above diagram is based upon the example of the Contractor failing to comply with Sub-Clause 8.2.
3. The Defects Notification Period is to be stated (in the Particular Conditions) as a number of days, to which is added any extensions under Sub-Clause 11.3.
4. Depending on the type of Works, Tests after Completion may also be required.

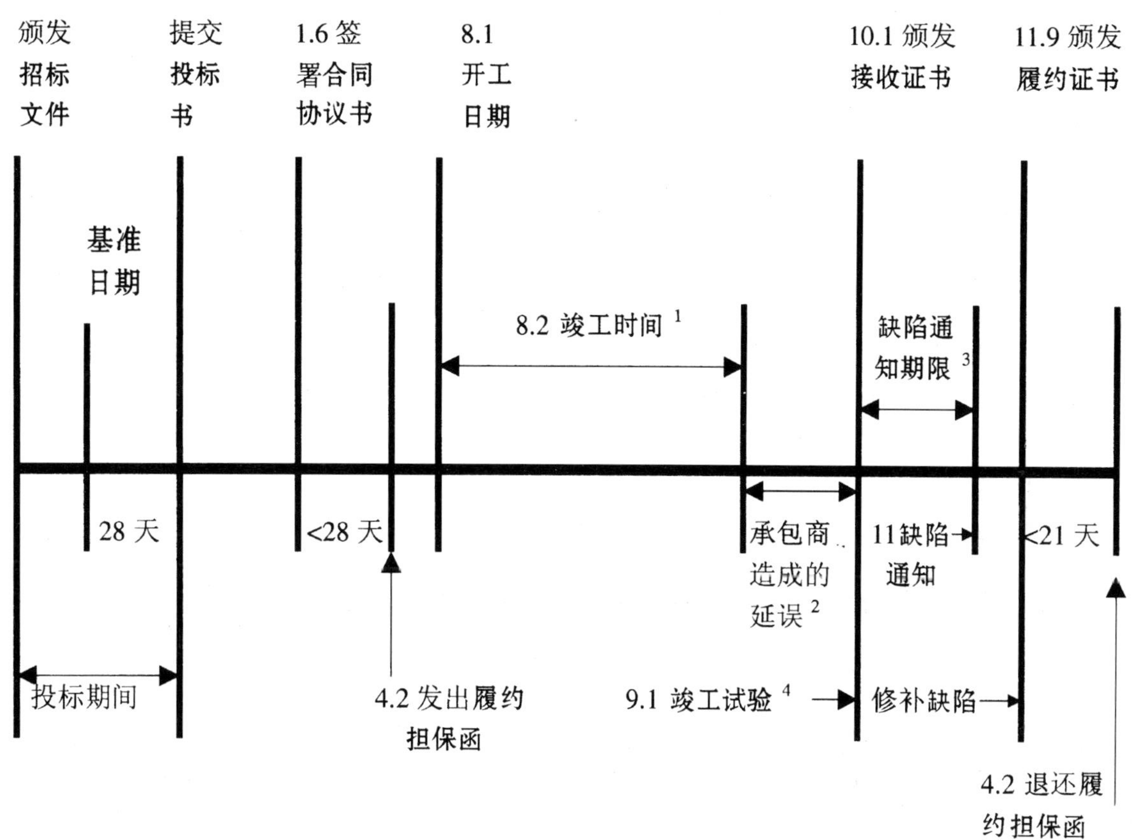

设计施工(EC)/交钥匙工程合同中主要事项的典型顺序

1. **竣工时间**(在**专用条件**中)用天数表示,加上根据**第 8.4 款**的任何延长期。

2. 为了表示事项的顺序，上图以**承包商**未能遵守**第 8.2 款**的规定为例。

3. **缺陷通知期限**(在**专用条件**中)用天数表示,加上根据**第 11.3 款**的任何延长期。

4. 根据**工程**的类型，可能还需要**竣工后试验**。

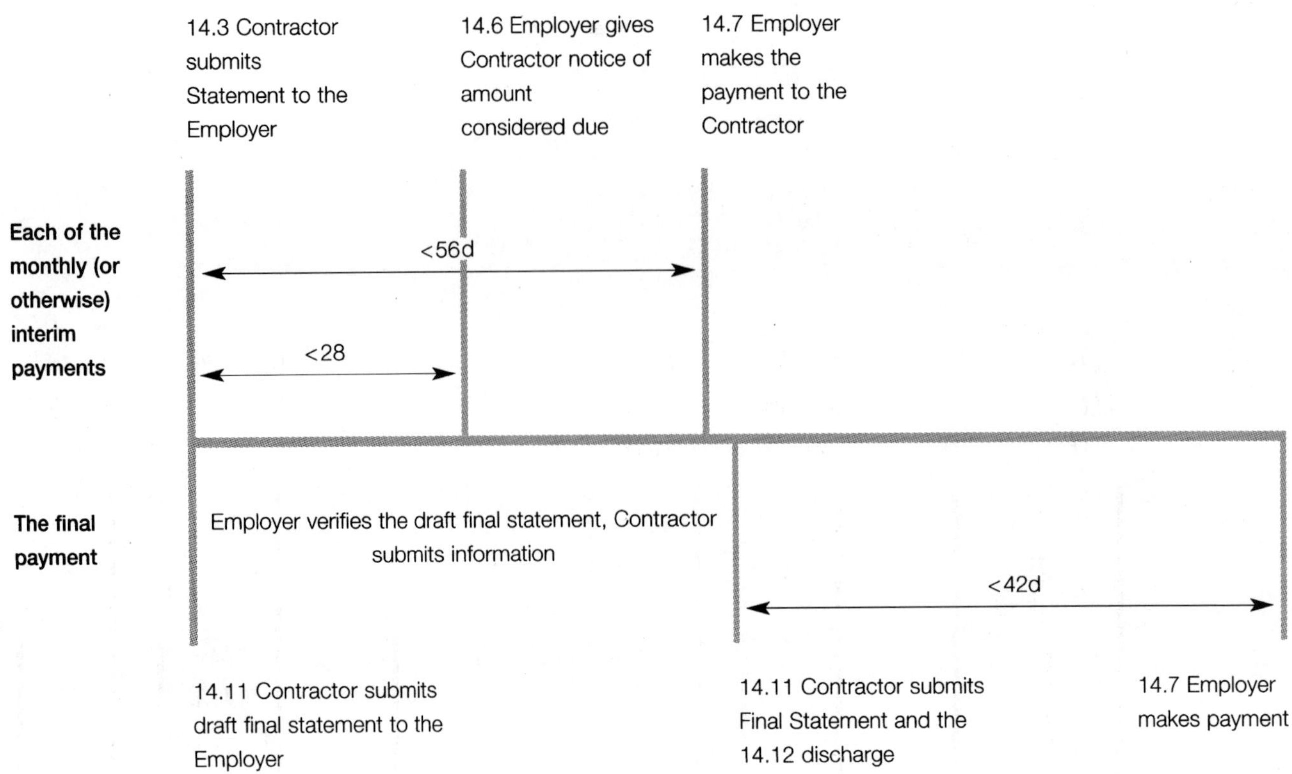

Typical sequence of Payment Events envisaged in Clause 14

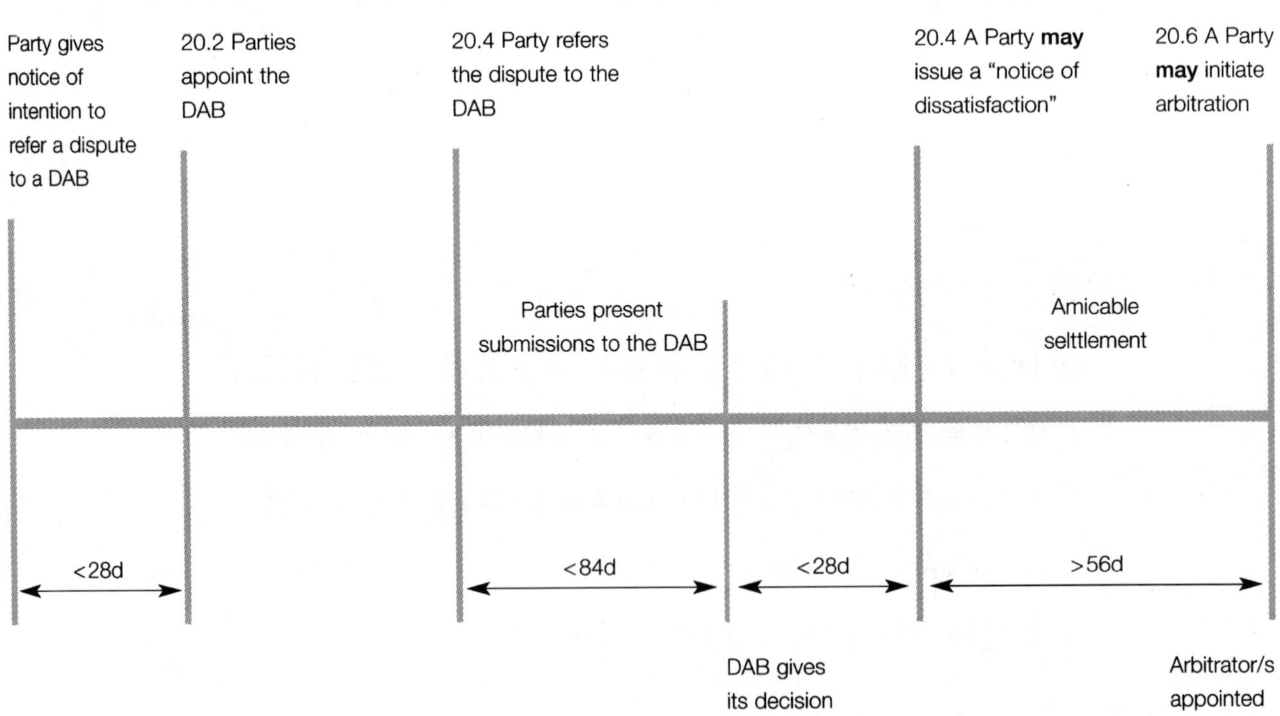

Typical sequence of Dispute Events envisaged in Clause 20

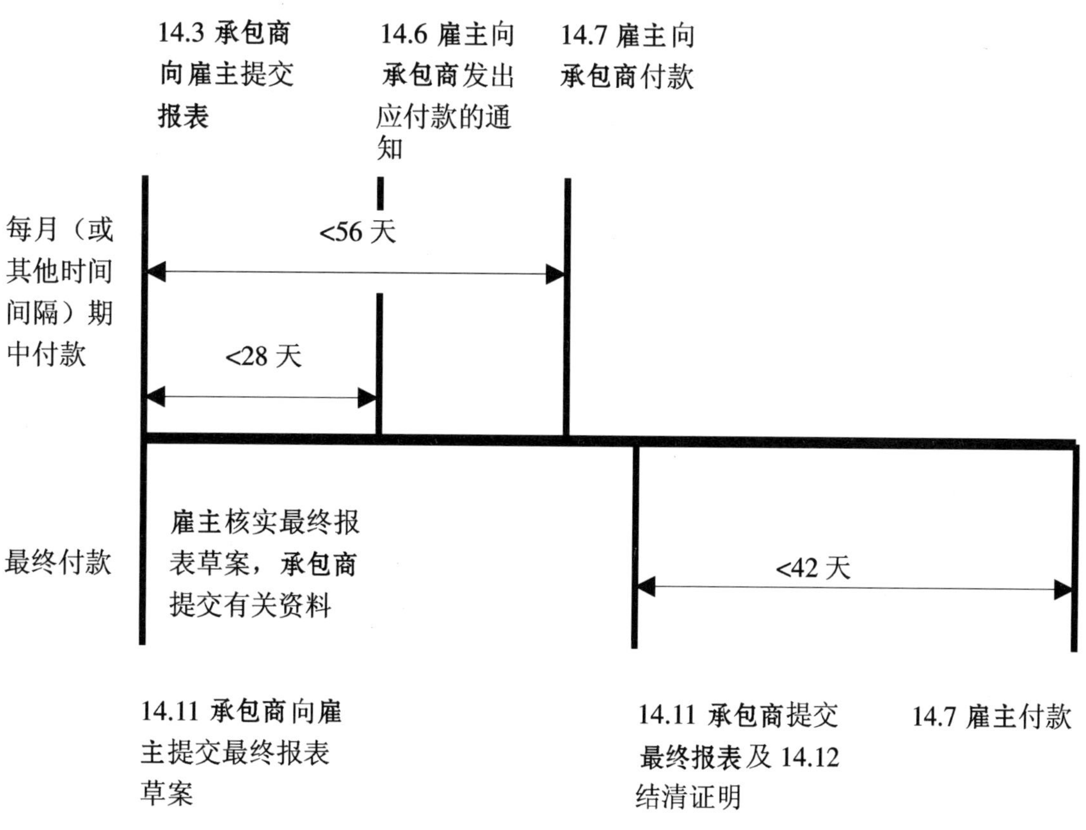

第 14 条中设想的付款事项的典型顺序

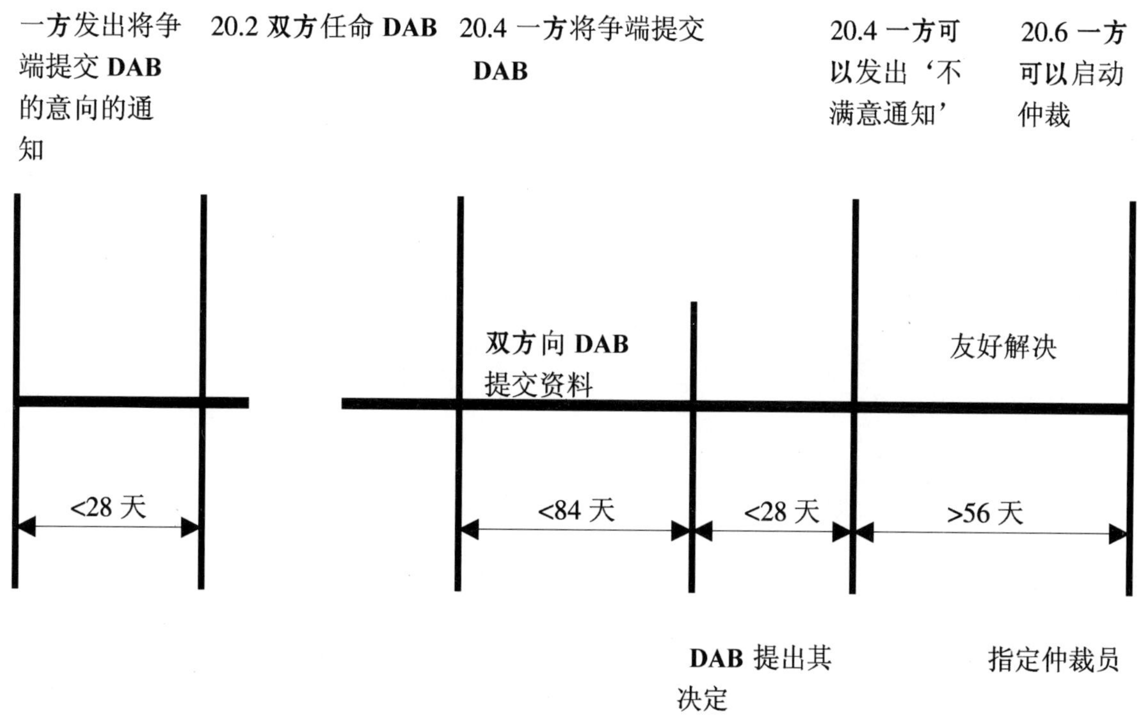

第 20 条中设想的解决争端事项的典型顺序

设计采购施工(EPC)/交钥匙工程合同条件

Conditions of Contract for **EPC/Turnkey Projects**

通用条件
GENERAL CONDITIONS

专用条件编写指南
GUIDANCE FOR THE PREPARATION OF PARTICULAR CONDITIONS

投标函、合同协议书和争端裁决协议书格式
FORMS OF LETTER OF TENDER, CONTRACT AGREEMENT AND DISPUTE ADJUDICATION AGREEMENT

通用条件
General Conditions

国 际 咨 询 工 程 师 联 合 会

FEDERATION INTERNATIONALE DES INGENIEURS-CONSEILS
INTERNATIONAL FEDERATION OF CONSULTING ENGINEERS
INTERNATIONALE VEREINIGUNG BERATENDER INGENIEURE
FEDERACION INTERNACIONAL DE INGENIEROS CONSOLTORES

General Conditions

CONTENTS

通 用 条 件

目　　录

Definitions listed alphabetically

1.1.3.1 Base Date
1.1.3.2 Commencement Date
1.1.1.1 Contract
1.1.1.2 Contract Agreement
1.1.4.1 Contract Price
1.1.2.3 Contractor
1.1.6.1 Contractor's Documents
1.1.5.1 Contractor's Equipment
1.1.2.7 Contractor's Personnel
1.1.2.5 Contractor's Representative
1.1.4.2 Cost
1.1.6.2 Country
1.1.2.9 DAB
1.1.3.9 day
1.1.3.7 Defects Notification Period
1.1.2.2 Employer
1.1.6.3 Employer's Equipment
1.1.2.6 Employer's Personnel
1.1.2.4 Employer's Representative
1.1.1.3 Employer's Requirements
1.1.2.10 FIDIC
1.1.4.3 Final Statement
1.1.6.4 Force Majeure
1.1.4.4 Foreign Currency
1.1.5.2 Goods
1.1.6.5 Laws
1.1.4.5 Local Currency
1.1.5.3 Materials
1.1.2.1 Party
1.1.3.8 Performance Certificate
1.1.1.5 Performance Guarantees
1.1.6.6 Performance Security
1.1.5.4 Permanent Works
1.1.5.5 Plant
1.1.4.6 Provisional Sum
1.1.4.7 Retention Money
1.1.1.5 Schedule of Payments
1.1.5.6 Section
1.1.6.7 Site
1.1.4.8 Statement
1.1.2.8 Subcontractor
1.1.3.5 Taking-Over Certificate
1.1.5.7 Temporary Works
1.1.1.4 Tender
1.1.3.6 Tests after Completion
1.1.3.4 Tests on Completion
1.1.3.3 Time for Completion
1.1.6.8 Variation
1.1.5.8 Works
1.1.3.9 year

按字母顺序排列的定义词语表

(原文按英文字母顺序排列,中译文按汉语拼音字母顺序排列)

1.1.4.7　保留金

1.1.4.8　报表

1.1.6.8　变更

1.1.6.4　不可抗力

1.1.5.3　材料

1.1.4.2　成本(费用)

1.1.2.3　承包商

1.1.2.5　承包商代表

1.1.2.7　承包商人员

1.1.5.1　承包商设备

1.1.6.1　承包商文件

1.1.5.6　单位工程

1.1.4.4　当地货币

1.1.2.1　当事方

1.1.6.5　法律

1.1.2.10　菲迪克

1.1.2.8　分包商

1.1.1.5　付款计划表

1.1.5.8　工程

1.1.6.2　工程所在国

1.1.2.2　雇主

1.1.2.4　雇主代表

1.1.2.6　雇主人员

1.1.6.3　雇主设备

1.1.1.3　雇主要求

1.1.1.1　合同

1.1.4.1　合同价格

1.1.1.2　合同协议书

1.1.5.2　货物

1.1.3.1　基准日期

1.1.3.5　接收证书

1.1.3.6　竣工后试验

1.1.3.3　竣工时间

1.1.3.4　竣工试验

1.1.3.2　开工日期

1.1.5.7　临时工程

1.1.1.5　履约保证

1.1.6.6　履约担保

1.1.3.8　履约证书

1.1.3.9　年

1.1.3.7　缺陷通知期限

1.1.3.9　日

1.1.5.5　生产设备

1.1.1.4　投标书

1.1.4.4　外币

1.1.6.7　现场

1.1.5.4　永久工程

1.1.4.6　暂列金额

1.1.2.9　争端裁决委员会

1.1.4.3　最终报表

General Conditions

1 General Provisions

1.1
Definitions

In the Conditions of Contract ("these Conditions"), which include Particular Conditions and these General Conditions, the following words and expressions shall have the meanings stated. Words indicating persons or parties include corporations and other legal entities, except where the context requires otherwise.

1.1.1
The Contract

1.1.1.1 "**Contract**" means the Contract Agreement, these Conditions, the Employer's Requirements, the Tender, and the further documents (if any) which are listed in the Contract Agreement.

1.1.1.2 "**Contract Agreement**" means the contract agreement referred to in Sub-Clause 1.6 [*Contract Agreement*], including any annexed memoranda.

1.1.1.3 "**Employer's Requirements**" means the document entitled employer's requirements, as included in the Contract, and any additions and modifications to such document in accordance with the Contract. Such document specifies the purpose, scope, and/or design and/or other technical criteria, for the Works.

1.1.1.4 "**Tender**" means the Contractor's signed offer for the Works and all other documents which the Contractor submitted therewith (other than these Conditions and the Employer's Requirements, if so submitted), as included in the Contract.

1.1.1.5 "**Performance Guarantees**" and "**Schedule of Payments**" mean the documents so named (if any), as included in the Contract.

1.1.2
Parties and Persons

1.1.2.1 "**Party**" means the Employer or the Contractor, as the context requires.

1.1.2.2 "**Employer**" means the person named as employer in the Contract Agreement and the legal successors in title to this person.

1.1.2.3 "**Contractor**" means the person(s) named as contractor in the Contract Agreement and the legal successors in title to this person(s).

1.1.2.4 "**Employer's Representative**" means the person named by the Employer in the Contract or appointed from time to time by the Employer under Sub-Clause 3.1 [*The Employer's Representative*], who acts on behalf of the Employer.

1.1.2.5 "**Contractor's Representative**" means the person named by the Contractor in the Contract or appointed from time to time by the Contractor under Sub-Clause 4.3 [*Contractor's Representative*], who acts on behalf of the Contractor.

1.1.2.6 "**Employer's Personnel**" means the Employer's Representative, the assistants referred to in Sub-Clause 3.2 [*Other Employer's Personnel*]

通 用 条 件

1 一般规定

1.1
定义

在**合同条件**（“本**条件**”），包括**专用条件**和本**通用条件**中，下列词语和措辞应具有以下所述的含义。除上下文另有要求外，文中人员或当事各方等词语包括公司和其他合法实体。

1.1.1
合同

1.1.1.1 **“合同”**系指**合同协议书**、本**条件**、**雇主要求**、**投标书**和**合同协议书**列出的其他文件(如果有)。

1.1.1.2 **“合同协议书”**系指**第 1.6 款**[*合同协议书*]中所述的合同协议书及所附各项备忘录。

1.1.1.3 **“雇主要求”**系指**合同**中包括的，题为雇主要求的文件，其中列明工程的目标、范围、和(或)设计和(或)其他技术标准，以及按合同对此项文件所作的任何补充和修改。

1.1.1.4 **“投标书”**系指包含在**合同**中的由**承包商**提交的为完成**工程**签署的报价，以及随同提交的所有其他文件(本**条件**和**雇主要求**除外，如同时提交)。

1.1.1.5 **“履约保证”**和**“付款计划表”**系指**合同**中包括的具有上述名称的文件(如果有)。

1.1.2
各方和人员

1.1.2.1 **“当事方(或一方)”**根据上下文需要，或指**雇主**，或指**承包商**。

1.1.2.2 **“雇主”**系指在**合同协议书**中被称为雇主的当事人及其财产所有权的合法继承人。

1.1.2.3 **“承包商”**系指**合同协议书**中被称为承包商的当事人及其财产所有权的合法继承人。

1.1.2.4 **“雇主代表”**系指由**雇主**在**合同**中指名的人员，或有时由**雇主**根据**第 3.1 款**[*雇主代表*]的规定任命为其代表的人员。

1.1.2.5 **“承包商代表”**系指由**承包商**在**合同**中指名的人员，或有时由**承包商**根据**第 4.3 款**[*承包商代表*]的规定任命为其代表的人员。

1.1.2.6 **“雇主人员”**系指**雇主代表**、**第 3.2 款**[*其他雇主人员*]中提到的

GENERAL CONDITIONS

GUIDANCE

FORMS

and all other staff, labour and other employees of the Employer and of the Employer's Representative; and any other personnel notified to the Contractor, by the Employer or the Employer's Representative, as Employer's Personnel.

1.1.2.7 "**Contractor's Personnel**" means the Contractor's Representative and all personnel whom the Contractor utilises on Site, who may include the staff, labour and other employees of the Contractor and of each Subcontractor; and any other personnel assisting the Contractor in the execution of the Works.

1.1.2.8 "**Subcontractor**" means any person named in the Contract as a subcontractor, or any person appointed as a subcontractor, for a part of the Works; and the legal successors in title to each of these persons.

1.1.2.9 "**DAB**" means the person or three persons so named in the Contract, or other person(s) appointed under Sub-Clause 20.2 [*Appointment of the Dispute Adjudication Board*] or Sub-Clause 20.3 [*Failure to Agree Dispute Adjudication Board*].

1.1.2.10 "**FIDIC**" means the Fédération Internationale des Ingénieurs-Conseils, the international federation of consulting engineers.

1.1.3
Dates, Tests, Periods and Completion

1.1.3.1 "**Base Date**" means the date 28 days prior to the latest date for submission of the Tender.

1.1.3.2 "**Commencement Date**" means the date notified under Sub-Clause 8.1 [*Commencement of Works*], unless otherwise defined in the Contract Agreement.

1.1.3.3 "**Time for Completion**" means the time for completing the Works or a Section (as the case may be) under Sub-Clause 8.2 [*Time for Completion*], as stated in the Particular Conditions (with any extension under Sub-Clause 8.4 [*Extension of Time for Completion*]), calculated from the Commencement Date.

1.1.3.4 "**Tests on Completion**" means the tests which are specified in the Contract or agreed by both Parties or instructed as a Variation, and which are carried out under Clause 9 [*Tests on Completion*] before the Works or a Section (as the case may be) are taken over by the Employer.

1.1.3.5 "**Taking-Over Certificate**" means a certificate issued under Clause 10 [*Employer's Taking Over*].

1.1.3.6 "**Tests after Completion**" means the tests (if any) which are specified in the Contract and which are carried out under Clause 12 [*Tests after Completion*] after the Works or a Section (as the case may be) are taken over by the Employer.

1.1.3.7 "**Defects Notification Period**" means the period for notifying defects in the Works or a Section (as the case may be) under Sub-Clause 11.1 [*Completion of Outstanding Work and Remedying Defects*], as stated in the Particular Conditions (with any extension under Sub-Clause 11.3 [*Extension of Defects Notification Period*]), calculated from the date on which the Works or Section is completed as certified under Sub-Clause

助手、以及**雇主**和**雇主代表**的所有其他职员、工人和其他雇员，以及**雇主**或**雇主代表**通知**承包商**作为**雇主人员**的任何其他人员。

1.1.2.7 **“承包商人员”**系指**承包商代表**和**承包商**在**现场**聘用的所有人员，包括**承包商**和每个**分包商**的职员、工人和其他雇员，以及所有其他帮助**承包商**实施**工程**的人员。

1.1.2.8 **“分包商”**系指为完成部分**工程**，在**合同**中指名为分包商、或被任命为分包商的任何人员，以及这些人员财产所有权的合法继承人。

1.1.2.9 **“DAB（争端裁决委员会）”**系指在**合同**中如此指名的一名或三名人员，或根据**第20.2款**[**争端裁决委员会的任命**]或**第20.3款**[**对争端裁决委员会未能取得一致**]的规定任命的其他人员。

1.1.2.10 **“菲迪克（FIDIC）”**系指**国际咨询工程师联合会**。

1.1.3
日期、试验、期限和竣工

1.1.3.1 **“基准日期”**系指递交**投标书**截止日期前28天的日期。

1.1.3.2 **“开工日期”**系指根据**第8.1款**[**工程的开工**]的规定通知的日期，除非**合同协议书**中另有规定。

1.1.3.3 **“竣工时间”**系指**专用条件**中规定的，自**开工日期**算起至**工程**或某**单位工程**（视情况而定）根据**第8.2款**[**竣工时间**]规定的要求竣工（连同根据**第8.4款**[**竣工时间的延长**]的规定提出的任何延长期）的全部时间。

1.1.3.4 **“竣工试验”**系指在**合同**中规定或双方商定的，或按指示作为一项**变更**的，在**工程**或某**单位工程**（视情况而定）被**雇主**接收前，根据**第9条**[**竣工试验**]的要求，进行的试验。

1.1.3.5 **“接收证书”**系指根据**第10条**[**雇主接收**]的规定颁发的证书。

1.1.3.6 **“竣工后试验”**系指在**合同**中规定的，在**工程**或某**单位工程**（视情况而定）被**雇主**接收后，根据**第12条**[**竣工后试验**]的要求，进行的试验（如果有）。

1.1.3.7 **“缺陷通知期限”**系指**专用条件**中规定的，自**工程**或某**单位工程**（视情况而定）根据**第10.1款**[**工程和单位工程的接收**]的规定证明的竣工日期算起，至根据**第11.1款**[**完成扫尾工作和修补缺陷**]的规定通知**工程**或**单位工程**存在缺陷的期限（连同根据**第11.3款**[**缺陷通知期限的延长**]的规定提出的任何延长期）。如果**专用**

GENERAL CONDITIONS

GUIDANCE

FORMS

10.1 [*Taking Over of the Works and Sections*]. If no such period is stated in the Particular Conditions, the period shall be one year.

1.1.3.8 "**Performance Certificate**" means the certificate issued under Sub-Clause 11.9 [*Performance Certificate*].

1.1.3.9 "**day**" means a calendar day and "**year**" means 365 days.

1.1.4
Money and Payments

1.1.4.1 "**Contract Price**" means the agreed amount stated in the Contract Agreement for the design, execution and completion of the Works and the remedying of any defects, and includes adjustments (if any) in accordance with the Contract.

1.1.4.2 "**Cost**" means all expenditure reasonably incurred (or to be incurred) by the Contractor, whether on or off the Site, including overhead and similar charges, but does not include profit.

1.1.4.3 "**Final Statement**" means the statement defined in Sub-Clause 14.11 [*Application for Final Payment*].

1.1.4.4 "**Foreign Currency**" means a currency in which part (or all) of the Contract Price is payable, but not the Local Currency.

1.1.4.5 "**Local Currency**" means the currency of the Country.

1.1.4.6 "**Provisional Sum**" means a sum (if any) which is specified in the Contract as a provisional sum, for the execution of any part of the Works or for the supply of Plant, Materials or services under Sub-Clause 13.5 [*Provisional Sums*].

1.1.4.7 "**Retention Money**" means the accumulated retention moneys which the Employer retains under Sub-Clause 14.3 [*Application for Interim Payments*] and pays under Sub-Clause 14.9 [*Payment of Retention Money*].

1.1.4.8 "**Statement**" means a statement submitted by the Contractor as part of an application for payment under Clause 14 [*Contract Price and Payment*].

1.1.5
Works and Goods

1.1.5.1 "**Contractor's Equipment**" means all apparatus, machinery, vehicles and other things required for the execution and completion of the Works and the remedying of any defects. However, Contractor's Equipment excludes Temporary Works, Employer's Equipment (if any), Plant, Materials and any other things intended to form or forming part of the Permanent Works.

1.1.5.2 "**Goods**" means Contractor's Equipment, Materials, Plant and Temporary Works, or any of them as appropriate.

1.1.5.3 "**Materials**" means things of all kinds (other than Plant) intended to form or forming part of the Permanent Works, including the supply-only materials (if any) to be supplied by the Contractor under the Contract.

1.1.5.4 "**Permanent Works**" means the permanent works to be designed and executed by the Contractor under the Contract.

条件中没有提出这一期限，该期限应为一年。

1.1.3.8 **“履约证书”**系指根据**第 11.9 款**[**履约证书**]的规定颁发的证书。

1.1.3.9 **“日(天)”**系指一个日历日，**“年”**系指 365 天。

1.1.4 款项与付款

1.1.4.1 **“合同价格”**系指在**合同协议书**中写明的、经商定的**工程**设计、施工、竣工和缺陷修补的款额，包括按照**合同**做出的调整（如果有）。

1.1.4.2 **“成本(费用)”**系指**承包商**在**现场**内外所发生(或将发生)的所有合理开支，包括管理费用及类似的支出，但不包括利润。

1.1.4.3 **“最终报表”**系指**第 14.11 款**[**最终付款的申请**]规定的报表。

1.1.4.4 **“外币”**系指可用于支付**合同价格**中部分(或全部)款项的**当地货币**以外的某种货币。

1.1.4.5 **“当地货币”**系指**工程所在国**的货币。

1.1.4.6 **“暂列金额”**系指**合同**中规定作为暂列金额的一笔款额(如果有)，根据**第 13.5 款**[**暂列金额**]的规定，用于**工程**某一部分的实施，或用于提供**生产设备**、**材料**或服务。

1.1.4.7 **“保留金”**系指**雇主**根据**第 14.3 款**[**期中付款的申请**]的规定扣留的保留金累计金额，根据**第 14.9 款**[**保留金的支付**]的规定进行支付。

1.1.4.8 **“报表”**系指**承包商**根据**第 14 条**[**合同价格和付款**]的规定提交的作为付款申请的组成部分的报表。

1.1.5 工程和货物

1.1.5.1 **“承包商设备”**系指为实施和完成**工程**、以及修补任何缺陷需要的所有仪器、机械、车辆和其他物品。但**承包商设备**不包括**临时工程**、**雇主设备**(如果有)、以及拟构成或正构成**永久工程**一部分的**生产设备**、**材料**和其他任何物品。

1.1.5.2 **“货物”**系指**承包商设备**、**材料**、**生产设备**和**临时工程**，或视情况其中任何一种。

1.1.5.3 **“材料”**系指拟构成或正构成**永久工程**一部分的各类物品(**生产设备**除外)，包括根据**合同**要由**承包商**供应的只供材料(如果有)。

1.1.5.4 **“永久工程”**系指根据**合同承包商**要进行设计和施工的永久性工程。

1.1.5.5 "**Plant**" means the apparatus, machinery and vehicles intended to form or forming part of the Permanent Works.

1.1.5.6 "**Section**" means a part of the Works specified in the Particular Conditions as a Section (if any).

1.1.5.7 "**Temporary Works**" means all temporary works of every kind (other than Contractor's Equipment) required on Site for the execution and completion of the Permanent Works and the remedying of any defects.

1.1.5.8 "**Works**" mean the Permanent Works and the Temporary Works, or either of them as appropriate.

1.1.6
Other Definitions

1.1.6.1 "**Contractor's Documents**" means the calculations, computer programs and other software, drawings, manuals, models and other documents of a technical nature supplied by the Contractor under the Contract; as described in Sub-Clause 5.2 [*Contractor's Documents*].

1.1.6.2 "**Country**" means the country in which the Site (or most of it) is located, where the Permanent Works are to be executed.

1.1.6.3 "**Employer's Equipment**" means the apparatus, machinery and vehicles (if any) made available by the Employer for the use of the Contractor in the execution of the Works, as stated in the Employer's Requirements; but does not include Plant which has not been taken over by the Employer.

1.1.6.4 "**Force Majeure**" is defined in Clause 19 [*Force Majeure*].

1.1.6.5 "**Laws**" means all national (or state) legislation, statutes, ordinances and other laws, and regulations and by-laws of any legally constituted public authority.

1.1.6.6 "**Performance Security**" means the security (or securities, if any) under Sub-Clause 4.2 [*Performance Security*].

1.1.6.7 "**Site**" means the places where the Permanent Works are to be executed and to which Plant and Materials are to be delivered, and any other places as may be specified in the Contract as forming part of the Site.

1.1.6.8 "**Variation**" means any change to the Employer's Requirements or the Works, which is instructed or approved as a variation under Clause 13 [*Variations and Adjustments*].

1.2
Interpretation

In the Contract, except where the context requires otherwise:

(a) words indicating one gender include all genders;
(b) words indicating the singular also include the plural and words indicating the plural also include the singular;
(c) provisions including the word "agree", "agreed" or "agreement" require the agreement to be recorded in writing, and
(d) "written" or "in writing" means hand-written, type-written, printed or electronically made, and resulting in a permanent record.

1.1.5.5 **“生产设备”**系指拟构成或正构成**永久工程**一部分的仪器、机械和车辆。

1.1.5.6 **“单位工程”***系指在**专用条件**中确定为**单位工程**(如果有)的**工程**组成部分。

1.1.5.7 **“临时工程”**系指为实施和完成**永久工程**及修补任何缺陷，在现场所需的所有各类临时性工程(**承包商设备**除外)。

1.1.5.8 **“工程”**系指**永久工程**和**临时工程**，或视情况指二者之一。

1.1.6
其他定义

1.1.6.1 **“承包商文件”**系指**第5.2款**[**承包商文件**]中所述的，**承包商**根据**合同**提交的所有计算书、计算机程序和其他软件、图纸、手册、模型、以及其他技术性文件。

1.1.6.2 **“工程所在国”**系指实施**永久工程**的现场(或其大部分)所在的国家。

1.1.6.3 **“雇主设备”**系指**雇主要求**中所述的，由**雇主**提供的供**承包商**在实施**工程**中使用的仪器、机械和车辆(如果有)，但不包括**雇主**尚未接收的**生产设备**。

1.1.6.4 **“不可抗力”**见**第19条**[**不可抗力**]的定义。

1.1.6.5 **“法律”**系指所有全国性(或州的)法律、条例、法令和其他法律，以及任何合法建立的公共当局制定的规则和细则等。

1.1.6.6 **“履约担保”**系指根据**第4.2款**[**履约担保**]规定的担保(或各项担保,如果有)。

1.1.6.7 **“现场”**系指将实施**永久工程**和运送**生产设备**与**材料**到达的地点，以及**合同**中可能指定为**现场**组成部分的任何其他场所。

1.1.6.8 **“变更”**系指按照**第13条**[**变更和调整**]的规定，经指示或批准作为变更的，对**雇主要求**或**工程**所做的任何更改。

1.2
解释

在**合同**中，除上下文另有需要外：

(a) 表示某一性别的词，包括所有性别；
(b) 单数形式的词也包括复数含义，反之亦然；
(c) 包括“同意(商定)”、“已达成(取得)一致”、或“协议”等词的各项规定都要求用书面记载；
(d) “书面”或“用书面”系指手写、打字、印刷、或电子制作，并形成永久性记录。

* 原文“Section”一词系指菲迪克(FIDIC)合同条件或投标书附录中专门定义的能够单独接收使用的部分工程。本译文参照我国建设项目统计划分，选译为“单位工程”，但其含义与我国统计规定的确解释不尽相同。

The marginal words and other headings shall not be taken into consideration in the interpretation of these Conditions.

1.3

Communications

Wherever these Conditions provide for the giving or issuing of approvals, certificates, consents, determinations, notices and requests, these communications shall be:

(a) in writing and delivered by hand (against receipt), sent by mail or courier, or transmitted using any of the agreed systems of electronic transmission as stated in the Particular Conditions; and
(b) delivered, sent or transmitted to the address for the recipient's communications as stated in the Contract. However:

  (i) if the recipient gives notice of another address, communications shall thereafter be delivered accordingly; and
  (ii) if the recipient has not stated otherwise when requesting an approval or consent, it may be sent to the address from which the request was issued.

Approvals, certificates, consents and determinations shall not be unreasonably withheld or delayed.

1.4

Law and Language

The Contract shall be governed by the law of the country (or other jurisdiction) stated in the Particular Conditions.

If there are versions of any part of the Contract which are written in more than one language, the version which is in the ruling language stated in the Particular Conditions shall prevail.

The language for communications shall be that stated in the Particular Conditions. If no language is stated there, the language for communications shall be the language in which the Contract (or most of it) is written.

1.5

Priority of Documents

The documents forming the Contract are to be taken as mutually explanatory of one another. For the purposes of interpretation, the priority of the documents shall be in accordance with the following sequence:

(a) the Contract Agreement,
(b) the Particular Conditions,
(c) these General Conditions,
(d) the Employer's Requirements,
(e) the Tender and any other documents forming part of the Contract.

1.6

Contract Agreement

The Contract shall come into full force and effect on the date stated in the Contract Agreement. The costs of stamp duties and similar charges (if any) imposed by law in connection with entry into the Contract Agreement shall be borne by the Employer.

1.7

Assignment

Neither Party shall assign the whole or any part of the Contract or any benefit or interest in or under the Contract. However, either Party:

(a) may assign the whole or any part with the prior agreement of the other Party, at the sole discretion of such other Party, and

旁注和其他标题在本**条件**的解释中不应考虑。

1.3

通信交流

本**条件**不论在何种场合规定给予或颁发批准、证明、同意、确定、通知和请求时，这些通信信息都应：

(a) 采用书面形式，由人面交(取得对方收据)，通过邮寄或信差传送，或用**专用条件**中提出的任何商定的电子传输方式发送；以及

(b) 交付、传送或传输到**合同**中注明的接收人的地址。但

(i) 如接收人通知了另外地址时，随后通信信息应按新址发送；

(ii) 如接收人在请求批准、同意时没有另外说明，可按请求发出的地址发送。

批准、证明、同意和确定不得无故被扣压或拖延。

1.4

法律和语言

合同应受**专用条件**中所述国家(或其他司法管辖区)的法律管辖。

当**合同**任何部分的文本采用一种以上语言编写时，应以**专用条件**中指定的主导语言文本为准。

通信交流应使用**专用条件**中指定的语言，如未指定，应使用**合同**(或其大部分)编写用的语言。

1.5

文件优先次序

构成**合同**的文件要认为是互作说明的。为了解释的目的，文件的优先次序如下：

(a) **合同协议书**，
(b) **专用条件**，
(c) **本通用条件**，
(d) **雇主要求**，
(e) **投标书**和构成**合同**组成部分的其他文件。

1.6

合同协议书

合同自**合同协议书**规定的日期起全面实施和生效。为签定**合同协议书**，依法征收的印花税和类似的费用(如果有)应由**雇主**承担。

1.7

权益转让

任**一方**都不应将**合同**的全部或任何部分，或**合同**中或根据**合同**所具有的任何利益或权益转让他人。但任**一方**：

(a) 在另**一方**完全自主决定的情况下，事先征得其同意后，可以将全部或部分转让；

(b) may, as security in favour of a bank or financial institution, assign its right to any moneys due, or to become due, under the Contract.

1.8

Care and Supply of Documents

Each of the Contractor's Documents shall be in the custody and care of the Contractor, unless and until taken over by the Employer. Unless otherwise stated in the Contract, the Contractor shall supply to the Employer six copies of each of the Contractor's Documents.

The Contractor shall keep, on the Site, a copy of the Contract, publications named in the Employer's Requirements, the Contractor's Documents, and Variations and other communications given under the Contract. The Employer's Personnel shall have the right of access to all these documents at all reasonable times.

If a Party becomes aware of an error or defect of a technical nature in a document which was prepared for use in executing the Works, the Party shall promptly give notice to the other Party of such error or defect.

1.9

Confidentiality

Both Parties shall treat the details of the Contract as private and confidential, except to the extent necessary to carry out obligations under it or to comply with applicable Laws. The Contractor shall not publish, permit to be published, or disclose any particulars of the Works in any trade or technical paper or elsewhere without the previous agreement of the Employer.

1.10

Employer's Use of Contractor's Documents

As between the Parties, the Contractor shall retain the copyright and other intellectual property rights in the Contractor's Documents and other design documents made by (or on behalf of) the Contractor.

The Contractor shall be deemed (by signing the Contract) to give to the Employer a non-terminable transferable non-exclusive royalty-free licence to copy, use and communicate the Contractor's Documents, including making and using modifications of them. This licence shall:

(a) apply throughout the actual or intended working life (whichever is longer) of the relevant parts of the Works,
(b) entitle any person in proper possession of the relevant part of the Works to copy, use and communicate the Contractor's Documents for the purposes of completing, operating, maintaining, altering, adjusting, repairing and demolishing the Works, and
(c) in the case of Contractor's Documents which are in the form of computer programs and other software, permit their use on any computer on the Site and other places as envisaged by the Contract, including replacements of any computers supplied by the Contractor.

The Contractor's Documents and other design documents made by (or on behalf of) the Contractor shall not, without the Contractor's consent, be used, copied or communicated to a third party by (or on behalf of) the Employer for purposes other than those permitted under this Sub-Clause.

1.11

Contractor's Use of Employer's Documents

As between the Parties, the Employer shall retain the copyright and other intellectual property rights in the Employer's Requirements and other documents made by (or on behalf of) the Employer. The Contractor may, at his cost, copy, use, and obtain communication of these documents for the purposes of the Contract.

(b) 可以作为以银行或金融机构为受款人的担保，转让其根据**合同**规定的任何到期或将到期应得款项的权利。

1.8

文件的照管和提供

每份**承包商文件**都应由**承包商**保存和照管，除非并直到被**雇主**接收为止。除非**合同**中另有规定，**承包商**应向**雇主**提供**承包商文件**一式六份。

承包商应在**现场**保存一份**合同**、**雇主要求**、**承包商文件**、**变更**、以及根据**合同**发出的其他往来文书。**雇主人员**有权在所有合理的时间使用所有这些文件。

如果**一方**发现为实施**工程**准备的文件中有技术性错误或缺陷，应立即将该错误或缺陷通知**另一方**。

1.9

保密性

除了根据**合同**履行义务和遵守适用**法律**的需要以外，**双方**应将**合同**的详情视为私人的和秘密的。没有**雇主**事先同意，**承包商**不得在任何商业或技术论文或其他场合发表或允许发表、或透露**工程**的任何细节。

1.10

雇主使用承包商文件

就各**当事方**间而言，由**承包商**(或以其名义)编制的**承包商**文件及其他设计文件，其版权和其他知识产权应归**承包商**所有。

承包商(通过签署**合同**)应被认为已给予**雇主**无限期的、可转让的、不排他的、免版税的，复制、使用和传送**承包商文件**的许可，包括对它们做出修改和使用修改后的文件的许可。这项许可应：

(a) 适用于**工程**相关部分的实际或预期寿命期(取较长的)；

(b) 允许具有**工程**相关部分正当占有权的任何人，为了完成、操作、维修、更改、调整、修复和拆除**工程**的目的，复制、使用和传送**承包商文件**；

(c) 在**承包商文件**是计算机程序或其他软件形式的情况下，允许它们在**现场**和**合同**中设想的其他场所的任何计算机上使用，包括对**承包商**提供的任何计算机进行替换。

未经**承包商**同意，**雇主**(或以其名义)不得在本款允许以外，为其他目的使用、复制由**承包商**(或以其名义)编制的**承包商文件**和其他设计文件，或将其传送给第三方。

1.11

承包商使用雇主文件

就各**当事方**间而言，由**雇主**(或以其名义)编制的**雇主要求**及其他文件，其版权和其他知识产权应归**雇主**所有。**承包商**因**合同**的目的，可自费复制、使

They shall not, without the Employer's consent, be copied, used or communicated to a third party by the Contractor, except as necessary for the purposes of the Contract.

1.12

Confidential Details

The Contractor shall not be required to disclose, to the Employer, any information which the Contractor described in the Tender as being confidential. The Contractor shall disclose any other information which the Employer may reasonably require in order to verify the Contractor's compliance with the Contract.

1.13

Compliance with Laws

The Contractor shall, in performing the Contract, comply with applicable Laws. Unless otherwise stated in the Particular Conditions:

(a) the Employer shall have obtained (or shall obtain) the planning, zoning or similar permission for the Permanent Works, and any other permissions described in the Employer's Requirements as having been (or being) obtained by the Employer; and the Employer shall indemnify and hold the Contractor harmless against and from the consequences of any failure to do so; and

(b) the Contractor shall give all notices, pay all taxes, duties and fees, and obtain all permits, licences and approvals, as required by the Laws in relation to the design, execution and completion of the Works and the remedying of any defects; and the Contractor shall indemnify and hold the Employer harmless against and from the consequences of any failure to do so.

1.14

Joint and Several Liability

If the Contractor constitutes (under applicable Laws) a joint venture, consortium or other unincorporated grouping of two or more persons:

(a) these persons shall be deemed to be jointly and severally liable to the Employer for the performance of the Contract;

(b) these persons shall notify the Employer of their leader who shall have authority to bind the Contractor and each of these persons; and

(c) the Contractor shall not alter its composition or legal status without the prior consent of the Employer.

2 The Employer

2.1

Right of Access to the Site

The Employer shall give the Contractor right of access to, and possession of, all parts of the Site within the time (or times) stated in the Particular Conditions. The right and possession may not be exclusive to the Contractor. If, under the Contract, the Employer is required to give (to the Contractor) possession of any foundation, structure, plant or means of access, the Employer shall do so in the time and manner stated in the Employer's Requirements. However, the Employer may withhold any such right or possession until the Performance Security has been received.

If no such time is stated in the Particular Conditions, the Employer shall give the Contractor right of access to, and possession of, the Site with effect from the Commencement Date.

If the Contractor suffers delay and/or incurs Cost as a result of a failure by the Employer to give any such right or possession within such time, the Contractor shall

用和传送上述文件。除**合同**需要外，未经**雇主**同意，**承包商**不得复制、使用上述文件，或将其传送给第三方。

1.12

保密事项

不得要求**承包商**向**雇主**透露他在**投标书**中称为是秘密的任何信息。对**雇主**为了证实**承包商**遵守**合同**的情况，合理需要的其他信息，**承包商**应当透露。

1.13

遵守法律

承包商在履行**合同**期间，应遵守适用**法律**。除非**专用条件**中另有规定：

(a) **雇主**应已(或将)为**永久工程**取得规划、区域划定、或类似的许可，以及在**雇主要求**中所述的雇主已(或将)取得的任何其他许可；**雇主**应保障并保持使**承包商**免受因未能完成上述工作带来的损害；

(b) **承包商**应发出所有通知，缴纳各项税费，按照**法律**关于工程设计、实施和竣工、以及修补任何缺陷等方面的要求，办理并领取所需要的全部许可、执照或批准；**承包商**应保障并保持使**雇主**免受因未能完成上述工作带来的损害。

1.14

共同的和各自的责任

如果**承包商**是由两个或两个以上当事人(依照适用**法律**)组成的联营体、联合体，或其他未立案的组合：

(a) 这些当事人应被认为在履行**合同**上对**雇主**负有共同的和各自的责任；

(b) 这些当事人应将有权约束**承包商**及每个当事人的负责人通知**雇主**；

(c) 未经**雇主**事先同意，**承包商**不得改变其组成或法律地位。

---

2 雇主

2.1

现场进入权

雇主应在**专用条件**中规定的时间(或几个时间)内，给**承包商**进入和占用**现场**各部分的权利。此项进入和占用权可不为**承包商**独享。如果根据**合同**，要求**雇主**(向**承包商**)提供任何基础、结构、生产设备或进入手段的占用权，**雇主**应按**雇主要求**中规定的时间和方式提供。但**雇主**在收到**履约担保**前，可保留上述任何进入或占用权，暂不给予。

如果在**专用条件**中没有规定上述时间，**雇主**应自**开工日期**起给**承包商**进入和占用**现场**的权利。

如果**雇主**未能及时给予**承包商**上述进入和占用的权利，使**承包商**遭受延误和(或)招致增加费用，**承包商**应向**雇主**发出通知，根据**第20.1款**[承包商的

give notice to the Employer and shall be entitled subject to Sub-Clause 20.1 [*Contractor's Claims*] to:

(a) an extension of time for any such delay, if completion is or will be delayed, under Sub-Clause 8.4 [*Extension of Time for Completion*], and
(b) payment of any such Cost plus reasonable profit, which shall be added to the Contract Price.

After receiving this notice, the Employer shall proceed in accordance with Sub-Clause 3.5 [*Determinations*] to agree or determine these matters.

However, if and to the extent that the Employer's failure was caused by any error or delay by the Contractor, including an error in, or delay in the submission of, any of the Contractor's Documents, the Contractor shall not be entitled to such extension of time, Cost or profit.

2.2

Permits, Licences or Approvals

The Employer shall (where he is in a position to do so) provide reasonable assistance to the Contractor at the request of the Contractor:

(a) by obtaining copies of the Laws of the Country which are relevant to the Contract but are not readily available, and
(b) for the Contractor's applications for any permits, licences or approvals required by the Laws of the Country:

  (i) which the Contractor is required to obtain under Sub-Clause 1.13 [*Compliance with Laws*],
  (ii) for the delivery of Goods, including clearance through customs, and
  (iii) for the export of Contractor's Equipment when it is removed from the Site.

2.3

Employer's Personnel

The Employer shall be responsible for ensuring that the Employer's Personnel and the Employer's other contractors on the Site:

(a) co-operate with the Contractor's efforts under Sub-Clause 4.6 [*Co-operation*], and
(b) take actions similar to those which the Contractor is required to take under sub-paragraphs (a), (b) and (c) of Sub-Clause 4.8 [*Safety Procedures*] and under Sub-Clause 4.18 [*Protection of the Environment*].

2.4

Employer's Financial Arrangements

The Employer shall submit, within 28 days after receiving any request from the Contractor, reasonable evidence that financial arrangements have been made and are being maintained which will enable the Employer to pay the Contract Price (as estimated at that time) in accordance with Clause 14 [*Contract Price and Payment*]. If the Employer intends to make any material change to his financial arrangements, the Employer shall give notice to the Contractor with detailed particulars.

2.5

Employer's Claims

If the Employer considers himself to be entitled to any payment under any Clause of these Conditions or otherwise in connection with the Contract, and/or to any extension of the Defects Notification Period, he shall give notice and particulars to the Contractor. However, notice is not required for payments due under Sub-Clause 4.19 [*Electricity, Water and Gas*], under Sub-Clause 4.20 [*Employer's Equipment and Free-Issue Material*], or for other services requested by the Contractor.

索赔]的规定有权要求：

(a) 根据**第 8.4 款**[**竣工时间的延长**]的规定，如果竣工已或将受到延误，对任何此类延误，给予延长期；
(b) 任何此类**费用**和合理利润，应加入**合同价格**，给予支付。

在收到此通知后，**雇主**应按照**第 3.5 款**[**确定**]的规定，就这些事项进行商定或确定。

但是，如果出现**雇主**的违约是由于**承包商**的任何错误或延误，包括在任何**承包商文件**中的错误或提交延误造成的情况，**承包商**应无权得到此类延长期、费用或利润。

2.2

许可、执照或批准

雇主应(按其所能)根据**承包商**的请求，应对其提供以下合理的协助：

(a) 取得与**合同**有关，但不易得到的**工程所在国**的**法律**文本；

(b) 协助**承包商**申办**工程所在国法律**要求的以下任何许可、执照或批准：

ⅰ) 根据**第 1.13 款**[**遵守法律**]的规定，**承包商**需要得到的，

ⅱ) 为运送**货物**，包括结关需要的，
ⅲ) 当**承包商设备**运离**现场**出口时需要的。

2.3

雇主人员

雇主应负责保证在**现场**的**雇主人员**和其他承包商做到：

(a) 根据**第 4.6 款**[**合作**]的规定，与**承包商**的各项努力进行合作；

(b) 采取与根据**第 4.8 款**[**安全程序**](a)(b)(c)项和**第 4.18 款**[**环境保护**]要求**承包商**采取的类似行动。

2.4

雇主的资金安排

雇主应在收到**承包商**的任何要求28 天内，提出其已做并将维持的资金安排的合理证明，说明**雇主**能够按照**第 14 条**[**合同价格和付款**]的规定，支付**合同价格**(按当时估算)。如果**雇主**拟对其资金安排做任何重要变更，应将其变更的详细情况通知**承包商**。

2.5

雇主的索赔

如果**雇主**认为，根据本**条件**任何条款、或**合同**有关的另外事项，他有权得到任何付款，和(或)**缺陷通知期限**的任何延长，他应向**承包商**发出通知，说明细节。但对**承包商**根据**第 4.19 款**[**电、水和燃气**]和**第 4.20 款**[**雇主的设备和免费供应的材料**]规定的到期应付款，或**承包商**要求的其他服务的应付款，不需发出通知。

The notice shall be given as soon as practicable after the Employer became aware of the event or circumstances giving rise to the claim. A notice relating to any extension of the Defects Notification Period shall be given before the expiry of such period.

The particulars shall specify the Clause or other basis of the claim, and shall include substantiation of the amount and/or extension to which the Employer considers himself to be entitled in connection with the Contract. The Employer shall then proceed in accordance with Sub-Clause 3.5 [*Determinations*] to agree or determine (i) the amount (if any) which the Employer is entitled to be paid by the Contractor, and/or (ii) the extension (if any) of the Defects Notification Period in accordance with Sub-Clause 11.3 [*Extension of Defects Notification Period*].

The Employer may deduct this amount from any moneys due, or to become due, to the Contractor. The Employer shall only be entitled to set off against or make any deduction from an amount due to the Contractor, or to otherwise claim against the Contractor, in accordance with this Sub-Clause or with sub-paragraph (a) and/or (b) of Sub-Clause 14.6 [*Interim Payments*].

3 The Employer's Administration

3.1
The Employer's Representative

The Employer may appoint an Employer's Representative to act on his behalf under the Contract. In this event, he shall give notice to the Contractor of the name, address, duties and authority of the Employer's Representative.

The Employer's Representative shall carry out the duties assigned to him, and shall exercise the authority delegated to him, by the Employer. Unless and until the Employer notifies the Contractor otherwise, the Employer's Representative shall be deemed to have the full authority of the Employer under the Contract, except in respect of Clause 15 [*Termination by Employer*].

If the Employer wishes to replace any person appointed as Employer's Representative, the Employer shall give the Contractor not less than 14 days' notice of the replacement's name, address, duties and authority, and of the date of appointment.

3.2
Other Employer's Personnel

The Employer or the Employer's Representative may from time to time assign duties and delegate authority to assistants, and may also revoke such assignment or delegation. These assistants may include a resident engineer, and/or independent inspectors appointed to inspect and/or test items of Plant and/or Materials. The assignment, delegation or revocation shall not take effect until a copy of it has been received by the Contractor.

Assistants shall be suitably qualified persons, who are competent to carry out these duties and exercise this authority, and who are fluent in the language for communications defined in Sub-Clause 1.4 [*Law and Language*].

3.3
Delegated Persons

All these persons, including the Employer's Representative and assistants, to whom duties have been assigned or authority has been delegated, shall only be authorised to issue instructions to the Contractor to the extent defined by the delegation. Any approval, check, certificate, consent, examination, inspection, instruction, notice, proposal, request, test, or similar act by a delegated person, in accordance with the delegation, shall have the same effect as though the act had been an act of the Employer. However:

通知应在**雇主**了解引起索赔的事件或情况后尽快发出。关于**缺陷通知期限**任何延长的通知，应在该期限到期前发出。

通知的细节应说明提出索赔根据的**条款**或其他依据，还应包括**雇主**认为根据**合同**他有权得到的索赔金额和(或)延长期的事实根据。然后，**雇主**应按照**第 3.5 款**[**确定**]的要求，商定或确定(ⅰ)**雇主**有权得到**承包商**支付的金额(如果有)，和(或)(ⅱ)按照**第 11.3 款**[**缺陷通知期限的延长**]的规定，得到**缺陷通知期限**的延长期(如果有)。

雇主可将上述金额在给**承包商**的到期或将到期的任何应付款中扣减。**雇主**应仅有权根据本**款**或**第 14.6 款**[**期中付款**](a)和(或)(b)项的规定，从给**承包商**的应付款中冲销或做任何扣减，或另外对**承包商**提出索赔。

3 雇主的管理

3.1

雇主代表

雇主可任命 1 名**雇主代表**，代表他根据**合同**进行工作。在此情况下，他应将**雇主代表**的姓名、地址、任务和权力通知**承包商**。

雇主代表应完成指派给他的任务，履行**雇主**付托给他的权力。除非和直到**雇主**另行通知**承包商**，**雇主代表**将被认为具有**雇主**根据**合同**规定的全部权力，涉及**第 15 条**[**由雇主终止**]规定的权力除外。

如果**雇主**希望替换任何已任命的**雇主代表**，应在不少于 14 天前将替换人的姓名、地址、任务和权力、以及任命的日期通知**承包商**。

3.2

其他雇主人员

雇主或**雇主代表**可随时对一些助手指派和付托一定的任务和权力，也可撤消这些指派或付托。这些助手可包括驻地工程师和(或)担任检验、和(或)试验各项**生产设备**和(或)**材料**的独立检查员。以上指派、付托或撤销，在**承包商**收到抄件后生效。

助手应为具有适当资质的人员、能履行这些任务，行使这些权力的能力，并能流利地使用**第1.4 款**[**法律和语言**]规定的交流语言。

3.3

受托人员

所有这些人员包括已被指派任务或付托权力的**雇主代表**和助手，应只被授权在付托规定的范围内向**承包商**发布指示。由受托人员根据付托做出的任何批准、校核、证明、同意、检查、检验、指示、通知、建议、要求、试验、或类似行动，应如同**雇主**采取的一样有效。但是：

(a) unless otherwise stated in the delegated person's communication relating to such act, it shall not relieve the Contractor from any responsibility he has under the Contract, including responsibility for errors, omissions, discrepancies and non-compliances;
(b) any failure to disapprove any work, Plant or Materials shall not constitute approval, and shall therefore not prejudice the right of the Employer to reject the work, Plant or Materials; and
(c) if the Contractor questions any determination or instruction of a delegated person, the Contractor may refer the matter to the Employer, who shall promptly confirm, reverse or vary the determination or instruction.

3.4
Instructions

The Employer may issue to the Contractor instructions which may be necessary for the Contractor to perform his obligations under the Contract. Each instruction shall be given in writing and shall state the obligations to which it relates and the Sub-Clause (or other term of the Contract) in which the obligations are specified. If any such instruction constitutes a Variation, Clause 13 [*Variations and Adjustments*] shall apply.

The Contractor shall take instructions from the Employer, or from the Employer's Representative or an assistant to whom the appropriate authority has been delegated under this Clause.

3.5
Determinations

Whenever these Conditions provide that the Employer shall proceed in accordance with this Sub-Clause 3.5 to agree or determine any matter, the Employer shall consult with the Contractor in an endeavour to reach agreement. If agreement is not achieved, the Employer shall make a fair determination in accordance with the Contract, taking due regard of all relevant circumstances.

The Employer shall give notice to the Contractor of each agreement or determination, with supporting particulars. Each Party shall give effect to each agreement or determination, unless the Contractor gives notice, to the Employer, of his dissatisfaction with a determination within 14 days of receiving it. Either Party may then refer the dispute to the DAB in accordance with Sub-Clause 20.4 [*Obtaining Dispute Adjudication Board's Decision*].

4 The Contractor

4.1
Contractor's General Obligations

The Contractor shall design, execute and complete the Works in accordance with the Contract, and shall remedy any defects in the Works. When completed, the Works shall be fit for the purposes for which the Works are intended as defined in the Contract.

The Contractor shall provide the Plant and Contractor's Documents specified in the Contract, and all Contractor's Personnel, Goods, consumables and other things and services, whether of a temporary or permanent nature, required in and for this design, execution, completion and remedying of defects.

The Works shall include any work which is necessary to satisfy the Employer's Requirements, or is implied by the Contract, and all works which (although not mentioned in the Contract) are necessary for stability or for the completion, or safe and proper operation, of the Works.

(a) 除非在受托人员关于上述行动的信函中另有说明，该行动不解除**承包商**根据**合同**应承担的任何职责，包括对错误、遗漏、误差和未遵办的职责；

(b) 未对任何工作、**生产设备**或**材料**提出否定意见不应构成批准，因而不应影响**雇主**拒绝该工作、**生产设备**或**材料**的权利；

(c) 如果**承包商**对受托人员的确定或指示提出质疑，**承包商**可将此事项提交给**雇主**，**雇主**应迅速对该确定或指示进行确认、取消或更改。

3.4

指示

雇主可向**承包商**发出为**承包商**根据**合同**履行义务所需要的指示。每项指示都应是书面的，并说明其有关的义务，以及规定这些义务的**条款**(或**合同**的其他条款)。如果任何此类指示构成一项**变更**时，应按照**第 13 条**[**变更和调整**]的规定办理。

承包商应接受**雇主**或**雇主代表**或根据本条受托相应权力的助手的指示。

3.5

确定

每当本**条件**规定**雇主**应按照**第 3.5 款**对任何事项进行商定或确定时，**雇主**应与**承包商**协商尽量达成协议。如果达不成协议，**雇主**应对有关情况给予应有的考虑，按照**合同**作出公正的确定。

雇主应将每项商定或确定，连同依据的细节通知**承包商**。各方都应履行每项商定或确定，除非**承包商**在收到通知14 天内向**雇主**发出通知，对某项确定表示不满。这时，任一方可依照**第 20.4 款**[**取得争端裁决委员会决定**]的规定，将争端提交 DAB。

4 承包商

4.1

承包商的一般义务

承包商应按照**合同**设计、实施和完成**工程**，并修补**工程**中的任何缺陷。完成后，**工程**应能满足**合同**规定的**工程**预期目的。

承包商应提供**合同**规定的**生产设备**和**承包商文件**，以及设计、施工、竣工和修补缺陷所需的所有临时性或永久性的**承包商人员**、**货物**、消耗品及其他物品和服务。

工程应包括为满足**雇主要求**或**合同**隐含要求的任何工作，以及(**合同**虽未提及但)为**工程**的稳定、或完成、或安全和有效运行所需的所有工作。

The Contractor shall be responsible for the adequacy, stability and safety of all Site operations, of all methods of construction and of all the Works.

The Contractor shall, whenever required by the Employer, submit details of the arrangements and methods which the Contractor proposes to adopt for the execution of the Works. No significant alteration to these arrangements and methods shall be made without this having previously been notified to the Employer.

4.2

Performance Security

The Contractor shall obtain (at his cost) a Performance Security for proper performance, in the amount and currencies stated in the Particular Conditions. If an amount is not stated in the Particular Conditions, this Sub-Clause shall not apply.

The Contractor shall deliver the Performance Security to the Employer within 28 days after both Parties have signed the Contract Agreement. The Performance Security shall be issued by an entity and from within a country (or other jurisdiction) approved by the Employer, and shall be in the form annexed to the Particular Conditions or in another form approved by the Employer.

The Contractor shall ensure that the Performance Security is valid and enforceable until the Contractor has executed and completed the Works and remedied any defects. If the terms of the Performance Security specify its expiry date, and the Contractor has not become entitled to receive the Performance Certificate by the date 28 days prior to the expiry date, the Contractor shall extend the validity of the Performance Security until the Works have been completed and any defects have been remedied.

The Employer shall not make a claim under the Performance Security, except for amounts to which the Employer is entitled under the Contract in the event of:

(a) failure by the Contractor to extend the validity of the Performance Security as described in the preceding paragraph, in which event the Employer may claim the full amount of the Performance Security,
(b) failure by the Contractor to pay the Employer an amount due, as either agreed by the Contractor or determined under Sub-Clause 2.5 [*Employer's Claims*] or Clause 20 [*Claims, Disputes and Arbitration*], within 42 days after this agreement or determination,
(c) failure by the Contractor to remedy a default within 42 days after receiving the Employer's notice requiring the default to be remedied, or
(d) circumstances which entitle the Employer to termination under Sub-Clause 15.2 [*Termination by Employer*], irrespective of whether notice of termination has been given.

The Employer shall indemnify and hold the Contractor harmless against and from all damages, losses and expenses (including legal fees and expenses) resulting from a claim under the Performance Security to the extent to which the Employer was not entitled to make the claim.

The Employer shall return the Performance Security to the Contractor within 21 days after the Contractor has become entitled to receive the Performance Certificate.

4.3

Contractor's Representative

The Contractor shall appoint the Contractor's Representative and shall give him all authority necessary to act on the Contractor's behalf under the Contract.

承包商应对所有**现场**作业、所有施工方法和全部**工程**的完备性、稳定性和安全性承担责任。

当**雇主**提出要求时，**承包商**应提交其建议采用的为**工程**施工的安排和方法的细节。事先未通知**雇主**，对这些安排和方法不得做重要改变。

4.2

履约担保

承包商应对严格履约(自费)取得**履约担保**，保证金额与币种应符合**专用条件**中的规定。**专用条件**中没有规定保证金额的，**本款**应不适用。

承包商应在**双方**签署**合同协议书**后28天内，将**履约担保**交给**雇主**。**履约担保**应由**雇主**批准的国家(或其他司法管辖区)内的实体提供，并采用**专用条件**所附格式或采用**雇主**批准的其他格式。

承包商应确保**履约担保**直到其完成**工程**的施工、竣工和修补完任何缺陷前持续有效和可执行。如果在**履约担保**的条款中规定了其期满日期，而**承包商**在该期满日期28天前尚无权拿到**履约证书**，**承包商**应将**履约担保**的有效期延至**工程**竣工和修补完任何缺陷时为止。

除出现以下情况**雇主**根据**合同**有权获得的金额外，**雇主**不应根据**履约担保**提出索赔：

(a) **承包商**未能按前一段所述延长**履约担保**的有效期，这时**雇主**可以索赔**履约担保**的全部金额；

(b) **承包商**未能在商定或确定后42天内，将**承包商**同意的，或按照**第2.5款**[*雇主的索赔*]或**第20条**[*索赔、争端和仲裁*]的规定确定的**承包商**应付金额付给**雇主**；

(c) **承包商**未能在收到**雇主**要求纠正违约的通知后42天内进行纠正；或

(d) **雇主**根据**第15.2款**[*由雇主终止*]的规定有权终止的情况，不管是否已发出终止通知。

雇主应保障并保持**承包商**免受因**雇主**根据**履约担保**提出的超出其本无权索赔范围的索赔引起的所有损害赔偿费、损失和开支(包括法律费用和开支)的损害。

雇主应在**承包商**有权获得**履约证书**后21天内，将**履约担保**退还**承包商**。

4.3

承包商代表

承包商应任命**承包商代表**，并授予他代表**承包商**根据**合同**采取行动所需要的全部权力。

GENERAL CONDITIONS

GUIDANCE

FORMS

Unless the Contractor's Representative is named in the Contract, the Contractor shall, prior to the Commencement Date, submit to the Employer for consent the name and particulars of the person the Contractor proposes to appoint as Contractor's Representative. If consent is withheld or subsequently revoked, or if the appointed person fails to act as Contractor's Representative, the Contractor shall similarly submit the name and particulars of another suitable person for such appointment.

The Contractor shall not, without the prior consent of the Employer, revoke the appointment of the Contractor's Representative or appoint a replacement.

The Contractor's Representative shall, on behalf of the Contractor, receive instructions under Sub-Clause 3.4 [*Instructions*].

The Contractor's Representative may delegate any powers, functions and authority to any competent person, and may at any time revoke the delegation. Any delegation or revocation shall not take effect until the Employer has received prior notice signed by the Contractor's Representative, naming the person and specifying the powers, functions and authority being delegated or revoked.

The Contractor's Representative and all these persons shall be fluent in the language for communications defined in Sub-Clause 1.4 [*Law and Language*].

4.4

Subcontractors

The Contractor shall not subcontract the whole of the Works.

The Contractor shall be responsible for the acts or defaults of any Subcontractor, his agents or employees, as if they were the acts or defaults of the Contractor. Where specified in the Particular Conditions, the Contractor shall give the Employer not less than 28 days' notice of:

(a) the intended appointment of the Subcontractor, with detailed particulars which shall include his relevant experience,
(b) the intended commencement of the Subcontractor's work, and
(c) the intended commencement of the Subcontractor's work on the Site.

4.5

Nominated Subcontractors

In this Sub-Clause, "nominated Subcontractor" means a Subcontractor whom the Employer, under Clause 13 [*Variations and Adjustments*], instructs the Contractor to employ as a Subcontractor. The Contractor shall not be under any obligation to employ a nominated Subcontractor against whom the Contractor raises reasonable objection by notice to the Employer as soon as practicable, with supporting particulars.

4.6

Co-operation

The Contractor shall, as specified in the Contract or as instructed by the Employer, allow appropriate opportunities for carrying out work to:

(a) the Employer's Personnel,
(b) any other contractors employed by the Employer, and
(c) the personnel of any legally constituted public authorities,

who may be employed in the execution on or near the Site of any work not included in the Contract.

Any such instruction shall constitute a Variation if and to the extent that it causes the Contractor to incur Cost in an amount which was not reasonably foreseeable by an

除非**合同**中已写明了**承包商代表**的姓名，**承包商**应在**开工日期**前，将其拟任命为**承包商代表**的人员姓名和详细资料提交**雇主**取得同意。如果未获同意，或随后撤销了同意，或任命的人不能担任**承包商代表**，**承包商**应同样地提交另外适合人选的姓名、详细资料，以取得该项任命。

未经**雇主**事先同意，**承包商**不应撤销**承包商代表**的任命，或任命何替代人员。

承包商代表应代表**承包商**接受根据**第 3.4 款**[**指示**]规定的指示。

承包商代表可向任何胜任的人员付托任何职权、任务和权力，并可随时撤销付托。任何付托或撤销应在**雇主**收到**承包商**代表签发的指明人员姓名、并说明付托或撤销的职权、任务和权力的事先通知后生效。

承包商代表和所有这些人员应能流利地使用**第 1.4 款**[**法律和语言**]规定的交流语言。

4.4

分包商

承包商不得将整个**工程**分包出去。

承包商应对任何**分包商**、其代理人或雇员的行为或违约，如同**承包商**自己的行为或违约一样地负责。对**专用条件**中有规定的，**承包商**应在不少于 28 天前向**雇主**通知以下事项：

(a) 拟雇用的**分包商**，并附包括其相关经验的详细资料，

(b) **分包商**承担工作的拟定开工日期，
(c) **分包商**承担现场工作的拟定开工日期。

4.5

指定的分包商

本**款**中，“指定的**分包商**”系指**雇主**根据**第 13 条**[**变更和调整**]的规定，指示**承包商**雇用的**分包商**。如果**承包商**对指定的**分包商**尽快向**雇主**发出通知，提出合理的反对意见，并附有详细的依据资料，**承包商**不应有任何雇用义务。

4.6

合作

承包商应依据**合同**的规定或**雇主**的指示，为可能被雇用在**现场**或其附近从事本**合同**未包括的任何工作的下列人员进行工作提供适当的机会：

(a) **雇主人员**，
(b) **雇主**雇用的任何其他**承包商**，和
(c) 任何合法建立的公共当局的人员。

如果任何此类指示导致**承包商**增加费用，达到一个有经验的承包商在提交**投标书**时不能合理预见的数额时，该指示应构成一项**变更**。为这些人员和

其他承包商的服务，可包括使用**承包商设备**、以及由**承包商**负责的**临时工程**或进入的安排。

experienced contractor by the date for submission of the Tender. Services for these personnel and other contractors may include the use of Contractor's Equipment, Temporary Works or access arrangements which are the responsibility of the Contractor.

The Contractor shall be responsible for his construction activities on the Site, and shall co-ordinate his own activities with those of other contractors to the extent (if any) specified in the Employer's Requirements.

If, under the Contract, the Employer is required to give to the Contractor possession of any foundation, structure, plant or means of access in accordance with Contractor's Documents, the Contractor shall submit such documents to the Employer in the time and manner stated in the Employer's Requirements.

4.7

Setting Out

The Contractor shall set out the Works in relation to original points, lines and levels of reference specified in the Contract. The Contractor shall be responsible for the correct positioning of all parts of the Works, and shall rectify any error in the positions, levels, dimensions or alignment of the Works.

4.8

Safety Procedures

The Contractor shall:

(a) comply with all applicable safety regulations,
(b) take care for the safety of all persons entitled to be on the Site,
(c) use reasonable efforts to keep the Site and Works clear of unnecessary obstruction so as to avoid danger to these persons,
(d) provide fencing, lighting, guarding and watching of the Works until completion and taking over under Clause 10 [*Employer's Taking Over*], and
(e) provide any Temporary Works (including roadways, footways, guards and fences) which may be necessary, because of the execution of the Works, for the use and protection of the public and of owners and occupiers of adjacent land.

4.9

Quality Assurance

The Contractor shall institute a quality assurance system to demonstrate compliance with the requirements of the Contract. The system shall be in accordance with the details stated in the Contract. The Employer shall be entitled to audit any aspect of the system.

Details of all procedures and compliance documents shall be submitted to the Employer for information before each design and execution stage is commenced. When any document of a technical nature is issued to the Employer, evidence of the prior approval by the Contractor himself shall be apparent on the document itself.

Compliance with the quality assurance system shall not relieve the Contractor of any of his duties, obligations or responsibilities under the Contract.

4.10

Site Data

The Employer shall have made available to the Contractor for his information, prior to the Base Date, all relevant data in the Employer's possession on subsurface and hydrological conditions at the Site, including environmental aspects. The Employer shall similarly make available to the Contractor all such data which come into the Employer's possession after the Base Date.

The Contractor shall be responsible for verifying and interpreting all such data. The Employer shall have no responsibility for the accuracy, sufficiency or completeness of such data, except as stated in Sub-Clause 5.1 [*General Design Responsibilities*].

承包商应对其在**现场**的施工活动负责，并应按照**雇主要求**中规定的范围(如果有)协调其自己与其他承包商的活动。

如果根据**合同**，要求**雇主**按照**承包商文件**向**承包商**提供任何基础、结构、生产设备、或进入手段的占用权，**承包商**应按**雇主要求**中提出的时间和方式，向**雇主**提交此类文件。

4.7

放线

承包商应根据**合同**中规定的原始基准点、基准线和基准标高，给**工程**放线。**承包商**应负责对**工程**的所有部分正确定位，并应纠正**工程**的位置、标高、尺寸或定线中的任何差错。

4.8

安全程序

承包商应：

(a) 遵守所有适用的安全规则；
(b) 照料有权在**现场**的所有人员的安全；
(c) 尽合理的努力保持**现场**和**工程**消除不需要的障碍物，以避免对这些人员造成危险；
(d) 在**工程**竣工和按照**第10条**[*雇主的接收*]的规定移交前，提供围栏、照明，保卫和看守；
(e) 因实施**工程**，为公众和邻近土地的所有人、占用人使用和对其保护，提供可能需要的任何**临时工程**(包括道路、人行路、防护物和围栏等)。

4.9

质量保证

承包商应建立质量保证体系，以论证遵照**合同**要求。该体系应符合**合同**的详细规定。**雇主**有权对体系的任何方面进行审查。

承包商应在每一设计和实施阶段开始前，向**雇主**提交所有程序和如何贯彻要求的文件的细节，供其参考。向**雇主**发送任何技术性文件时，文件本身应有经**承包商**本人事先批准的明显证据。

遵守质量保证体系，不应解除**合同**规定的**承包商**的任何任务、义务和职责。

4.10

现场数据

雇主应在**基准日期**前，将其取得的**现场**地下、水文条件及环境方面的所有有关资料，提供给**承包商**。同样地，**雇主**在**基准日期**后得到的所有此类资料，也应提供给**承包商**。

承包商应负责核实和解释所有此类资料。除**第5.1款**[*设计义务一般要求*]提出的情况以外，**雇主**对这些资料的准确性、充分性和完整性不承担责任。

GENERAL CONDITIONS

GUIDANCE

FORMS

4.11
Sufficiency of the Contract Price

The Contractor shall be deemed to have satisfied himself as to the correctness and sufficiency of the Contract Price.

Unless otherwise stated in the Contract, the Contract Price covers all the Contractor's obligations under the Contract (including those under Provisional Sums, if any) and all things necessary for the proper design, execution and completion of the Works and the remedying of any defects.

4.12
Unforeseeable Difficulties

Except as otherwise stated in the Contract:

(a) the Contractor shall be deemed to have obtained all necessary information as to risks, contingencies and other circumstances which may influence or affect the Works;
(b) by signing the Contract, the Contractor accepts total responsibility for having foreseen all difficulties and costs of successfully completing the Works; and
(c) the Contract Price shall not be adjusted to take account of any unforeseen difficulties or costs.

4.13
Rights of Way and Facilities

The Contractor shall bear all costs and charges for special and/or temporary rights-of-way which he may require, including those for access to the Site. The Contractor shall also obtain, at his risk and cost, any additional facilities outside the Site which he may require for the purposes of the Works.

4.14
Avoidance of Interference

The Contractor shall not interfere unnecessarily or improperly with:

(a) the convenience of the public, or
(b) the access to and use and occupation of all roads and footpaths, irrespective of whether they are public or in the possession of the Employer or of others.

The Contractor shall indemnify and hold the Employer harmless against and from all damages, losses and expenses (including legal fees and expenses) resulting from any such unnecessary or improper interference.

4.15
Access Route

The Contractor shall be deemed to have been satisfied as to the suitability and availability of access routes to the Site. The Contractor shall use reasonable efforts to prevent any road or bridge from being damaged by the Contractor's traffic or by the Contractor's Personnel. These efforts shall include the proper use of appropriate vehicles and routes.

Except as otherwise stated in these Conditions:

(a) the Contractor shall (as between the Parties) be responsible for any maintenance which may be required for his use of access routes;
(b) the Contractor shall provide all necessary signs or directions along access routes, and shall obtain any permission which may be required from the relevant authorities for his use of routes, signs and directions;
(c) the Employer shall not be responsible for any claims which may arise from the use or otherwise of any access route,
(d) the Employer does not guarantee the suitability or availability of particular access routes, and
(e) Costs due to non-suitability or non-availability, for the use required by the Contractor, of access routes shall be borne by the Contractor.

4.11
合同价格的充分性

承包商应被认为已确信**合同价格**的正确性和充分性。

除非**合同**另有规定，**合同价格**包括**承包商**根据**合同**所承担的全部义务(包括根据**暂列金额**所承担的义务,如果有)，以及为正确设计、实施和完成**工程**、并修补任何缺陷所需的全部有关事项的费用。

4.12
不可预见的困难

除**合同**另有说明外：

(a) **承包商**应被认为已取得了对**工程**可能产生影响或作用的有关风险、意外事件和其他情况的全部必要资料；

(b) 通过签署**合同**，**承包商**接受对预见到的为顺利完成**工程**的所有困难和费用的全部职责；

(c) **合同价格**对任何未预见到的困难和费用不应考虑予以调整。

4.13
道路通行权与设施

承包商应为其所需要的专用和(或)临时道路包括**进场**道路的通行权，承担全部费用和开支。**承包商**还应自担风险和费用，取得为**工程**目的可能需要的**现场**以外的任何附加设施。

4.14
避免干扰

承包商应避免对以下事项产生不必要或不当的干扰：

(a) 公众的方便，或

(b) 所有道路和人行道的进入、使用和占用，不论它们是公共的，或是**雇主**或其他人所有的。

承包商应保障并保持**雇主**免受因任何此类不必要或不当的干扰造成任何损害赔偿费、损失和开支(包括法律费用和开支)的损害。

4.15
进场通路

承包商应被认为已对现场的进入通路的适宜性和可用性感到满意。**承包商**应尽合理的努力，防止任何道路或桥梁因**承包商**的通行或**承包商人员**受到损坏。这些努力应包括正确使用适宜的车辆和通路。

除本**条件**另有规定外：

(a) **承包商**应(就各方间言)负责因他使用进场通路所需要的任何维护；

(b) **承包商**应提供进场通路的所有必需的标志或方向指示，还应为其使用这些通路、标志和方向指示取得必要的有关当局的许可；

(c) **雇主**不应对由于任何进场通路的使用或其他原因引起的索赔负责；

(d) **雇主**不保证特定进场通路的适宜性和可用性；

(e) 因进场通路对**承包商**的使用要求不适宜、不可用而发生的费用应由**承包商**负担。

GENERAL CONDITIONS

GUIDANCE

FORMS

4.16
Transport of Goods

Unless otherwise stated in the Particular Conditions:

(a) the Contractor shall give the Employer not less than 21 days' notice of the date on which any Plant or a major item of other Goods will be delivered to the Site;
(b) the Contractor shall be responsible for packing, loading, transporting, receiving, unloading, storing and protecting all Goods and other things required for the Works; and
(c) the Contractor shall indemnify and hold the Employer harmless against and from all damages, losses and expenses (including legal fees and expenses) resulting from the transport of Goods, and shall negotiate and pay all claims arising from their transport.

4.17

Contractor's Equipment

The Contractor shall be responsible for all Contractor's Equipment. When brought on to the Site, Contractor's Equipment shall be deemed to be exclusively intended for the execution of the Works.

4.18

Protection of the Environment

The Contractor shall take all reasonable steps to protect the environment (both on and off the Site) and to limit damage and nuisance to people and property resulting from pollution, noise and other results of his operations.

The Contractor shall ensure that emissions, surface discharges and effluent from the Contractor's activities shall not exceed the values indicated in the Employer's Requirements, and shall not exceed the values prescribed by applicable Laws.

4.19

Electricity, Water and Gas

The Contractor shall, except as stated below, be responsible for the provision of all power, water and other services he may require.

The Contractor shall be entitled to use for the purposes of the Works such supplies of electricity, water, gas and other services as may be available on the Site and of which details and prices are given in the Employer's Requirements. The Contractor shall, at his risk and cost, provide any apparatus necessary for his use of these services and for measuring the quantities consumed.

The quantities consumed and the amounts due (at these prices) for such services shall be agreed or determined in accordance with Sub-Clause 2.5 [*Employer's Claims*] and Sub-Clause 3.5 [*Determinations*]. The Contractor shall pay these amounts to the Employer.

4.20

Employer's Equipment and Free-Issue Material

The Employer shall make the Employer's Equipment (if any) available for the use of the Contractor in the execution of the Works in accordance with the details, arrangements and prices stated in the Employer's Requirements. Unless otherwise stated in the Employer's Requirements:

(a) the Employer shall be responsible for the Employer's Equipment, except that
(b) the Contractor shall be responsible for each item of Employer's Equipment whilst any of the Contractor's Personnel is operating it, driving it, directing it or in possession or control of it.

The appropriate quantities and the amounts due (at such stated prices) for the use of Employer's Equipment shall be agreed or determined in accordance with Sub-Clause 2.5 [*Employer's Claims*] and Sub-Clause 3.5 [*Determinations*]. The Contractor shall pay these amounts to the Employer.

4.16
货物运输

除非**专用条件**中另有规定：

(a) **承包商**应在不少于 21 天前，将任何**生产设备**或每项其他主要**货物**将运到**现场**的日期，通知**雇主**；
(b) **承包商**应负责**工程**需要的所有**货物**和其他物品的包装、装货、运输、接收、卸货、存储和保护；

(c) **承包商**应保障并保持**雇主**免受因**货物**运输引起的所有损害赔偿费、损失和开支(包括法律费用和开支)的损害，并应协商和支付由于**货物**运输引起的所有索赔。

4.17
承包商设备

承包商应负责所有**承包商设备**。**承包商设备**运到**现场**后，应视作准备为**工程**施工专用。

4.18
环境保护

承包商应采取一切适当措施，保护(**现场**内外)环境，限制由其施工作业引起的污染、噪音和其他后果对公众和财产造成的损害和妨害。

承包商应确保因其活动产生的气体排放、地面排水及排污等，不超过**雇主要求**中规定的数值，也不超过适用**法律**规定的数值。

4.19
电、水和燃气

除下述情况外，**承包商**应负责供应其所需的所有电、水和其他服务。

承包商应有权因**工程**的需要使用**现场**可供的电、水、燃气和其他服务,其详细规定和价格见**雇主要求**。**承包商**应自担风险和费用，提供他使用这些服务和计量所需要的任何仪器。

这些服务的耗用数量和应付金额(按其价格)，应根据**第 2.5 款**[*雇主的索赔*]和**第 3.5 款**[*确定*]的要求商定或确定。**承包商**应向**雇主**支付此金额。

4.20
雇主设备和免费供应的材料

雇主应准备**雇主设备**(如果有)，供**承包商**按照**雇主要求**中规定的细节、安排和价格，在**工程**实施中使用。除非**雇主要求**中另有说明：

(a) 除下列(b)项所列情况外，**雇主**应对**雇主设备**负责，
(b) 当任何**承包商人员**操作、驾驶、指挥、或占用或控制某项**雇主设备**时，**承包商**应对该项**设备**负责。

使用**雇主设备**的适当数量和应付费用金额(按规定价格)，应按**第 2.5 款**[*雇主的索赔*]和**第 3.5 款**[*确定*]的要求商定或确定。**承包商**应向**雇主**支付此金额。

The Employer shall supply, free of charge, the "free-issue materials" (if any) in accordance with the details stated in the Employer's Requirements. The Employer shall, at his risk and cost, provide these materials at the time and place specified in the Contract. The Contractor shall then visually inspect them, and shall promptly give notice to the Employer of any shortage, defect or default in these materials. Unless otherwise agreed by both Parties, the Employer shall immediately rectify the notified shortage, defect or default.

After this visual inspection, the free-issue materials shall come under the care, custody and control of the Contractor. The Contractor's obligations of inspection, care, custody and control shall not relieve the Employer of liability for any shortage, defect or default not apparent from a visual inspection.

4.21

Progress Reports

Unless otherwise stated in the Particular Conditions, monthly progress reports shall be prepared by the Contractor and submitted to the Employer in six copies. The first report shall cover the period up to the end of the first calendar month following the Commencement Date. Reports shall be submitted monthly thereafter, each within 7 days after the last day of the period to which it relates.

Reporting shall continue until the Contractor has completed all work which is known to be outstanding at the completion date stated in the Taking-Over Certificate for the Works.

Each report shall include:

(a) charts and detailed descriptions of progress, including each stage of design, Contractor's Documents, procurement, manufacture, delivery to Site, construction, erection, testing, commissioning and trial operation;
(b) photographs showing the status of manufacture and of progress on the Site;
(c) for the manufacture of each main item of Plant and Materials, the name of the manufacturer, manufacture location, percentage progress, and the actual or expected dates of:

    (i) commencement of manufacture,
    (ii) Contractor's inspections,
    (iii) tests, and
    (iv) shipment and arrival at the Site;

(d) the details described in Sub-Clause 6.10 [*Records of Contractor's Personnel and Equipment*];
(e) copies of quality assurance documents, test results and certificates of Materials;
(f) list of Variations, notices given under Sub-Clause 2.5 [*Employer's Claims*] and notices given under Sub-Clause 20.1 [*Contractor's Claims*];
(g) safety statistics, including details of any hazardous incidents and activities relating to environmental aspects and public relations; and
(h) comparisons of actual and planned progress, with details of any events or circumstances which may jeopardize the completion in accordance with the Contract, and the measures being (or to be) adopted to overcome delays.

4.22

Security of the Site

Unless otherwise stated in the Particular Conditions:

(a) the Contractor shall be responsible for keeping unauthorised persons off the Site, and

雇主应按照**雇主要求**中规定的细节，免费提供“免费供应的材料”（如果有）。**雇主**应自行承担风险和费用，按照**合同**规定的时间和地点供应这些材料。随后，**承包商**应对其进行目视检查，并将这些材料的短少、缺陷或缺项迅速通知**雇主**。除非**双方**另有协议，**雇主**应立即改正通知指出的短少、缺陷或缺项。

目视检查后，这些免费供应的材料应由**承包商**照管、监护和控制。**承包商**的检查、照管、监护和控制的义务，不应解除**雇主**对目视检查难发现的任何短少、缺陷或缺项所负的责任。

4.21 进度报告

除非**专用条件**中另有规定，**承包商**应编制月进度报告，一式六份，提交给**雇主**。第一次报告所包含的期间，应自**开工日期**起至当月的月底止。以后应每月报告一次，在每次报告期最后一天后 7 日内报出。

报告应持续到**承包商**完成**工程移交证书**注明的竣工日期时所有未完扫尾工作为止。

每次报告应包括：

(a) 设计、**承包商文件**、采购、制造、货物运达**现场**、施工、安装、试验、投产准备和试运行等每一阶段进展情况的图表和详细说明；

(b) 反映制造情况和**现场**进展情况的照片；

(c) 关于每项主要**工程设备**和**材料**的生产、制造商名称、制造地点、进度百分比，以及下列事项的实际或预计日期：

（ⅰ）开始制造，
（ⅱ）**承包商**检验，
（ⅲ）试验，
（ⅳ）发货和运抵**现场**；

(d) **第 6.10 款**[*承包商的人员和设备的记录*]中所述的细节；

(e) **材料**的质量保证文件、试验结果及合格证的副本；

(f) **变更**、根据**第 2.5 款**[*雇主的索赔*]的规定发出的通知和根据**第 20.1 款**[*承包商的索赔*]的规定发出的通知的清单；

(g) 安全统计，包括对环境和公共关系有危害的任何事件和活动的详细情况；

(h) 实际进度与计划进度的对比，包括可能影响按**合同**竣工的任何事件或情况的详情，以及为消除延误正在(或准备)采取的措施。

4.22 现场保安

除非**专用条件**中另有规定：

(a) **承包商**应负责阻止未经授权的人员进入**现场**；

GENERAL CONDITIONS

GUIDANCE

FORMS

(b) authorised persons shall be limited to the Contractor's Personnel and the Employer's Personnel; and to any other personnel notified to the Contractor, by (or on behalf of) the Employer, as authorised personnel of the Employer's other contractors on the Site.

4.23

Contractor's Operations on Site

The Contractor shall confine his operations to the Site, and to any additional areas which may be obtained by the Contractor and agreed by the Employer as working areas. The Contractor shall take all necessary precautions to keep Contractor's Equipment and Contractor's Personnel within the Site and these additional areas, and to keep them off adjacent land.

During the execution of the Works, the Contractor shall keep the Site free from all unnecessary obstruction, and shall store or dispose of any Contractor's Equipment or surplus materials. The Contractor shall clear away and remove from the Site any wreckage, rubbish and Temporary Works which are no longer required.

Upon the issue of the Taking-Over Certificate for the Works, the Contractor shall clear away and remove all Contractor's Equipment, surplus material, wreckage, rubbish and Temporary Works. The Contractor shall leave the Site and the Works in a clean and safe condition. However, the Contractor may retain on Site, during the Defects Notification Period, such Goods as are required for the Contractor to fulfil obligations under the Contract.

4.24

Fossils

All fossils, coins, articles of value or antiquity, and structures and other remains or items of geological or archaeological interest found on the Site shall be placed under the care and authority of the Employer. The Contractor shall take reasonable precautions to prevent Contractor's Personnel or other persons from removing or damaging any of these findings.

The Contractor shall, upon discovery of any such finding, promptly give notice to the Employer, who shall issue instructions for dealing with it. If the Contractor suffers delay and/or incurs Cost from complying with the instructions, the Contractor shall give a further notice to the Employer and shall be entitled subject to Sub-Clause 20.1 [*Contractor's Claims*] to:

(a) an extension of time for any such delay, if completion is or will be delayed, under Sub-Clause 8.4 [*Extension of Time for Completion*], and

(b) payment of any such Cost, which shall be added to the Contract Price.

After receiving this further notice, the Employer shall proceed in accordance with Sub-Clause 3.5 [*Determinations*] to agree or determine these matters.

5 Design

5.1

General Design Obligations

The Contractor shall be deemed to have scrutinised, prior to the Base Date, the Employer's Requirements (including design criteria and calculations, if any). The Contractor shall be responsible for the design of the Works and for the accuracy of *such Employer's Requirements (including design criteria and calculations)*, except as stated below.

(b) 授权人员应仅限于**承包商人员**和**雇主人员**、以及由(或代表)**雇主**通知**承包商**，作为**雇主**在**现场**的其他承包商的授权人员的任何其他人员。

4.23 承包商的现场作业

承包商应将其作业限制在**现场**、以及**承包商**可得到并经**雇主**同意作为工作场地的任何附加区域内。**承包商**应采取一切必要的预防措施，以保持**承包商设备**和**承包商人员**处在**现场**和此类附加区域内，避免他们进入邻近地区。

在**工程**施工期间，**承包商**应保持**现场**没有一切不必要的障碍物，并应妥善存放和处置**承包商设备**或剩余的材料。**承包商**应从**现场**清除并运走任何残物、垃圾和不再需要的**临时工程**。

在颁发**工程接收证书**后，**承包商**应清除并运走所有**承包商设备**、剩余材料、残物、垃圾和**临时工程**。**承包商**应使**现场**和**工程**处于清洁和安全的状况。但在**缺陷通知期限**内，**承包商**可在**现场**保留其根据**合同**完成规定义务所需要的此类**货物**。

4.24 化石

在**现场**发现的所有化石、硬币、有价值的物品或古物、以及具有地质或考古意义的结构物和其他遗迹或物品，应置于**雇主**的照管和权限下。**承包商**应采取合理预防措施，防止**承包商人员**或其他人员移动或损坏任何这类发现物。

一旦发现任何上述物品，**承包商**应迅速通知**雇主**。**雇主**应就处理上述物品发出指示。如果**承包商**因执行这些指示遭受延误和(或)招致**费用**，**承包商**应向**雇主**再次发出通知，有权根据**第 20.1 款**[*承包商的索赔*]的规定提出：

(a) 根据**第 8.4 款**[*竣工时间的延长*]的规定，如果竣工已或将受到延误对任何此类延误给予延长期；
(b) 任何此类**费用**应加入**合同价格**，给予支付。

雇主收到上述再次通知后，应按照**第 3.5 款**[*确定*]的要求，商定或确定这些事项。

5 设计

5.1 设计义务一般要求

承包商应被视为，在**基准日期**前已仔细审查了**雇主要求**(包括设计标准和计算，如果有)。**承包商**应负责**工程**的设计，并在除下列**雇主**应负责的部分外，对**雇主要求**(包括设计标准和计算)的正确性负责。

The Employer shall not be responsible for any error, inaccuracy or omission of any kind in the Employer's Requirements as originally included in the Contract and shall not be deemed to have given any representation of accuracy or completeness of any data or information, except as stated below. Any data or information received by the Contractor, from the Employer or otherwise, shall not relieve the Contractor from his responsibility for the design and execution of the Works.

However, the Employer shall be responsible for the correctness of the following portions of the Employer's Requirements and of the following data and information provided by (or on behalf of) the Employer:

(a) portions, data and information which are stated in the Contract as being immutable or the responsibility of the Employer,
(b) definitions of intended purposes of the Works or any parts thereof,
(c) criteria for the testing and performance of the completed Works, and
(d) portions, data and information which cannot be verified by the Contractor, except as otherwise stated in the Contract.

5.2

Contractor's Documents

The Contractor's Documents shall comprise the technical documents specified in the Employer's Requirements, documents required to satisfy all regulatory approvals, and the documents described in Sub-Clause 5.6 [*As-Built Documents*] and Sub-Clause 5.7 [*Operation and Maintenance Manuals*]. Unless otherwise stated in the Employer's Requirements, the Contractor's Documents shall be written in the language for communications defined in Sub-Clause 1.4 [*Law and Language*].

The Contractor shall prepare all Contractor's Documents, and shall also prepare any other documents necessary to instruct the Contractor's Personnel.

If the Employer's Requirements describe the Contractor's Documents which are to be submitted to the Employer for review, they shall be submitted accordingly, together with a notice as described below. In the following provisions of this Sub-Clause, (i) "review period" means the period required by the Employer for review, and (ii) "Contractor's Documents" exclude any documents which are not specified as being required to be submitted for review.

Unless otherwise stated in the Employer's Requirements, each review period shall not exceed 21 days, calculated from the date on which the Employer receives a Contractor's Document and the Contractor's notice. This notice shall state that the Contractor's Document is considered ready, both for review in accordance with this Sub-Clause and for use. The notice shall also state that the Contractor's Document complies with the Contract, or the extent to which it does not comply.

The Employer may, within the review period, give notice to the Contractor that a Contractor's Document fails (to the extent stated) to comply with the Contract. If a Contractor's Document so fails to comply, it shall be rectified, resubmitted and reviewed in accordance with this Sub-Clause, at the Contractor's cost.

For each part of the Works, and except to the extent that the Parties otherwise agree:

(a) execution of such part of the Works shall not commence prior to the expiry of the review periods for all the Contractor's Documents which are relevant to its design and execution;
(b) execution of such part of the Works shall be in accordance with these Contractor's Documents, as submitted for review; and

除下述情况外，**雇主**不应对原包括在**合同**内的**雇主要求**中的任何错误、不准确、或遗漏负责，并不应被认为，对任何数据或资料给出了任何准确性或完整性的表示。**承包商**从**雇主**或其他方面收到任何数据或资料，不应解除**承包商**对设计和**工程**施工承担的职责。

但是，**雇主**应对**雇主要求**中的下列部分，以及由(或代表)**雇主**提供的下列数据和资料的正确性负责：

(a) 在**合同**中规定的由**雇主**负责的、或不可变的部分、数据和资料，

(b) 对**工程**或其任何部分的预期目的的说明，
(c) 竣工**工程**的试验和性能的标准，
(d) 除**合同**另有说明外，**承包商**不能核实的部分、数据和资料。

5.2 承包商文件

承包商文件应包括**雇主要求**中规定的技术文件、为满足所有规章要求报批的文件、以及**第 5.6 款**[**竣工文件**]和**第 5.7 款**[**操作和维修手册**]中所述的文件。除非**雇主要求**中另有说明，**承包商文件**应使用**第 1.4 款**[**法律和语言**]中规定的交流语言书写。

承包商应编制所有**承包商文件**，还应编制指导**承包商人员**所需要的任何其他文件。

如果**雇主要求**中描述了要提交**雇主**审核的**承包商文件**，这些文件应依照要求，连同下文叙述的通知一并上报。在**本款**下列规定中，(ⅰ)“审核期”系指**雇主**审核需要的期限，以及(ⅱ)“**承包商文件**”不包括未规定要提交审核的任何文件。

除非**雇主要求**中另有说明，每项审核期，从**雇主**收到一份**承包商文件**和**承包商**通知的日期算起不应超过 21 天。该通知应说明，本**承包商文件**是已可供按照**本款**进行审核和使用。通知还应说明本**承包商文件**符合**合同**规定的情况，或在哪些范围不符合。

雇主在审核期可向**承包商**发出通知，指出**承包商文件**(在说明的范围)不符合**合同**的规定。如果**承包商文件**确实如此不符合，该文件应由**承包商**承担费用，按照**本款**修正，重新上报，并审核。

除**双方**另有协议的范围外，对**工程**每一部分都应：

(a) 在有关该部分的设计和施工的**承包商文件**的审核期尚未期满前，不得开工；

(b) 该部分的实施，应按上报审核的**承包商文件**进行；

(c) if the Contractor wishes to modify any design or document which has previously been submitted for review, the Contractor shall immediately give notice to the Employer. Thereafter, the Contractor shall submit revised documents to the Employer in accordance with the above procedure.

Any such agreement (under the preceding paragraph) or any review (under this Sub-Clause or otherwise) shall not relieve the Contractor from any obligation or responsibility.

5.3

Contractor's Undertaking

The Contractor undertakes that the design, the Contractor's Documents, the execution and the completed Works will be in accordance with:

(a) the Laws in the Country, and
(b) the documents forming the Contract, as altered or modified by Variations.

5.4

Technical Standards and Regulations

The design, the Contractor's Documents, the execution and the completed Works shall comply with the Country's technical standards, building, construction and environmental Laws, Laws applicable to the product being produced from the Works, and other standards specified in the Employer's Requirements, applicable to the Works, or defined by the applicable Laws.

All these Laws shall, in respect of the Works and each Section, be those prevailing when the Works or Section are taken over by the Employer under Clause 10 [*Employer's Taking Over*]. References in the Contract to published standards shall be understood to be references to the edition applicable on the Base Date, unless stated otherwise.

If changed or new applicable standards come into force in the Country after the Base Date, the Contractor shall give notice to the Employer and (if appropriate) submit proposals for compliance. In the event that:

(a) the Employer determines that compliance is required, and
(b) the proposals for compliance constitute a variation,

then the Employer shall initiate a Variation in accordance with Clause 13 [*Variations and Adjustments*].

5.5

Training

The Contractor shall carry out the training of Employer's Personnel in the operation and maintenance of the Works to the extent specified in the Employer's Requirements. If the Contract specifies training which is to be carried out before taking-over, the Works shall not be considered to be completed for the purposes of taking-over under Sub-Clause 10.1 [*Taking Over of the Works and Sections*] until this training has been completed.

5.6

As-Built Documents

The Contractor shall prepare, and keep up-to-date, a complete set of "as-built" records of the execution of the Works, showing the exact as-built locations, sizes and details of the work as executed. These records shall be kept on the Site and shall be used exclusively for the purposes of this Sub-Clause. Two copies shall be supplied to the Employer prior to the commencement of the Tests on Completion.

In addition, the Contractor shall supply to the Employer as-built drawings of the Works, showing all Works as executed, and submit them to the Employer for review

(c) 如果**承包商**希望对已送审的设计或文件进行修改，应立即通知**雇主**。然后，**承包商**应按照上述程序将修改后的文件提交**雇主**。

(根据前一段的)任何协议，或(根据**本款**或其他条款的)任何审核，都不应解除**承包商**的任何义务或职责。

5.3 承包商的承诺

承包商承诺其设计、**承包商文件**、实施和竣工的**工程**符合：

(a) **工程所在国**的**法律**，
(b) 经过**变更**做出更改或修正时，构成**合同**的各项文件。

5.4 技术标准和法规

设计、**承包商文件**、施工和竣工**工程**，均应符合**工程所在国**的技术标准、建筑、施工与环境方面的**法律**、适用于**工程**将生产的产品的**法律**、以及**雇主要求**中提出的适用于**工程**、或适用**法律**规定的其他标准。

所有这些关于**工程**和其各**单位工程**的法规，应是在**雇主**根据**第 10 条**[**雇主的接收**]的规定接收**工程**或**单位工程**时通行的。除非另有说明，**合同**中提到的各项已公布的标准，应视为在**基准日期**适用的版本。

如果在**基准日期**后，上述版本有修改或有新的标准生效，**承包商**应通知**雇主**，并(如适宜)提交遵守新标准的建议书。如果：

(a) **雇主**确定需要遵守，
(b) 遵守新标准的建议书构成一项**变更**时，

雇主应按照**第 13 条**[**变更和调整**]的规定着手做出**变更**。

5.5 培训

承包商应按照**雇主要求**中规定的范围，对**雇主人员**进行工程操作和维修培训。如果**合同**规定了工程接收前要进行培训，在此项培训结束前，不应认为**工程**已按照**第 10.1 款**[**工程和单位工程的接收**]规定的接收要求竣工。

5.6 竣工文件

承包商应编制并随时更新一套完整的**工程**施工“竣工”记录，如实记载竣工的准确位置、尺寸和已实施工作的详细说明。上述竣工记录应保存在**现场**，并仅限用于本款的目的。应在**竣工试验**开始前，提交两套副本给**雇主**。

此外，**承包商**应负责绘制并向**雇主**提供**工程**的竣工图，表明整个**工程**的施工完毕的实际情况，提交**雇主**根据**第 5.2 款**[**承包商文件**]的规定进行审核。

under Sub-Clause 5.2 [*Contractor's Documents*]. The Contractor shall obtain the consent of the Employer as to their size, the referencing system, and other relevant details.

Prior to the issue of any Taking-Over Certificate, the Contractor shall supply to the Employer the specified numbers and types of copies of the relevant as-built drawings, in accordance with the Employer's Requirements. The Works shall not be considered to be completed for the purposes of taking-over under Sub-Clause 10.1 [*Taking Over of the Works and Sections*] until the Employer has received these documents.

5.7

Operation and Maintenance Manuals

Prior to commencement of the Tests on Completion, the Contractor shall supply to the Employer provisional operation and maintenance manuals in sufficient detail for the Employer to operate, maintain, dismantle, reassemble, adjust and repair the Plant.

The Works shall not be considered to be completed for the purposes of taking-over under Sub-Clause 10.1 [*Taking Over of the Works and Sections*] until the Employer has received final operation and maintenance manuals in such detail, and any other manuals specified in the Employer's Requirements for these purposes.

5.8

Design Error

If errors, omissions, ambiguities, inconsistencies, inadequacies or other defects are found in the Contractor's Documents, they and the Works shall be corrected at the Contractor's cost, notwithstanding any consent or approval under this Clause.

6 Staff and Labour

6.1

Engagement of Staff and Labour

Except as otherwise stated in the Employer's Requirements, the Contractor shall make arrangements for the engagement of all staff and labour, local or otherwise, and for their payment, housing, feeding and transport.

6.2

Rates of Wages and Conditions of Labour

The Contractor shall pay rates of wages, and observe conditions of labour, which are not lower than those established for the trade or industry where the work is carried out. If no established rates or conditions are applicable, the Contractor shall pay rates of wages and observe conditions which are not lower than the general level of wages and conditions observed locally by employers whose trade or industry is similar to that of the Contractor.

6.3

Persons in the Service of Employer

The Contractor shall not recruit, or attempt to recruit, staff and labour from amongst the Employer's Personnel.

6.4

Labour Laws

The Contractor shall comply with all the relevant labour Laws applicable to the Contractor's Personnel, including Laws relating to their employment, health, safety, welfare, immigration and emigration, and shall allow them all their legal rights.

The Contractor shall require his employees to obey all applicable Laws, including those concerning safety at work.

6.5

Working Hours

No work shall be carried out on the Site on locally recognised days of rest, or outside normal working hours, unless:

承包商应取得**雇主**对它们的尺寸、基准体系、及其他相关细节的同意。

在颁发任何**接收证书**前，**承包商**应按照**雇主要求**中规定的份数和复制形式，向**雇主**提交上述相关的竣工图。在**雇主**收到这些文件前，不应认为**工程**已经按照**第 10.1 款**[**工程和单位工程的接收**]规定的接收要求竣工。

5.7

操作和维修手册

在**竣工试验**开始前，**承包商**应向**雇主**提供暂行的操作和维修手册，上述操作和维修手册的详细程度，应能满足**雇主**操作、维修、拆卸、重新组装、调整和修复**生产设备**的需要。

在**雇主**收到足够详细的最后的操作和维修手册和**雇主要求**中为此类目的规定的其他手册前，不应认为**工程**已经按照**第 10.1 款**[**工程和单位工程的接收**]规定的接收要求竣工。

5.8

设计错误

如果在**承包商文件**中发现有错误、遗漏、含糊、不一致、不适当或其他缺陷，尽管根据本**条**做出了任何同意或批准，**承包商**仍应自费对这些缺陷和其带来的**工程**问题进行改正。

6 员工

6.1

员工的雇用

除**雇主要求**中另有说明外，**承包商**应安排从当地或其他地方雇用所有的员工，并负责他们的报酬、住宿、膳食和交通。

6.2

工资标准和劳动条件

承包商所付的工资标准及遵守的劳动条件，应不低于实施工作的地区该工种或行业制订的标准和条件。如果没有现成的标准和条件可以引用，**承包商**所付的工资标准及遵守的劳动条件，应不低于当地与**承包商**类似的工种或行业雇主所付的一般工资标准及遵守的劳动条件。

6.3

为雇主服务的人员

承包商不应从**雇主人员**中招收或试图招收员工。

6.4

劳动法

承包商应遵守所有适用于**承包商人员**的相关劳动**法律**，包括有关他们的雇用、健康、安全、福利、入境和出境等**法律**，并应允许他们享有所有合法权利。

承包商应要求其雇员遵守所有适用的**法律**，包括有关工作安全的**法律**。

6.5

工作时间

除非出现下列情况，在当地公认的休息日，或在正常工作时间以外，不应在**现场**进行工作：

(a) otherwise stated in the Contract,
(b) the Employer gives consent, or
(c) the work is unavoidable, or necessary for the protection of life or property or for the safety of the Works, in which case the Contractor shall immediately advise the Employer.

6.6

Facilities for Staff and Labour

Except as otherwise stated in the Employer's Requirements, the Contractor shall provide and maintain all necessary accommodation and welfare facilities for the Contractor's Personnel. The Contractor shall also provide facilities for the Employer's Personnel as stated in the Employer's Requirements.

The Contractor shall not permit any of the Contractor's Personnel to maintain any temporary or permanent living quarters within the structures forming part of the Permanent Works.

6.7

Health and Safety

The Contractor shall at all times take all reasonable precautions to maintain the health and safety of the Contractor's Personnel. In collaboration with local health authorities, the Contractor shall ensure that medical staff, first aid facilities, sick bay and ambulance service are available at all times at the Site and at any accommodation for Contractor's and Employer's Personnel, and that suitable arrangements are made for all necessary welfare and hygiene requirements and for the prevention of epidemics.

The Contractor shall appoint an accident prevention officer at the Site, responsible for maintaining safety and protection against accidents. This person shall be qualified for this responsibility, and shall have the authority to issue instructions and take protective measures to prevent accidents. Throughout the execution of the Works, the Contractor shall provide whatever is required by this person to exercise this responsibility and authority.

The Contractor shall send, to the Employer, details of any accident as soon as practicable after its occurrence. The Contractor shall maintain records and make reports concerning health, safety and welfare of persons, and damage to property, as the Employer may reasonably require.

6.8

Contractor's Superintendence

Throughout the design and execution of the Works, and as long thereafter as is necessary to fulfil the Contractor's obligations, the Contractor shall provide all necessary superintendence to plan, arrange, direct, manage, inspect and test the work.

Superintendence shall be given by a sufficient number of persons having adequate knowledge of the language for communications (defined in Sub-Clause 1.4 [*Law and Language*]) and of the operations to be carried out (including the methods and techniques required, the hazards likely to be encountered and methods of preventing accidents), for the satisfactory and safe execution of the Works.

6.9

Contractor's Personnel

The Contractor's Personnel shall be appropriately qualified, skilled and experienced in their respective trades or occupations. The Employer may require the Contractor to remove (or cause to be removed) any person employed on the Site or Works, including the Contractor's Representative if applicable, who:

(a) persists in any misconduct or lack of care,
(b) carries out duties incompetently or negligently,

(a) **合同**中另有规定，
(b) **雇主**同意，或
(c) 为保护生命或财产、或为**工程**的安全不可避免或必需的工作，在此情况下**承包商**应立即通知**雇主**。

6.6

为员工提供设施

除**雇主要求**中另有说明外，**承包商**应为**承包商人员**提供和保持一切必要的食宿和福利设施。**承包商**还应按**雇主要求**中的规定为**雇主人员**提供设施。

承包商不应允许**承包商人员**中的任何人，在构成**永久工程**一部分的构筑物内，保留任何临时或永久的居住场所。

6.7

健康和安全

承包商应始终采取合理的预防措施，维护**承包商人员**的健康和安全。**承包商**应与当地卫生部门合作，始终确保在**现场**，以及**承包商**人员和**雇主人员**的任何住地，配备医务人员、急救设施、病房及救护车服务，并应对所有必需的福利和卫生要求、以及预防传染病做出适当安排。

承包商应在**现场**指派一名事故预防员，负责维护安全和事故预防工作。该人员应能胜任此项职责，并应有权发布指示及采取防止事故的保护措施。在**工程**实施过程中，**承包商**应提供该人员履行其职责和权力所需要的任何事项。

任何事故发生后，**承包商**应立即将事故详情通报**雇主**。**承包商**应按**雇主**可能提出的合理要求，保持记录，并写出有关人员健康、安全和福利、以及财产损坏等情况的报告。

6.8

承包商的监督

在设计和**工程**实施过程中，以及其后为了完成**承包商**的义务所需要的期间内，**承包商**应对工作的规划、安排、指导、管理、检验和试验，提供一切必要的监督。

此类监督应由足够的人员执行，他们应具有交流所用语言(**第1.4款**[**法律和语言**]所规定的）、以及合乎要求地、安全地实施**工程**各项作业所需的足够的知识(包括需要的方法和技术、可能遇到的危险和预防事故的方法)。

6.9

承包商人员

承包商人员都应是在他们各自工种或职业内，具有相应资质、技能和经验的人员。**雇主**可要求**承包商**撤换(或促使撤换)受雇于**现场**或**工程**的，有下列行为的任何人员，适当时也包括**承包商代表**：

(a) 经常行为不当，或工作漫不经心；
(b) 无能力履行义务或玩忽职守；

GENERAL CONDITIONS | GUIDANCE | FORMS

(c) fails to conform with any provisions of the Contract, or
(d) persists in any conduct which is prejudicial to safety, health, or the protection of the environment.

If appropriate, the Contractor shall then appoint (or cause to be appointed) a suitable replacement person.

6.10

Records of Contractor's Personnel and Equipment

The Contractor shall submit, to the Employer, details showing the number of each class of Contractor's Personnel and of each type of Contractor's Equipment on the Site. Details shall be submitted each calendar month, in a form approved by the Employer, until the Contractor has completed all work which is known to be outstanding at the completion date stated in the Taking-Over Certificate for the Works.

6.11

Disorderly Conduct

The Contractor shall at all times take all reasonable precautions to prevent any unlawful, riotous or disorderly conduct by or amongst the Contractor's Personnel, and to preserve peace and protection of persons and property on and near the Site.

7 Plant, Materials and Workmanship

7.1

Manner of Execution

The Contractor shall carry out the manufacture of Plant, the production and manufacture of Materials, and all other execution of the Works:

(a) in the manner (if any) specified in the Contract,
(b) in a proper workmanlike and careful manner, in accordance with recognised good practice, and
(c) with properly equipped facilities and non-hazardous Materials, except as otherwise specified in the Contract.

7.2

Samples

The Contractor shall submit samples to the Employer, for review in accordance with the procedures for Contractor's Documents described in Sub-Clause 5.2 [*Contractor's Documents*], as specified in the Contract and at the Contractor's cost. Each sample shall be labelled as to origin and intended use in the Works.

7.3

Inspection

The Employer's Personnel shall at all reasonable times:

(a) have full access to all parts of the Site and to all places from which natural Materials are being obtained, and
(b) during production, manufacture and construction (at the Site and, to the extent specified in the Contract, elsewhere), be entitled to examine, inspect, measure and test the materials and workmanship, and to check the progress of manufacture of Plant and production and manufacture of Materials.

The Contractor shall give the Employer's Personnel full opportunity to carry out these activities, including providing access, facilities, permissions and safety equipment. No such activity shall relieve the Contractor from any obligation or responsibility.

In respect of the work which Employer's Personnel are entitled to examine, inspect, measure and/or test, the Contractor shall give notice to the Employer whenever any such work is ready and before it is covered up, put out of sight, or packaged for

(c) 不遵守**合同**的任何规定；或
(d) 坚持有损安全、健康或有损环境保护的行为。

如果适宜，**承包商**随后应指派(或促使指派)合适的替代人员。

6.10

承包商人员和设备的记录

承包商应向**雇主**提交说明**现场**各类**承包商人员**的人数和各类**承包商设备**数量的详细资料。应按**雇主**批准的格式，每月填报，直到**承包商**完成了**工程接收证书**上写明的竣工日期时的全部扫尾工作为止。

6.11

无序行为

承包商应始终采取各种合理的预防措施，防止**承包商人员**或其内部发生任何非法的、骚乱的或无序的行为，以保持安定，保护**现场**及邻近人员和财产的安全。

7 生产设备、材料和工艺

7.1

实施方法

承包商应按以下方法进行**生产设备**的制造、**材料**的生产加工、以及**工程**的所有其他实施作业：

(a) 按照**合同**规定的方法(如果有)；
(b) 按照公认的良好惯例，使用恰当、精巧、仔细的方法；

(c) 除**合同**另有规定外，使用适当配备的设施和无危险的**材料**。

7.2

样品

承包商应根据**合同**规定，按照**第 5.2 款**[**承包商文件**]中所述的对**承包商文件**的送审程序，自费向**雇主**提交样品，供其审核。每件样品应标明其原产地、及其在**工程**中预期的用处。

7.3

检验

雇主人员应在所有合理的时间内：

(a) 有充分机会进入**现场**的所有部分以及获得天然**材料**的所有地点；

(b) 有权在生产、加工和施工期间(在**现场**和**合同**规定的其他范围)，对材料和工艺进行检查、检验、测量和试验，并对**生产设备**的制造和**材料**的加工生产进度进行检查。

承包商应为**雇主人员**进行上述活动提供一切机会，包括提供进入条件、设施、许可和安全装备。此类活动不应解除**承包商**的任何义务和职责。

对于**雇主人员**有权检查、检验、测量和(或)试验的工作，每当任何工作已经准备好，在覆盖、掩蔽、包装以便储存或运输前，**承包商**应通知**雇主**。

storage or transport. The Employer shall then either carry out the examination, inspection, measurement or testing without unreasonable delay, or promptly give notice to the Contractor that the Employer does not require to do so. If the Contractor fails to give the notice, he shall, if and when required by the Employer, uncover the work and thereafter reinstate and make good, all at the Contractor's cost.

7.4

Testing

This Sub-Clause shall apply to all tests specified in the Contract, other than the Tests after Completion (if any).

The Contractor shall provide all apparatus, assistance, documents and other information, electricity, equipment, fuel, consumables, instruments, labour, materials, and suitably qualified and experienced staff, as are necessary to carry out the specified tests efficiently. The Contractor shall agree, with the Employer, the time and place for the specified testing of any Plant, Materials and other parts of the Works.

The Employer may, under Clause 13 [*Variations and Adjustments*], vary the location or details of specified tests, or instruct the Contractor to carry out additional tests. If these varied or additional tests show that the tested Plant, Materials or workmanship is not in accordance with the Contract, the cost of carrying out this Variation shall be borne by the Contractor, notwithstanding other provisions of the Contract.

The Employer shall give the Contractor not less than 24 hours' notice of the Employer's intention to attend the tests. If the Employer does not attend at the time and place agreed, the Contractor may proceed with the tests, unless otherwise instructed by the Employer, and the tests shall then be deemed to have been made in the Employer's presence.

If the Contractor suffers delay and/or incurs Cost from complying with these instructions or as a result of a delay for which the Employer is responsible, the Contractor shall give notice to the Employer and shall be entitled subject to Sub-Clause 20.1 [*Contractor's Claims*] to:

(a) an extension of time for any such delay, if completion is or will be delayed, under Sub-Clause 8.4 [*Extension of Time for Completion*], and

(b) payment of any such Cost plus reasonable profit, which shall be added to the Contract Price.

After receiving this notice, the Employer shall proceed in accordance with Sub-Clause 3.5 [*Determinations*] to agree or determine these matters.

The Contractor shall promptly forward to the Employer duly certified reports of the tests. When the specified tests have been passed, the Employer shall endorse the Contractor's test certificate, or issue a certificate to him, to that effect. If the Employer has not attended the tests, he shall be deemed to have accepted the readings as accurate.

7.5

Rejection

If, as a result of an examination, inspection, measurement or testing, any Plant, Materials, design or workmanship is found to be defective or otherwise not in accordance with the Contract, the Employer may reject the Plant, Materials, design or workmanship by giving notice to the Contractor, with reasons. The Contractor shall then promptly make good the defect and ensure that the rejected item complies with the Contract.

If the Employer requires this Plant, Materials, design or workmanship to be retested, the tests shall be repeated under the same terms and conditions. If the rejection and

这时，**雇主**应及时进行检查、检验、测量或试验，不得无故拖延，或立即通知**承包商**无需进行这些工作。如果**承包商**没有发出此类通知，而当**雇主**提出要求时，**承包商**应除去物件上的覆盖，并随后恢复完好，所需费用由**承包商**负担。

7.4

试验

本款适用于**竣工后试验**(如果有)以外的**合同**规定的所有试验。

为有效进行规定的试验，**承包商**应提供所需的所有仪器、帮助、文件和其他资料、电力、装备、燃料、消耗品、工具、劳力、材料，以及具有适当资质和经验的人员。对任何**生产设备**、**材料**和**工程**其他部分进行规定的试验，其时间和地点，应由**承包商**和**雇主**商定。

根据**第 13 条**[**变更和调整**]的规定，**雇主**可以改变进行规定试验的位置或细节，或指示**承包商**进行附加的试验。如果这些变更或附加的试验表明，经过试验的**生产设备**、**材料**、或工艺不符合**合同**要求，不管**合同**有何其他规定，**承包商**应负担进行本项**变更**的费用。

雇主应至少提前 24 小时将参加试验的意图通知**承包商**。如果**雇主**没有在商定的时间和地点参加试验，除非**雇主**另有指示，**承包商**可以自行进行试验，这些试验应被视为是在**雇主**在场情况下进行的。

如果由于服从这些指示或因**雇主**应负责的延误的结果，使**承包商**遭受延误和(或)招致**费用**，**承包商**应向**雇主**发出通知，并有权根据**第 20.1 款**[**承包商的索赔**]的规定要求：

(a) 根据**第 8.4 款**[**竣工时间的延长**]的规定，如果竣工已或将受到延误，对任何此类延误给予延长期；
(b) 任何此类**费用**加合理利润应加入**合同价格**，给予支付。

雇主收到此通知后，应按照**第 3.5 款**[**确定**]的规定对这些事项进行商定或确定。

承包商应迅速向**雇主**提交充分证实的试验报告。当规定的试验通过时，**雇主**应在**承包商**的试验证书上签字认可，或向**承包商**颁发等效的证书。如果**雇主**未参加试验，他应被视为已经认可试验示数是准确的。

7.5

拒收

如果检查、检验、测量或试验结果，发现任何**生产设备**、**材料**、设计或工艺有缺陷，或不符合**合同**要求，**雇主**可向**承包商**发出通知，并说明理由，拒收该**生产设备**、**材料**、设计或工艺。**承包商**应迅速修复缺陷，并保证上述被拒收的项目符合**合同**规定。

如果**雇主**要求对上述**生产设备**、**材料**、设计或工艺再次进行试验，这些试验应按相同的条款和条件重新进行。如果此项拒收和再次试验使**雇主**增加

retesting cause the Employer to incur additional costs, the Contractor shall subject to Sub-Clause 2.5 [*Employer's Claims*] pay these costs to the Employer.

7.6

Remedial Work

Notwithstanding any previous test or certification, the Employer may instruct the Contractor to:

(a) remove from the Site and replace any Plant or Materials which is not in accordance with the Contract,
(b) remove and re-execute any other work which is not in accordance with the Contract, and
(c) execute any work which is urgently required for the safety of the Works, whether because of an accident, unforeseeable event or otherwise.

If the Contractor fails to comply with any such instruction, which complies with Sub-Clause 3.4 [*Instructions*], the Employer shall be entitled to employ and pay other persons to carry out the work. Except to the extent that the Contractor would have been entitled to payment for the work, the Contractor shall subject to Sub-Clause 2.5 [*Employer's Claims*] pay to the Employer all costs arising from this failure.

7.7

Ownership of Plant and Materials

Each item of Plant and Materials shall, to the extent consistent with the Laws of the Country, become the property of the Employer at whichever is the earlier of the following times, free from liens and other encumbrances:

(a) when it is delivered to the Site;
(b) when the Contractor is entitled to payment of the value of the Plant and Materials under Sub-Clause 8.10 [*Payment for Plant and Materials in Event of Suspension*].

7.8

Royalties

Unless otherwise stated in the Employer's Requirements, the Contractor shall pay all royalties, rents and other payments for:

(a) natural Materials obtained from outside the Site, and
(b) the disposal of material from demolitions and excavations and of other surplus material (whether natural or man-made), except to the extent that disposal areas within the Site are specified in the Contract.

8 Commencement, Delays and Suspension

8.1
Commencement of Works

Unless otherwise stated in the Contract Agreement:

(a) the Employer shall give the Contractor not less than 7 days' notice of the Commencement Date; and
(b) the Commencement Date shall be within 42 days after the date on which the Contract comes into full force and effect under Sub-Clause 1.6 [*Contract Agreement*].

The Contractor shall commence the design and execution of the Works as soon as is reasonably practicable after the Commencement Date, and shall then proceed with the Works with due expedition and without delay.

了费用，**承包商**应按照**第 2.5 款**[*雇主的索赔*]的规定，向**雇主**支付这笔费用。

7.6 修补工作

尽管已有先前的任何试验或证书，**雇主**仍可指示**承包商**进行以下工作：

(a) 将不符合**合同**要求的任何**生产设备**或**材料**移出现场，并进行更换；

(b) 去除不符合**合同**的任何其他工作并重新实施；

(c) 实施因意外、不可预见的事件或其他原因引起的、为**工程**的安全迫切需要的任何工作。

如果**承包商**未能遵从任何此类符合**第 3.4 款**[*指示*]要求的指示，**雇主**应有权雇用并付款给他人从事该工作。除**承包商**原有权从该工作所得付款的范围外，**承包商**应遵照**第 2.5 款**[*雇主的索赔*]的规定，向**雇主**支付因他未履行指示而使**雇主**支付的所有费用。

7.7 生产设备和材料的所有权

从下列二者中较早的时间起，在符合**工程所在国法律**规定范围内，每项**生产设备**和**材料**都应无扣押和其他阻碍地成为**雇主**的财产：

(a) 当上述**生产设备**、**材料**运至**现场**时；
(b) 当根据**第 8.10 款**[*暂停时对生产设备和材料的支付*]的规定，**承包商**有权得到按**生产设备**和**材料**价值的付款时。

7.8 土地(矿区)使用费

除非在**雇主要求**中另有说明，**承包商**应为以下事项支付所有的土地(矿区)使用费、租金和其他付款：

(a) 从**现场**以外地区得到的天然**材料**；
(b) 在**合同**规定的**现场**范围内的弃置区以外，弃置拆除、开挖的材料和其他剩余材料(不论是天然的或人工的)。

8 开工、延误和暂停

8.1 工程的开工

除非**合同协议书**另有说明：

(a) **雇主**应在不少于 7 天前向**承包商**发出**开工日期**的通知；

(b) **开工日期**应在**第 1.6 款**[*合同协议书*]规定的**合同**全面实施和生效日期后 42 天内。

承包商应在**开工日期**后，在合理可能情况下尽早开始**工程**的设计和施工，随后应以正当速度，不拖延地进行**工程**。

8.2
Time for Completion

The Contractor shall complete the whole of the Works, and each Section (if any), within the Time for Completion for the Works or Section (as the case may be), including:

(a) achieving the passing of the Tests on Completion, and
(b) completing all work which is stated in the Contract as being required for the Works or Section to be considered to be completed for the purposes of taking-over under Sub-Clause 10.1 [*Taking Over of the Works and Sections*].

8.3
Programme

The Contractor shall submit a time programme to the Employer within 28 days after the Commencement Date. The Contractor shall also submit a revised programme whenever the previous programme is inconsistent with actual progress or with the Contractor's obligations. Unless otherwise stated in the Contract, each programme shall include:

(a) the order in which the Contractor intends to carry out the Works, including the anticipated timing of each major stage of the Works,
(b) the periods for reviews under Sub-Clause 5.2 [*Contractor's Documents*],
(c) the sequence and timing of inspections and tests specified in the Contract, and
(d) a supporting report which includes:

    (i) a general description of the methods which the Contractor intends to adopt for the execution of each major stage of the Works, and
    (ii) the approximate number of each class of Contractor's Personnel and of each type of Contractor's Equipment for each major stage.

Unless the Employer, within 21 days after receiving a programme, gives notice to the Contractor stating the extent to which it does not comply with the Contract, the Contractor shall proceed in accordance with the programme, subject to his other obligations under the Contract. The Employer's Personnel shall be entitled to rely upon the programme when planning their activities.

The Contractor shall promptly give notice to the Employer of specific probable future events or circumstances which may adversely affect or delay the execution of the Works. In this event, or if the Employer gives notice to the Contractor that a programme fails (to the extent stated) to comply with the Contract or to be consistent with actual progress and the Contractor's stated intentions, the Contractor shall submit a revised programme to the Employer in accordance with this Sub-Clause.

8.4
Extension of Time for Completion

The Contractor shall be entitled subject to Sub-Clause 20.1 [*Contractor's Claims*] to an extension of the Time for Completion if and to the extent that completion for the purposes of Sub-Clause 10.1 [*Taking Over of the Works and Sections*] is or will be delayed by any of the following causes:

(a) a Variation (unless an adjustment to the Time for Completion has been agreed under Sub-Clause 13.3 [*Variation Procedure*]),
(b) a cause of delay giving an entitlement to extension of time under a Sub-Clause of these Conditions, or
(c) any delay, impediment or prevention caused by or attributable to the Employer, the Employer's Personnel, or the Employer's other contractors on the Site.

If the Contractor considers himself to be entitled to an extension of the Time for Completion, the Contractor shall give notice to the Employer in accordance with Sub-

8.2

竣工时间

承包商应在工程或单位工程(视情况而定)的**竣工时间**内，完成整个工程和每个单位工程(如果有)，包括：

(a) **竣工试验**获得通过；

(b) 完成**合同**提出的、**工程**和单位**工程**按照**第 10.1 款**[**工程和单位工程的接收**]规定的接收要求竣工所需要的全部工作。

8.3

进度计划

承包商应在**开工日期**后 28 天内，向**雇主**提交一份进度计划。当原定进度计划与实际进度或**承包商**的义务不相符时，**承包商**还应提交一份修订的进度计划。除非**合同**另有说明，每份进度计划应包括：

(a) **承包商**计划实施**工程**的工作顺序，包括**工程**各主要阶段的预期时间安排；

(b) 根据**第 5.2 款**[**承包商文件**]规定的审核期限；

(c) **合同**中规定的各项检验和试验的顺序和时间安排；

(d) 一份支持报告，内容包括：

(ⅰ) **工程**实施中各主要阶段和**承包商**拟采用的方法的一般描述；

(ⅱ) 各主要阶段配备的各级**承包商人员**和各类型**承包商设备**的大概数量。

除非**雇主**在收到进度计划后 21 天内向**承包商**发出通知，指出其中不符合**合同**要求的部分，**承包商**即应按照该进度计划，并遵守**合同**规定的其他义务，进行工作。**雇主人员**应有权依照该进度计划安排他们的活动。

承包商应及时将未来可能对**工程**施工造成不利影响或延误的事件或情况通知**雇主**。在此情况下，或在**雇主**通知**承包商**指出进度计划(在指出的部分)不符合**合同**要求，或与实际进度或**承包商**提出的意向不一致时，**承包商**应遵照**本款**要求向**雇主**提交一份修订进度计划。

8.4

竣工时间的延长

如由于下列任何原因，致使达到按照**第 10.1 款**[**工程和单位工程的接收**]要求的竣工受到或将受到延误的程度，**承包商**有权按照**第 20.1 款**[**承包商的索赔**]的规定提出延长**竣工时间**：

(a) **变更**(除非已根据**第 13.3 款**[**变更程序**]的规定商定调整了**竣工时间**)；

(b) 根据本**条件**某款，有权获得延长期的原因；或

(c) 由**雇主**、**雇主人员**、或在**现场**的**雇主**的其他承包商造成或引起的任何延误、妨碍和阻碍。

如果**承包商**认为他有权提出延长**竣工时间**，应按照**第20.1款**[**承包商的索**

Clause 20.1 [*Contractor's Claims*]. When determining each extension of time under Sub-Clause 20.1, the Employer shall review previous determinations and may increase, but shall not decrease, the total extension of time.

8.5

Delays Caused by Authorities

If the following conditions apply, namely:

(a) the Contractor has diligently followed the procedures laid down by the relevant legally constituted public authorities in the Country,
(b) these authorities delay or disrupt the Contractor's work, and
(c) the delay or disruption was not reasonably foreseeable by an experienced contractor by the date for submission of the Tender,

then this delay or disruption will be considered as a cause of delay under sub-paragraph (b) of Sub-Clause 8.4 [*Extension of Time for Completion*].

8.6

Rate of Progress

If, at any time:

(a) actual progress is too slow to complete within the Time for Completion, and/or
(b) progress has fallen (or will fall) behind the current programme under Sub-Clause 8.3 [*Programme*],

other than as a result of a cause listed in Sub-Clause 8.4 [*Extension of Time for Completion*], then the Employer may instruct the Contractor to submit, under Sub-Clause 8.3 [*Programme*], a revised programme and supporting report describing the revised methods which the Contractor proposes to adopt in order to expedite progress and complete within the Time for Completion.

Unless the Employer notifies otherwise, the Contractor shall adopt these revised methods, which may require increases in the working hours and/or in the numbers of Contractor's Personnel and/or Goods, at the risk and cost of the Contractor. If these revised methods cause the Employer to incur additional costs, the Contractor shall subject to Sub-Clause 2.5 [*Employer's Claims*] pay these costs to the Employer, in addition to delay damages (if any) under Sub-Clause 8.7 below.

8.7

Delay Damages

If the Contractor fails to comply with Sub-Clause 8.2 [*Time for Completion*], the Contractor shall subject to Sub-Clause 2.5 [*Employer's Claims*] pay delay damages to the Employer for this default. These delay damages shall be the sum stated in the Particular Conditions, which shall be paid for every day which shall elapse between the relevant Time for Completion and the date stated in the Taking-Over Certificate. However, the total amount due under this Sub-Clause shall not exceed the maximum amount of delay damages (if any) stated in the Particular Conditions.

These delay damages shall be the only damages due from the Contractor for such default, other than in the event of termination under Sub-Clause 15.2 [*Termination by Employer*] prior to completion of the Works. These damages shall not relieve the Contractor from his obligation to complete the Works, or from any other duties, obligations or responsibilities which he may have under the Contract.

8.8

Suspension of Work

The Employer may at any time instruct the Contractor to suspend progress of part or all of the Works. During such suspension, the Contractor shall protect, store and secure such part or the Works against any deterioration, loss or damage.

赔]的规定，向**雇主**发出通知。**雇主**每次按照**第 20.1 款**确定延长时间时，应对以前所作的确定进行审查，可以增加，但不得减少总的延长时间。

8.5

当局造成的延误

如果符合下列条件，即：

(a) **承包商**已努力遵守了**工程所在国**依法成立的有关公共当局所制订的程序；
(b) 这些当局延误或打乱了**承包商**的工作；
(c) 延误或中废是一个有经验的**承包商**在递交**投标书**时无法合理预见的；

则上述延误或中断可视为根据**第 8.4 款**[***竣工时间的延长***](b)项规定的延误原因。

8.6

工程进度

如果在任何时候：

(a) 实际工程进度对于在**竣工时间**内完工过于迟缓，和(或)
(b) 进度已(或将)落后于根据**第 8.3 款**[***进度计划***]的规定制订的现行进度计划，

除由于**第 8.4 款**[***竣工时间的延长***]中列举的某项原因造成的结果外，**雇主**可指示**承包商**根据**第 8.3 款**[***进度计划***]的规定提交一份修订的进度计划，以及说明**承包商**为加快进度在**竣工时间**内竣工，建议采用的修订方法的补充报告。

除非**雇主**另有通知，**承包商**应采取这些修订方法，对可能需要增加工时、和(或)**承包商人员**和(或)**货物**的数量，**承包商**应自行承担风险和费用。如果这些修订方法使**雇主**招致附加费用，**承包商**应根据**第 2.5 款**[***雇主的索赔***]的要求，连同下述**第 8.7 款**中提出的误期损害赔偿费(如果有)，向**雇主**支付这些费用。

8.7

误期损害赔偿费

如果**承包商**未能遵守**第 8.2 款**[***竣工时间***]的要求，**承包商**应当为其违约行为，根据**第 2.5 款**[***雇主的索赔***]的要求向**雇主**支付误期损害赔偿费。这些项误期损害赔偿费应按**专用条件**中规定的每天应付金额，以**接收证书**注明的日期超过相应的**竣工时间**的天数计算。但按本**款**计算的赔偿总额，不得超过**专用条件**中规定的误期损害赔偿费的最高限额(如果有)。

除在**工程**竣工前根据**第 15.2 款**[***由雇主终止***]的规定终止的情况外，这些误期损害赔偿费应是**承包商**为此类违约应付的唯一损害赔偿费。这些损害赔偿费不应解除**承包商**完成**工程**的义务，或**合同**规定的其可能承担的其他责任、义务或职责。

8.8

暂时停工

雇主可以随时指示**承包商**暂停**工程**某一部分或全部的施工。在暂停期间，**承包商**应保护、保管，并保证该部分或全部**工程**不致产生任何变质、损失或损害。

GENERAL CONDITIONS

GUIDANCE

FORMS

The Employer may also notify the cause for the suspension. If and to the extent that the cause is notified and is the responsibility of the Contractor, the following Sub-Clauses 8.9, 8.10 and 8.11 shall not apply.

8.9

Consequences of Suspension

If the Contractor suffers delay and/or incurs Cost from complying with the Employer's instructions under Sub-Clause 8.8 [*Suspension of Work*] and/or from resuming the work, the Contractor shall give notice to the Employer and shall be entitled subject to Sub-Clause 20.1 [*Contractor's Claims*] to:

(a) an extension of time for any such delay, if completion is or will be delayed, under Sub-Clause 8.4 [*Extension of Time for Completion*], and
(b) payment of any such Cost, which shall be added to the Contract Price.

After receiving this notice, the Employer shall proceed in accordance with Sub-Clause 3.5 [*Determinations*] to agree or determine these matters.

The Contractor shall not be entitled to an extension of time for, or to payment of the Cost incurred in, making good the consequences of the Contractor's faulty design, workmanship or materials, or of the Contractor's failure to protect, store or secure in accordance with Sub-Clause 8.8 [*Suspension of Work*].

8.10

Payment for Plant and Materials in Event of Suspension

The Contractor shall be entitled to payment of the value (as at the date of suspension) of Plant and/or Materials which have not been delivered to Site, if:

(a) the work on Plant or delivery of Plant and/or Materials has been suspended for more than 28 days, and
(b) the Contractor has marked the Plant and/or Materials as the Employer's property in accordance with the Employer's instructions.

8.11

Prolonged Suspension

If the suspension under Sub-Clause 8.8 [*Suspension of Work*] has continued for more than 84 days, the Contractor may request the Employer's permission to proceed. If the Employer does not give permission within 28 days after being requested to do so, the Contractor may, by giving notice to the Employer, treat the suspension as an omission under Clause 13 [*Variations and Adjustments*] of the affected part of the Works. If the suspension affects the whole of the Works, the Contractor may give notice of termination under Sub-Clause 16.2 [*Termination by Contractor*].

8.12

Resumption of Work

After the permission or instruction to proceed is given, the Parties shall jointly examine the Works and the Plant and Materials affected by the suspension. The Contractor shall make good any deterioration or defect in or loss of the Works or Plant or Materials, which has occurred during the suspension.

9 Tests on Completion

9.1
Contractor's Obligations

The Contractor shall carry out the Tests on Completion in accordance with this Clause and Sub-Clause 7.4 [*Testing*], after providing the documents in accordance with Sub-Clause 5.6 [*As-Built Documents*] and Sub-Clause 5.7 [*Operation and Maintenance Manuals*].

雇主可以通知暂停的原因。如果是已通知了原因，而且是由于**承包商**的职责造成的情况，则下列**第 8.9、8.10 和 8.11** 款应不适用。

8.9

暂停的后果

如果**承包商**因执行**雇主**根据**第 8.8 款**[**暂时停工**]的规定发出的指示，和(或)因为复工而遭受延误和(或)招致增加**费用**，**承包商**应向**雇主**发出通知，并有权依照**第 20.1 款**[**承包商的索赔**]的规定提出：

(a) 根据**第 8.4 款**[**竣工时间的延长**]的规定，如竣工已或将受到延误，应对任何此类延误给予延长期；
(b) 对任何**此类**费用应计入**合同价格**，给予支付。

雇主收到此通知后，应按照**第 3.5 款**[**确定**]的要求，对这些事项进行商定或确定。

为弥补因**承包商**有缺陷的设计、工艺或材料，或因**承包商**未能按照**第 8.8 款**[**暂时停工**]的规定保护、保管、或保证安全的后果，**承包商**应无权得到由其带来的延长期或招致**费用**的支付。

8.10

暂停时对生产设备和材料的付款

在下列条件下，**承包商**有权得到尚未运到**现场**的**生产设备**和(或)**材料**(按暂停开始日期时)的价值的付款：

(a) **生产设备**的生产、或**生产设备**和(或)**材料**的交付被暂停达到 28 天以上；
(b) **承包商**已按**雇主**的指示，标明上述**生产设备**和(或)**材料**为**雇主**的财产。

8.11

拖长的暂停

如果**第 8.8 款**[**暂时停工**]所述的暂停已持续 84 天以上，**承包商**可以要求**雇主**允许继续施工。如在提出这一要求后 28 天内，**雇主**没有给予许可，**承包商**可以通知**雇主**，将**工程**受暂停影响的部分视为根据**第 13 条**[**变更和调整**]规定的删减项目。如果暂停影响到整个**工程**，**承包商**可以根据**第 16.2 款**[**由承包商终止**]的规定发出终止的通知。

8.12

复工

在发出继续施工的许可或指示后，双方应共同对受暂停影响的**工程**、**生产设备**和**材料**进行检查。**承包商**应负责恢复在暂停期间发生的**工程**或**生产设备**或**材料**的任何变质、缺陷或损失。

9 竣工试验

9.1

承包商的义务

承包商应在按照**第 5.6 款**[**竣工文件**]和**第 5.7 款**[**操作和维修手册**]的要求，提供各种文件后，按照**本条**和**第 7.4 款**[**试验**]的要求进行**竣工试验**。

GENERAL CONDITIONS

GUIDANCE

FORMS

The Contractor shall give to the Employer not less than 21 days' notice of the date after which the Contractor will be ready to carry out each of the Tests on Completion. Unless otherwise agreed, Tests on Completion shall be carried out within 14 days after this date, on such day or days as the Employer shall instruct.

Unless otherwise stated in the Particular Conditions, the Tests on Completion shall be carried out in the following sequence:

(a) pre-commissioning tests, which shall include the appropriate inspections and ("dry" or "cold") functional tests to demonstrate that each item of Plant can safely under-take the next stage, (b);
(b) commissioning tests, which shall include the specified operational tests to demonstrate that the Works or Section can be operated safely and as specified, under all available operating conditions; and
(c) trial operation, which shall demonstrate that the Works or Section perform reliably and in accordance with the Contract.

During trial operation, when the Works are operating under stable conditions, the Contractor shall give notice to the Employer that the Works are ready for any other Tests on Completion, including performance tests to demonstrate whether the Works conform with criteria specified in the Employer's Requirements and with the Performance Guarantees.

Trial operation shall not constitute a taking-over under Clause 10 [*Employer's Taking Over*]. Unless otherwise stated in the Particular Conditions, any product produced by the Works during trial operation shall be the property of the Employer.

In considering the results of the Tests on Completion, appropriate allowances shall be made for the effect of any use of the Works by the Employer on the performance or other characteristics of the Works. As soon as the Works, or a Section, have passed each of the Tests on Completion described in sub-paragraph (a), (b) or (c), the Contractor shall submit a certified report of the results of these Tests to the Employer.

9.2 Delayed Tests

If the Tests on Completion are being unduly delayed by the Employer, Sub-Clause 7.4 [*Testing*] (fifth paragraph) and/or Sub-Clause 10.3 [*Interference with Tests on Completion*] shall be applicable.

If the Tests on Completion are being unduly delayed by the Contractor, the Employer may by notice require the Contractor to carry out the Tests within 21 days after receiving the notice. The Contractor shall carry out the Tests on such day or days within that period as the Contractor may fix and of which he shall give notice to the Employer

If the Contractor fails to carry out the Tests on Completion within the period of 21 days, the Employer's Personnel may proceed with the Tests at the risk and cost of the Contractor. These Tests on Completion shall then be deemed to have been carried out in the presence of the Contractor and the results of the Tests shall be accepted as accurate.

9.3 Retesting

If the Works, or a Section, fail to pass the Tests on Completion, Sub-Clause 7.5 [*Rejection*] shall apply, and the Employer or the Contractor may require the failed Tests, and Tests on Completion on any related work, to be repeated under the same terms and conditions.

承包商应提前 21 天将他可以进行每项**竣工试验**的日期通知**雇主**。除非另有商定，**竣工试验**应在此通知日期后的 14 天内，在**雇主**指示的某日或某几日内进行。

除非在**专用条件**中另有说明，**竣工试验**应按下列顺序进行：

(a) 启动前试验，应包括适当的检验和（"干"或"冷"）性能试验，以证明每项**生产设备**能够安全地承受下一阶段(b)项试验；

(b) 启动试验，应包括规定的操作试验，以证明**工程**或**单位工程**能够在所有可利用的操作条件下安全地操作。

(c) 试运行，应证明**工程**或**单位工程**运行可靠，符合**合同**要求。

在试运行期间，当**工程**正在稳定条件下运行时，**承包商**应通知**雇主**，告知**工程**已可以做任何其他**竣工试验**，包括各种性能试验，以证明**工程**是否符合**雇主要求**中规定的标准和**履约保证**。

试运行不应构成**第 10 条**[**雇主的接收**]规定的接收。除非**专用条件**中另有说明，**工程**在试运行期间生产的任何产品应属于**雇主**的财产。

在考虑**竣工试验**结果时，**雇主**应适当考虑到因**雇主**对**工程**的任何使用，对**工程**的性能或其他特性产生的影响。一旦**工程**或某**单位工程**通过了**本款**(a)、(b)或(c)项中的每项**竣工试验**，**承包商**应向**雇主**提供一份经证实的这些试验结果的报告。

9.2

延误的试验

如果**雇主**不当地延误**竣工试验**，应适用**第 7.4 款**[**试验**]（第 5 段）和（或）**第 10.3 款**[**对竣工试验的干扰**]的规定。

如果**承包商**不当地延误**竣工试验**，**雇主**可通知**承包商**，要求在接到通知后 21 天内进行**竣工试验**。**承包商**应在上述期限内的某日或某几日内进行**竣工试验**，并将该日期通知**雇主**。

如果**承包商**未在规定的 21 天内进行**竣工试验**，**雇主人员**可自行进行这些试验。试验的风险和费用应由**承包商**承担。这些**竣工试验**应被视为是**承包商**在场时进行的，试验结果应认为准确，予以认可。

9.3

重新试验

如果**工程**或某**单位工程**未能通过**竣工试验**，应适用**第 7.5 款**[**拒收**]的规定，**雇主**或**承包商**可要求按相同的条款和条件，重新进行此项未通过的试验和相关工程的**竣工试验**。

9.4
Failure to Pass Tests on Completion

If the Works, or a Section, fail to pass the Tests on Completion repeated under Sub-Clause 9.3 [*Retesting*], the Employer shall be entitled to:

(a) order further repetition of Tests on Completion under Sub-Clause 9.3;
(b) if the failure deprives the Employer of substantially the whole benefit of the Works or Section, reject the Works or Section (as the case may be), in which event the Employer shall have the same remedies as are provided in sub-paragraph (c) of Sub-Clause 11.4 [*Failure to Remedy Defects*]; or
(c) issue a Taking-Over Certificate.

In the event of sub-paragraph (c), the Contractor shall proceed in accordance with all other obligations under the Contract, and the Contract Price shall be reduced by such amount as shall be appropriate to cover the reduced value to the Employer as a result of this failure. Unless the relevant reduction for this failure is stated (or its method of calculation is defined) in the Contract, the Employer may require the reduction to be (i) agreed by both Parties (in full satisfaction of this failure only) and paid before this Taking-Over Certificate is issued, or (ii) determined and paid under Sub-Clause 2.5 [*Employer's Claims*] and Sub-Clause 3.5 [*Determinations*].

10 Employer's Taking Over

10.1
Taking Over of the Works and Sections

Except as stated in Sub-Clause 9.4 [*Failure to Pass Tests on Completion*], the Works shall be taken over by the Employer when (i) the Works have been completed in accordance with the Contract, including the matters described in Sub-Clause 8.2 [*Time for Completion*] and except as allowed in sub-paragraph (a) below, and (ii) a Taking-Over Certificate for the Works has been issued, or is deemed to have been issued in accordance with this Sub-Clause.

The Contractor may apply by notice to the Employer for a Taking-Over Certificate not earlier than 14 days before the Works will, in the Contractor's opinion, be complete and ready for taking over. If the Works are divided into Sections, the Contractor may similarly apply for a Taking-Over Certificate for each Section.

The Employer shall, within 28 days after receiving the Contractor's application:

(a) issue the Taking-Over Certificate to the Contractor, stating the date on which the Works or Section were completed in accordance with the Contract, except for any minor outstanding work and defects which will not substantially affect the use of the Works or Section for their intended purpose (either until or whilst this work is completed and these defects are remedied); or
(b) reject the application, giving reasons and specifying the work required to be done by the Contractor to enable the Taking-Over Certificate to be issued. The Contractor shall then complete this work before issuing a further notice under this Sub-Clause.

If the Employer fails either to issue the Taking-Over Certificate or to reject the Contractor's application within the period of 28 days, and if the Works or Section (as the case may be) are substantially in accordance with the Contract, the Taking-Over Certificate shall be deemed to have been issued on the last day of that period.

10.2
Taking Over of Parts of the Works

Parts of the Works (other than Sections) shall not be taken over or used by the Employer, except as may be stated in the Contract or as may be agreed by both Parties.

9.4
未能通过竣工试验

如果**工程**或某**单位工程**未能通过根据**第 9.3 款**[**重新试验**]的规定重新进行的**竣工试验，雇主**应有权：

(a) 下令根据**第 9.3 款**再次重复**竣工试验**；
(b) 如果此项试验未通过，使**雇主**实质上丧失了**工程**或**单位工程**的整个利益时，拒收**工程**或**单位工程**(视情况而定)，在此情况下，**雇主**应采取与**第 11.4 款**[**未能修补缺陷**](c)项规定的相同补救措施；或
(c) 颁发**接受证书**。

在采用(c)项办法的情况下，**承包商**应继续履行**合同**规定的所有其他义务。但**合同价格**应予减少，减少的金额应足以弥补此项试验未通过的后果给**雇主**带来的价值损失。除非对此项试验未通过相应减少的**合同价格**在**合同**中另有说明(或规定了计算方法)，**雇主**可以要求该减少额(i)经**双方**商定(仅限于满足此项试验未通过的要求)，并在此项**接收证书**颁发前支付，或(ii)根据**第 2.5 款**[**雇主的索赔**]和**第 3.5 款**[**确定**]的规定，确定并支付。

10 雇主的接收

10.1
工程和单位工程的接收

除**第 9.4 款**[**未能通过竣工试验**]中所述情况外，当(i)除下面(a)项允许的情况以外，**工程**已按**合同**规定，包括**第 8.2 款**[**竣工时间**]中提出的事项竣工，(ii)已按照本**款**规定颁发**工程接收证书**，或被认为已颁发时，**雇主**应接收**工程**。

承包商可在他认为**工程**将竣工并做好接收准备的日期前不少于 14 天，向**雇主**发出申请**接收证书**的通知。若**工程**分成若干个**单位工程**，**承包商**可类似地为每个**单位工程**申请**接收证书**。

雇主在收到**承包商**申请通知后 28 天内，应：

(a) 向**承包商**颁发**接收证书**，注明**工程**或**单位工程**按照**合同**要求竣工的日期，任何对**工程**或**单位工程**预期使用目的没有实质影响的少量收尾工作和缺陷(直到或当收尾工作和缺陷修补完成时)除外；或

(b) 拒绝申请，说明理由，并指出在能颁发**接收证书**前**承包商**需做的工作。**承包商**应在再次根据本**款**发出申请通知前，完成此项工作。

如果**雇主**在 28 天期限内既未颁发**接收证书**，又未拒绝**承包商**的申请，而**工程**或**单位工程**(视情况而定)实质上符合**合同**规定，**接收证书**应视为已在上述规定期限的最后一日颁发。

10.2
部分工程的接收

除**合同**中可能说明或可能经**双方**同意以外，任何部分**工程**(**单位工程**以外)，**雇主**均不得接收或使用。

10.3
Interference with Tests on Completion

If the Contractor is prevented, for more than 14 days, from carrying out the Tests on Completion by a cause for which the Employer is responsible, the Contractor shall carry out the Tests on Completion as soon as practicable.

If the Contractor suffers delay and/or incurs Cost as a result of this delay in carrying out the Tests on Completion, the Contractor shall give notice to the Employer and shall be entitled subject to Sub-Clause 20.1 [*Contractor's Claims*] to:

(a) an extension of time for any such delay, if completion is or will be delayed, under Sub-Clause 8.4 [*Extension of Time for Completion*], and
(b) payment of any such Cost plus reasonable profit, which shall be added to the Contract Price.

After receiving this notice, the Employer shall proceed in accordance with Sub-Clause 3.5 [*Determinations*] to agree or determine these matters.

11 Defects Liability

11.1
Completion of Outstanding Work and Remedying Defects

In order that the Works and Contractor's Documents, and each Section, shall be in the condition required by the Contract (fair wear and tear excepted) by the expiry date of the relevant Defects Notification Period or as soon as practicable thereafter, the Contractor shall:

(a) complete any work which is outstanding on the date stated in a Taking-Over Certificate, within such reasonable time as is instructed by the Employer, and
(b) execute all work required to remedy defects or damage, as may be notified by the Employer on or before the expiry date of the Defects Notification Period for the Works or Section (as the case may be).

If a defect appears or damage occurs, the Employer shall notify the Contractor accordingly.

11.2
Cost of Remedying Defects

All work referred to in sub-paragraph (b) of Sub-Clause 11.1 [*Completion of Outstanding Work and Remedying Defects*] shall be executed at the risk and cost of the Contractor, if and to the extent that the work is attributable to:

(a) the design of the Works,
(b) Plant, Materials or workmanship not being in accordance with the Contract,
(c) improper operation or maintenance which was attributable to matters for which the Contractor is responsible (under Sub-Clauses 5.5 to 5.7 or otherwise), or
(d) failure by the Contractor to comply with any other obligation.

If and to the extent that such work is attributable to any other cause, the Employer shall give notice to the Contractor accordingly, and Sub-Clause 13.3 [*Variation Procedure*] shall apply.

11.3
Extension of Defects Notification Period

The Employer shall be entitled subject to Sub-Clause 2.5 [*Employer's Claims*] to an extension of the Defects Notification Period for the Works or a Section if and to the extent that the Works, Section or a major item of Plant (as the case may be, and after taking over) cannot be used for the purposes for which they are intended by reason of a defect or damage. However, a Defects Notification Period shall not be extended by more than two years.

10.3
对竣工试验的干扰

如果由**雇主**应负责的原因妨碍**承包商**进行**竣工试验**达14天以上，**承包商**应尽快地进行**竣工试验**。

如果由于进行**竣工试验**的此项拖延，使**承包商**遭受延误和(或)招致增加**费用**，**承包商**应向**雇主**发出通知，并应有权根据**第20.1款**[*承包商的索赔*]的规定要求：

(a) 根据**第8.4款**[*竣工时间的延长*]的规定，如果竣工已或将受到延误，对任何此类延误给予延长期；
(b) 对任何此类**费用**，加合理的利润，应加入**合同价格**，给予支付。

雇主收到此通知后，应按照**第3.5款**[*确定*]的规定，对这些事项进行商定或确定。

11 缺陷责任

11.1
完成扫尾工作和修补缺陷

为了使**工程**、**承包商文件**和每个**单位工程**在相应**缺陷通知期限**期满日期或其后尽快达到**合同**要求(合理的损耗除外)，**承包商**应：

(a) 在**雇主**指示的合理时间内，完成**接收证书**注明日期时尚未完成的任何工作；
(b) 在**工程**或**单位工程**(视情况而定)的**缺陷通知期限**期满日期或其以前，按照**雇主**可能通知的要求，完成修补缺陷或损害所需要的所有工作。

如果出现缺陷，或发生损害，**雇主**应相应地，通知**承包商**。

11.2
修补缺陷的费用

第11.1款[*完成扫尾工作和修补缺陷*](b)项中提出的所有工作，如果在归因于下述原因的范围，其执行中的风险和费用应由**承包商**承担：

(a) **工程**的设计；
(b) **生产设备**、**材料**或工艺不符合**合同**要求；
(c) 由**承包商**(根据**第5.5至5.7款**或其他规定)负责的事项产生的不当的操作或维修；或
(d) **承包商**未能遵守任何其他义务。

如果此类工作在归因于任何其他原因的范围，**雇主**应根据情况通知**承包商**，并应适用**第13.3款**[*变更程序*]的规定。

11.3
缺陷通知期限的延长

如果因为某项缺陷或损害达到使**工程**、**单位工程**或某项主要**生产设备**(视情况而定，并在接收以后)不能按原定目的使用的程度，**雇主**应有权根据**第2.5款**[*雇主的索赔*]的规定对**工程**或某一**单位工程**的**缺陷通知期限**提出延长期。但**缺陷通知期限**的延长不得超过两年。

If delivery and/or erection of Plant and/or Materials was suspended under Sub-Clause 8.8 [*Suspension of Work*] or Sub-Clause 16.1 [*Contractor's Entitlement to Suspend Work*], the Contractor's obligations under this Clause shall not apply to any defects or damage occurring more than two years after the Defects Notification Period for the Plant and/or Materials would otherwise have expired.

11.4

Failure to Remedy Defects

If the Contractor fails to remedy any defect or damage within a reasonable time, a date may be fixed by (or on behalf of) the Employer, on or by which the defect or damage is to be remedied. The Contractor shall be given reasonable notice of this date.

If the Contractor fails to remedy the defect or damage by this notified date and this remedial work was to be executed at the cost of the Contractor under Sub-Clause 11.2 [*Cost of Remedying Defects*], the Employer may (at his option):

(a) carry out the work himself or by others, in a reasonable manner and at the Contractor's cost, but the Contractor shall have no responsibility for this work; and the Contractor shall subject to Sub-Clause 2.5 [*Employer's Claims*] pay to the Employer the costs reasonably incurred by the Employer in remedying the defect or damage;

(b) agree or determine a reasonable reduction in the Contract Price in accordance with Sub-Clause 3.5 [*Determinations*]; or

(c) if the defect or damage deprives the Employer of substantially the whole benefit of the Works or any major part of the Works, terminate the Contract as a whole, or in respect of such major part which cannot be put to the intended use. Without prejudice to any other rights, under the Contract or otherwise, the Employer shall then be entitled to recover all sums paid for the Works or for such part (as the case may be), plus financing costs and the cost of dismantling the same, clearing the Site and returning Plant and Materials to the Contractor.

11.5

Removal of Defective Work

If the defect or damage cannot be remedied expeditiously on the Site and the Employer gives consent, the Contractor may remove from the Site for the purposes of repair such items of Plant as are defective or damaged. This consent may require the Contractor to increase the amount of the Performance Security by the full replacement cost of these items, or to provide other appropriate security.

11.6

Further Tests

If the work of remedying of any defect or damage may affect the performance of the Works, the Employer may require the repetition of any of the tests described in the Contract, including Tests on Completion and/or Tests after Completion. The requirement shall be made by notice within 28 days after the defect or damage is remedied.

These tests shall be carried out in accordance with the terms applicable to the previous tests, except that they shall be carried out at the risk and cost of the Party liable, under Sub-Clause 11.2 [*Cost of Remedying Defects*], for the cost of the remedial work.

11.7

Right of Access

Until the Performance Certificate has been issued, the Contractor shall have the right of access to all parts of the Works and to records of the operation and performance of the Works, except as may be inconsistent with the Employer's reasonable security restrictions.

11.8

Contractor to Search

The Contractor shall, if required by the Employer, search for the cause of any defect, under the direction of the Employer. Unless the defect is to be remedied at the cost

当**生产设备**和(或)**材料**的交付和(或)安装，已根据**第 8.8 款**[**暂时停工**]或**第 16.1 款**[**承包商暂停工作的权利**]的规定暂停进行时，对于**生产设备**和(或)**材料**的**缺陷通知期限**原期满日期两年后发生的任何缺陷或损害，本**条**规定的**承包商**各项义务应不适用。

11.4 未能修补缺陷

如果**承包商**未能在合理的时间内修补任何缺陷和损害，**雇主**(或其代表)可确定一个日期，要求到或不迟于该日期修补好缺陷或损害。应将该日期向**承包商**发出合理的通知。

如果**承包商**到该通知的日期仍未修补好缺陷或损害，且此项修补工作根据**第 11.2 款**[**修补缺陷的费用**]的规定，应由**承包商**承担实施的费用，**雇主**可以(自行选择)：

(a) 以合理的方式由他自己或他人进行此项工作，由**承包商**承担费用，但**承包商**对此项工作将不再负责任；**承包商**应按照**第 2.5 款**[**雇主的索赔**]的规定，向**雇主**支付由**雇主**修补缺陷或损害而发生的合理费用；

(b) 按照**第 3.5 款**[**确定**]的规定，商定或确定**合同价格**的合理减少额；或

(c) 如果缺陷或损害使**雇主**实质上丧失了**工程**或**工程**的任何主要部分的整个利益时，终止整个**合同**或其有关不能按原定意图使用的该主要部分。**雇主**还应有权在不损害根据**合同**或其他规定所具有的任何其他权利的情况下，收回对**工程**或该部分**工程**(视情况而定)的全部支出总额，加上融资费用和拆除**工程**、清理**现场**、以及将**生产设备**和**材料**退还给**承包商**所支付的费用。

11.5 移出有缺陷的工程

如果缺陷或损害在**现场**无法迅速修复，**承包商**可经**雇主**同意，将此类有缺陷或损害的各项**生产设备**移出**现场**进行修复。**雇主**此项同意可要求**承包商**按该项设备的全部重置成本，增加**履约担保**的金额，或提供其他适宜的担保。

11.6 进一步试验

如果任何缺陷或损害的修补，可能对**工程**的性能产生影响，**雇主**可要求重新进行**合同**提出的任何试验，包括**竣工试验**和(或)**竣工后试验**。此要求应在缺陷或损害修补后 28 天内发出通知提出。

这些试验，除应根据**第 11.2 款**[**修补缺陷的费用**]的规定，由对修补费用负责的一**方**承担试验的风险和费用外，应按适用于先前试验的条款进行。

11.7 进入权

在颁发**履约证书**前，**承包商**应有进入**工程**的所有部分，使用**工程**的运行和工作记录的权力。但不符合**雇主**的合理保安限制的情况除外。

11.8 承包商调查

如果**雇主**要求**承包商**调查任何缺陷的原因，**承包商**应在**雇主**的指导下进行调查。除非根据**第 11.2 款**[**修补缺陷的费用**]的规定，应由**承包商**承担修补

of the Contractor under Sub-Clause 11.2 [*Cost of Remedying Defects*], the Cost of the search plus reasonable profit shall be agreed or determined in accordance with Sub-Clause 3.5 [*Determinations*] and shall be added to the Contract Price.

11.9

Performance Certificate

Performance of the Contractor's obligations shall not be considered to have been completed until the Employer has issued the Performance Certificate to the Contractor, stating the date on which the Contractor completed his obligations under the Contract.

The Employer shall issue the Performance Certificate within 28 days after the latest of the expiry dates of the Defects Notification Periods, or as soon thereafter as the Contractor has supplied all the Contractor's Documents and completed and tested all the Works, including remedying any defects. If the Employer fails to issue the Performance Certificate accordingly:

(a) the Performance Certificate shall be deemed to have been issued on the date 28 days after the date on which it should have been issued, as required by this Sub-Clause, and

(b) Sub-Clause 11.11 [*Clearance of Site*] and sub-paragraph (a) of Sub-Clause 14.14 [*Cessation of Employer's Liability*] shall be inapplicable.

Only the Performance Certificate shall be deemed to constitute acceptance of the Works.

11.10

Unfulfilled Obligations

After the Performance Certificate has been issued, each Party shall remain liable for the fulfilment of any obligation which remains unperformed at that time. For the purposes of determining the nature and extent of unperformed obligations, the Contract shall be deemed to remain in force.

11.11

Clearance of Site

Upon receiving the Performance Certificate, the Contractor shall remove any remaining Contractor's Equipment, surplus material, wreckage, rubbish and Temporary Works from the Site.

If all these items have not been removed within 28 days after the Employer issues the Performance Certificate, the Employer may sell or otherwise dispose of any remaining items. The Employer shall be entitled to be paid the costs incurred in connection with, or attributable to, such sale or disposal and restoring the Site.

Any balance of the moneys from the sale shall be paid to the Contractor. If these moneys are less than the Employer's costs, the Contractor shall pay the outstanding balance to the Employer.

12 Tests after Completion

12.1

Procedure for Tests after Completion

If Tests after Completion are specified in the Contract, this Clause shall apply. Unless otherwise stated in the Particular Conditions:

(a) the Employer shall provide all electricity, fuel and materials, and make the Employer's Personnel and Plant available;

(b) the Contractor shall provide any other plant, equipment and suitably qualified

费用的情况，调查**费用**加合理的利润，应按照**第 3.5 款**[*确定*]的要求商定或确定，并加入**合同价格**。

11.9

履约证书

直到**雇主**向**承包商**颁发**履约证书**，注明**承包商**完成**合同**规定的各项义务的日期后，才应认为**承包商**的义务已经完成。

履约证书应由**雇主**在最后一个**缺陷通知期限**期满日期后 28 天内颁发，或在**承包商**提供所有**承包商文件**、完成了所有**工程**的施工和试验，包括修补任何缺陷后尽快颁发。如果**雇主**未能按此要求颁发**履约证书**：

(a) 应认为**履约证书**已经在本**款**要求的应颁发日期后 28 天的日期颁发；

(b) **第 11.11 款**[*现场清理*]和**第 14.14 款**[*雇主责任的中止*](a)项的规定应不适用。

只有**履约证书**应被认为构成对**工程**的认可。

11.10

未履行的义务

颁发**履约证书**后，每一**方**仍应负责完成当时尚未履行的任何义务。为了确定这些未完义务的性质和范围，**合同**应被认为仍然有效。

11.11

现场清理

在收到**履约证书**时，**承包商**应从**现场**撤走任何剩余的**承包商设备**、多余材料、残余物、垃圾和**临时工程**等。

如果所有这些物品，在**雇主**颁发**履约证书**后 28 天内，尚未被运走，**雇主**可出售或另行处理任何这些剩余物品。**雇主**应有权收回有关或由于此类出售或处理、以及恢复**现场**所发生的费用。

此类出售的任何余款应付给**承包商**。如果出售收入少于**雇主**支出的费用，**承包商**应将差额付给**雇主**。

12 竣工后试验

12.1

竣工后试验的程序

如果**合同**规定了**竣工后试验**，应适用本**条**规定。除非**专用条件**中另有说明：

(a) **雇主**应提供全部电力、燃料和材料，并安排动用**雇主人员**和**生产设备**；

(b) **承包商**应提供有效进行**竣工后试验**所需要的所有其他设备、装备、以

and experienced staff, as are necessary to carry out the Tests after Completion efficiently; and

(c) the Contractor shall carry out the Tests after Completion in the presence of such Employer's and/or Contractor's Personnel as either Party may reasonably request.

The Tests after Completion shall be carried out as soon as is reasonably practicable after the Works or Section have been taken over by the Employer. The Employer shall give to the Contractor 21 days' notice of the date after which the Tests after Completion will be carried out. Unless otherwise agreed, these Tests shall be carried out within 14 days after this date, on the day or days determined by the Employer.

The results of the Tests after Completion shall be compiled and evaluated by the Contractor, who shall prepare a detailed report. Appropriate account shall be taken of the effect of the Employer's prior use of the Works.

12.2

Delayed Tests

If the Contractor incurs Cost as a result of any unreasonable delay by the Employer to the Tests after Completion, the Contractor shall (i) give notice to the Employer and (ii) be entitled subject to Sub-Clause 20.1 [*Contractor's Claims*] to payment of any such Cost plus reasonable profit, which shall be added to the Contract Price.

After receiving this notice, the Employer shall proceed in accordance with Sub-Clause 3.5 [*Determinations*] to agree or determine this Cost and profit.

If, for reasons not attributable to the Contractor, a Test after Completion on the Works or any Section cannot be completed during the Defects Notification Period (or any other period agreed upon by both Parties), then the Works or Section shall be deemed to have passed this Test after Completion.

12.3

Retesting

If the Works, or a Section, fail to pass the Tests after Completion:

(a) sub-paragraph (b) of Sub-Clause 11.1 [*Completion of Outstanding Work and Remedying of Defects*] shall apply, and
(b) either Party may then require the failed Tests, and the Tests after Completion on any related work, to be repeated under the same terms and conditions.

If and to the extent that this failure and retesting are attributable to any of the matters listed in sub-paragraphs (a) to (d) of Sub-Clause 11.2 [*Cost of Remedying Defects*] and cause the Employer to incur additional costs, the Contractor shall subject to Sub-Clause 2.5 [*Employer's Claims*] pay these costs to the Employer.

12.4

Failure to Pass Tests after Completion

If the following conditions apply, namely:

(a) the Works, or a Section, fail to pass any or all of the Tests after Completion,
(b) the relevant sum payable as non-performance damages for this failure is stated (or its method of calculation is defined) in the Contract, and
(c) the Contractor pays this relevant sum to the Employer during the Defects Notification Period,

then the Works or Section shall be deemed to have passed these Tests after Completion.

If the Works, or a Section, fail to pass a Test after Completion and the Contractor proposes to make adjustments or modifications to the Works or such Section, the Contractor may be instructed by (or on behalf of) the Employer that right of access to

及有适当资质和经验的人员；

(c) **承包商**应在任一**方**可能合理要求的**雇主**和(或)**承包商**的有关人员的参加下，进行**竣工后试验**。

竣工后试验应在**工程**或**单位工程**被**雇主**接收后的合理可行的时间内尽快进行。**雇主**应提前21天将开始进行**竣工后试验**的日期通知**承包商**。除非另有商定，这些试验应在该日期后14天内，在**雇主**确定的某日或某几日进行。

竣工后试验的结果应由**承包商**负责整理和评价，并编写一份详细报告。对**雇主**提前使用**工程**的影响应予适当考虑。

12.2

延误的试验

如果由于**雇主**对**竣工后试验**的无故延误，致使**承包商**增加**费用**，**承包商**应：(ⅰ)向**雇主**发出通知，(ⅱ)有权根据**第20.1款**[*承包商的索赔*]的规定提出对任何此类**费用**和合理利润应加入**合同价格**，给予支付。

雇主收到通知后，应按照**第3.5款**[*确定*]的要求商定或确定此项**费用**和利润。

如果**工程**或任何**单位工程**的**竣工后试验**，未能在**缺陷通知期限**(或**双方**商定的任何其他期限)内完成，且原因不在**承包商**方面，**工程**或**单位工程**应被视为已通过了**竣工后试验**。

12.3

重新试验

如果**工程**或**单位工程**未能通过**竣工后试验**：

(a) 应适用**第11.1款**[*完成扫尾工作和修补缺陷*](b)项；

(b) 任一**方**即可要求按相同条款和条件，重新进行此项未通过的**试验**和任何相关工程的**竣工后试验**。

如果此项未通过试验和重新试验是由**第11.2款**[*修补缺陷的费用*](a)至(d)项所列的任何事项造成的，达到致使**雇主**增加费用的程度，**承包商**应根据**第2.5款**[*雇主的索赔*]的规定，向**雇主**支付这些费用。

12.4

未能通过竣工后试验

如果下列条件成立，即：

(a) **工程**或某**单位工程**未能通过任何或全部**竣工后试验**；
(b) **合同**中已说明对此项未通过试验可作为未履约损害赔偿费支付的相应金额(或其计算方法已规定)；
(c) **承包商**已在**缺陷通知期限**内向雇主支付了此项相应金额；

则该**工程**或**单位工程**应被视为已通过了这些**竣工后试验**。

如果**工程**或某**单位工程**未通过某项**竣工后试验**，而**承包商**建议对**工程**或该**单位工程**进行调整或修正，**雇主**(或其代表)可指示**承包商**，到**雇主**方便时

the Works or Section cannot be given until a time that is convenient to the Employer. The Contractor shall then remain liable to carry out the adjustments or modifications and to satisfy this Test, within a reasonable period of receiving notice by (or on behalf of) the Employer of the time that is convenient to the Employer. However, if the Contractor does not receive this notice during the relevant Defects Notification Period, the Contractor shall be relieved of this obligation and the Works or Section (as the case may be) shall be deemed to have passed this Test after Completion.

If the Contractor incurs additional Cost as a result of any unreasonable delay by the Employer in permitting access to the Works or Plant by the Contractor, either to investigate the causes of a failure to pass a Test after Completion or to carry out any adjustments or modifications, the Contractor shall (i) give notice to the Employer and (ii) be entitled subject to Sub-Clause 20.1 [*Contractor's Claims*] to payment of any such Cost plus reasonable profit, which shall be added to the Contract Price.

After receiving this notice, the Employer shall proceed in accordance with Sub-Clause 3.5 [*Determinations*] to agree or determine this Cost and profit.

13 Variations and Adjustments

13.1
Right to Vary

Variations may be initiated by the Employer at any time prior to issuing the Taking-Over Certificate for the Works, either by an instruction or by a request for the Contractor to submit a proposal. A Variation shall not comprise the omission of any work which is to be carried out by others.

The Contractor shall execute and be bound by each Variation, unless the Contractor promptly gives notice to the Employer stating (with supporting particulars) that (i) the Contractor cannot readily obtain the Goods required for the Variation, (ii) it will reduce the safety or suitability of the Works, or (iii) it will have an adverse impact on the achievement of the Performance Guarantees. Upon receiving this notice, the Employer shall cancel, confirm or vary the instruction.

13.2
Value Engineering

The Contractor may, at any time, submit to the Employer a written proposal which (in the Contractor's opinion) will, if adopted, (i) accelerate completion, (ii) reduce the cost to the Employer of executing, maintaining or operating the Works, (iii) improve the efficiency or value to the Employer of the completed Works, or (iv) otherwise be of benefit to the Employer.

The proposal shall be prepared at the cost of the Contractor and shall include the items listed in Sub-Clause 13.3 [*Variation Procedure*].

13.3
Variation Procedure

If the Employer requests a proposal, prior to instructing a Variation, the Contractor shall respond in writing as soon as practicable, either by giving reasons why he cannot comply (if this is the case) or by submitting:

(a) a description of the proposed design and/or work to be performed and a programme for its execution,
(b) the Contractor's proposal for any necessary modifications to the programme according to Sub-Clause 8.3 [*Programme*] and to the Time for Completion, and
(c) the Contractor's proposal for adjustment to the Contract Price.

才能给予**工程**或**单位工程**的进入权。此时，**承包商**应在等待**雇主**(或其代表)关于**雇主**方便时间的通知的合理期限内，对进行调整或修正、并履行该项**试验**继续负责。但如果**承包商**在相关**缺陷通知期限**内未收到此项通知，**承包商**应解除上述义务，而**工程**或**单位工程**(视情况而定)应视为通过了该项**竣工后试验**。

如果对**承包商**为调查未通过某项**竣工后试验**的原因，或为进行任何调整或修正，要进入**工程**或**生产设备**，**雇主**无故延误给予许可，招致**承包商**增加**费用**，**承包商**应：(ⅰ)向**雇主**发出通知，(ⅱ)有权根据**第 20.1 款**[*承包商的索赔*]的规定，提出将任何此类**费用**和合理利润加入**合同价格**，给予支付。

雇主收到此通知后，应按照**第 3.5 款**[*确定*]的要求，对此项费用和利润进行商定或确定。

13 变更和调整

13.1 变更权

在颁发**工程接收证书**前的任何时间，**雇主**可通过发布指示或要求**承包商**提交建议书的方式，提出**变更**。**变更**不应包括准备交他人进行的任何工作的删减。

承包商应遵守并执行每项**变更**。除非**承包商**迅速向**雇主**发出通知，说明(附详细根据)：(ⅰ)**承包商**难以取得**变更**所需要的货物；(ⅱ)**变更**将降低**工程**的安全性或适用性；或(ⅲ)将对**履约保证**的完成产生不利的影响。**雇主**接到此类通知后，应取消、确认、或改变原指示。

13.2 价值工程

承包商可随时向**雇主**提交书面建议，提出(他认为)采纳后将：(ⅰ)加快竣工，(ⅱ)降低**雇主的工程**施工、维护、或运行的费用，(ⅲ)提高**雇主**的竣工**工程**的效率或价值，或(ⅳ)给**雇主**带来其他利益的建议。

此类建议书应由**承包商**自费编制，并应包括**第 13.3 款**[*变更程序*]所列内容。

13.3 变更程序

如果**雇主**在发出**变更**指示前要求**承包商**提出一份建议书，**承包商**应尽快做出书面回应，或提出他不能照办的理由(如果情况如此)，或提交：

(a) 对建议的设计和(或)要完成的工作的说明，以及实施的进度计划；

(b) 根据**第 8.3 款**[*进度计划*]和**竣工时间**的要求，**承包商**对进度计划做出必要修改的建议书；

(c) **承包商**对调整**合同价格**的建议书。

The Employer shall, as soon as practicable after receiving such proposal (under Sub-Clause 13.2 [*Value Engineering*] or otherwise), respond with approval, disapproval or comments. The Contractor shall not delay any work whilst awaiting a response.

Each instruction to execute a Variation, with any requirements for the recording of Costs, shall be issued by the Employer to the Contractor, who shall acknowledge receipt.

Upon instructing or approving a Variation, the Employer shall proceed in accordance with Sub-Clause 3.5 [*Determinations*] to agree or determine adjustments to the Contract Price and the Schedule of Payments. These adjustments shall include reasonable profit. and shall take account of the Contractor's submissions under Sub-Clause 13.2 [*Value Engineering*] if applicable.

13.4

Payment in Applicable Currencies

If the Contract provides for payment of the Contract Price in more than one currency, then whenever an adjustment is agreed, approved or determined as stated above, the amount payable in each of the applicable currencies shall be specified. For this purpose, reference shall be made to the actual or expected currency proportions of the Cost of the varied work, and to the proportions of various currencies specified for payment of the Contract Price.

13.5

Provisional Sums

Each Provisional Sum shall only be used, in whole or in part, in accordance with the Employer's instructions, and the Contract Price shall be adjusted accordingly. The total sum paid to the Contractor shall include only such amounts, for the work, supplies or services to which the Provisional Sum relates, as the Employer shall have instructed. For each Provisional Sum, the Employer may instruct:

(a) work to be executed (including Plant, Materials or services to be supplied) by the Contractor and valued under Sub-Clause 13.3 [*Variation Procedure*]; and/or

(b) Plant, Materials or services to be purchased by the Contractor, for which there shall be added to the Contract Price less the original Provisional Sums:

  (i) the actual amounts paid (or due to be paid) by the Contractor, and

  (ii) a sum for overhead charges and profit, calculated as a percentage of these actual amounts by applying the relevant percentage rate (if any) stated in the Contract.

The Contractor shall, when required by the Employer, produce quotations, invoices, vouchers and accounts or receipts in substantiation.

13.6

Daywork

For work of a minor or incidental nature, the Employer may instruct that a Variation shall be executed on a daywork basis. The work shall then be valued in accordance with the daywork schedule included in the Contract, and the following procedure shall apply. If a daywork schedule is not included in the Contract, this Sub-Clause shall not apply.

Before ordering Goods for the work, the Contractor shall submit quotations to the Employer. When applying for payment, the Contractor shall submit invoices, vouchers and accounts or receipts for any Goods.

Except for any items for which the daywork schedule specifies that payment is not due, the Contractor shall deliver each day to the Employer accurate statements in

雇主收到此类(根据**第 13.2 款**[**价值工程**]的规定或其他规定提出的）建议书后，应尽快给予批准、不批准、或提出意见的回复。在等待答复期间，**承包商**不应延误任何工作。

应由**雇主**向**承包商**发出执行每项**变更**并附做好各项费用记录的任何要求的指示，**承包商**应确认收到该指示。

为指示或批准一项**变更**，**雇主**应按照**第 3.5 款**[**确定**]的要求，商定或确定对**合同价格**和**付款计划表**的调整。这些调整应包括合理的利润，如果适用，并应考虑**承包商**根据**第 13.2 款**[**价值工程**]提交的建议。

13.4

以适用货币支付

如果**合同**规定**合同价格**以一种以上货币支付，在上述商定、批准或确定调整时，应规定以每种适用货币支付的款额。为此，应参考变更后工作**费用**的实际或预期的货币比例，和规定的**合同价格**支付中的各种货币比例。

13.5

暂列金额

每笔**暂列金额**只应按**雇主**指示全部或部分地使用，并对**合同价格**相应进行调整。付给**承包商**的总金额只应包括**雇主**已指示的，与**暂列金额**有关的工作、供货或服务的应付款项。对于每笔**暂列金额**，**雇主**可以指示用于下列支付：

(a) 根据**第 13.3 款**[**变更程序**]的规定进行估价的、要由**承包商**实施的工作(包括要提供的**生产设备**、**材料**、或服务)；和(或)

(b) 应加入扣除原列**暂列金额**后的**合同价格**的，要由**承包商**购买的**生产设备**、**材料**或服务的下列费用：

(i) **承包商**已付(或应付)的实际金额，

(ii) 以**合同**规定的有关百分率(如果有)计算的，这些实际金额的一个百分比，作为管理费和利润的金额。

当**雇主**要求时，**承包商**应出示报价单、发票、凭证、以及帐单或收据等证明。

13.6

计日工作

对于一些小的或附带性的工作，**雇主**可指示按计日工作实施**变更**。这时，工作应按照包括在**合同**中的计日工作计划表，并按下述程序进行估价。如果**合同**中未包括**计日工作计划表**，则**本款**不适用。

在为工作订购**货物**前，**承包商**应向**雇主**提交报价单。当申请支付时，**承包商**应提交任何**货物**的发票、凭证、以及帐单或收据。

除**计日工作计划表**中规定不应支付的任何项目外，**承包商**应向**雇主**提交每

duplicate which shall include the following details of the resources used in executing the previous day's work:

(a) the names, occupations and time of Contractor's Personnel,
(b) the identification, type and time of Contractor's Equipment and Temporary Works, and
(c) the quantities and types of Plant and Materials used.

One copy of each statement will, if correct, or when agreed, be signed by the Employer and returned to the Contractor. The Contractor shall then submit priced statements of these resources to the Employer, prior to their inclusion in the next Statement under Sub-Clause 14.3 [*Application for Interim Payments*].

13.7

Adjustments for Changes in Legislation

The Contract Price shall be adjusted to take account of any increase or decrease in Cost resulting from a change in the Laws of the Country (including the introduction of new Laws and the repeal or modification of existing Laws) or in the judicial or official governmental interpretation of such Laws, made after the Base Date, which affect the Contractor in the performance of obligations under the Contract.

If the Contractor suffers (or will suffer) delay and/or incurs (or will incur) additional Cost as a result of these changes in the Laws or in such interpretations, made after the Base Date, the Contractor shall give notice to the Employer and shall be entitled subject to Sub-Clause 20.1 [*Contractor's Claims*] to:

(a) an extension of time for any such delay, if completion is or will be delayed, under Sub-Clause 8.4 [*Extension of Time for Completion*], and
(b) payment of any such Cost, which shall be added to the Contract Price.

After receiving this notice, the Employer shall proceed in accordance with Sub-Clause 3.5 [*Determinations*] to agree or determine these matters.

13.8

Adjustments for Changes in Costs

If the Contract Price is to be adjusted for rises or falls in the cost of labour, Goods and other inputs to the Works, the adjustments shall be calculated in accordance with the provisions in the Particular Conditions.

14 Contract Price and Payment

14.1
The Contract Price

Unless otherwise stated in the Particular Conditions:

(a) payment for the Works shall be made on the basis of the lump sum Contract Price, subject to adjustments in accordance with the Contract; and
(b) the Contractor shall pay all taxes, duties and fees required to be paid by him under the Contract, and the Contract Price shall not be adjusted for any of these costs, except as stated in Sub-Clause 13.7 [*Adjustments for Changes in Legislation*].

14.2

Advance Payment

The Employer shall make an advance payment, as an interest-free loan for mobilization and design, when the Contractor submits a guarantee in accordance with this Sub-Clause including the details stated in the Particular Conditions. If the Particular Conditions does not state:

日的精确报表，一式二份，报表应包括前一日工作中使用的各项资源的详细资料：

(a) **承包商人员**的姓名、职业和使用时间；
(b) **承包商设备**和**临时工程**的标识、型号和使用时间；
(c) 所用的**生产设备**和**材料**的数量和型号。

报表如果正确或经同意，将由**雇主**签署并退回**承包商**一份。**承包商**应在将它们列入其后根据**第14.3款**[**期中支付的申请**]的规定提交的报表前，先向**雇主**提交关于这些资源的估价报表。

13.7

因法律改变的调整

对于**基准日期** **工程所在国**的**法律**有改变(包括施用新的**法律**，废除或修改现有**法律**)，或对此类**法律**的司法或政府解释有改变，影响**承包商**履行**合同**规定的义务的，**合同价格**应考虑由上述改变导致的任何费用增减进行调整。

如果由于这些**基准日期**后做出的**法律**或此类解释的改变，使**承包商**已(或将)遭受延误和(或)已(或将)招致增加**费用**，**承包商**应向**雇主**发出通知，并应有权根据**第20.1款**[**承包商的索赔**]的规定要求：

(a) 根据**第8.4款**[**竣工时间的延长**]的规定，如果竣工已(或)将受到延误，对任何此类延误给予延长期；
(b) 任何此类**费用**应计入**合同价格**，给予支付。

雇主收到此类通知后，应按照**第3.5款**[**确定**]的要求，对这些事项进行商定或确定。

13.8

因成本改变的调整

当**合同价格**要根据劳动力、**货物**、以及**工程**的其他投入的成本的升降进行调整时，应按照**专用条件**的规定进行计算。

14 合同价格和付款

14.1

合同价格

除非在**专用条件**中另有规定：

(a) **工程**款的支付应以总额**合同价格**为基础，按照**合同**规定进行调整；

(b) **承包商**应支付根据**合同**要求应由其支付的各项税费。除**第13.7款**[**因法律改变的调整**]说明的情况外，**合同价格**不应因任何这些费用进行调整。

14.2

预付款

当**承包商**按照本**款**，包括**专用条件**中提出的详细要求，提交保函后，**雇主**应支付一笔预付款作为用于动员和设计的无息贷款。如果**专用条件**没有说明：

(a) the amount of the advance payment, then this Sub-Clause shall not apply;
(b) the number and timing of instalments, then there shall be only one;
(c) the applicable currencies and proportions, then they shall be those in which the Contract Price is payable; and/or
(d) the amortisation rate for repayments, then it shall be calculated by dividing the total amount of the advance payment by the Contract Price stated in the Contract Agreement less Provisional Sums.

The Employer shall pay the first instalment after receiving (i) a Statement (under Sub-Clause 14.3 [*Application for Interim Payments*]), (ii) the Performance Security in accordance with Sub-Clause 4.2 [*Performance Security*], and (iii) a guarantee in amounts and currencies equal to the advance payment. This guarantee shall be issued by an entity and from within a country (or other jurisdiction) approved by the Employer, and shall be in the form annexed to the Particular Conditions or in another form approved by the Employer. Unless and until the Employer receives this guarantee, this Sub-Clause shall not apply.

The Contractor shall ensure that the guarantee is valid and enforceable until the advance payment has been repaid, but its amount may be progressively reduced by the amount repaid by the Contractor. If the terms of the guarantee specify its expiry date, and the advance payment has not been repaid by the date 28 days prior to the expiry date, the Contractor shall extend the validity of the guarantee until the advance payment has been repaid.

The advance payment shall be repaid through proportional deductions in interim payments. Deductions shall be made at the amortization rate stated in the Particular Conditions (or, if not so stated, as stated in sub-paragraph (d) above), which shall be applied to the amount otherwise due (excluding the advance payment and deductions and repayments of retention), until such time as the advance payment has been repaid.

If the advance payment has not been repaid prior to the issue of the Taking-Over Certificate for the Works or prior to termination under Clause 15 [*Termination by Employer*], Clause 16 [*Suspension and Termination by Contractor*] or Clause 19 [*Force Majeure*] (as the case may be), the whole of the balance then outstanding shall immediately become due and payable by the Contractor to the Employer.

14.3

Application for Interim Payments

The Contractor shall submit a Statement in six copies to the Employer after the end of the period of payment stated in the Contract (if not stated, after the end of each month), in a form approved by the Employer, showing in detail the amounts to which the Contractor considers himself to be entitled, together with supporting documents which shall include the relevant report on progress in accordance with Sub-Clause 4.21 [*Progress Reports*].

The Statement shall include the following items, as applicable, which shall be expressed in the various currencies in which the Contract Price is payable, in the sequence listed:

(a) the estimated contract value of the Works executed and the Contractor's Documents produced up to the end of the month (including Variations but excluding items described in sub-paragraphs (b) to (f) below);
(b) any amounts to be added and deducted for changes in legislation and changes in cost, in accordance with Sub-Clause 13.7 [*Adjustments for Changes in Legislation*] and Sub-Clause 13.8 [*Adjustments for Changes in Cost*];
(c) any amount to be deducted for retention, calculated by applying the percentage of retention stated in the Particular Conditions to the total of the

(a) 预付款的数量，则本**款**应不适用；
(b) 分期付款的期数和时间安排，则只应有一次；
(c) 预付款的适用货币及比例，则应按**合同价格**支付的货币比例支付；和(或)
(d) 预付款分期摊还比率，则应按预付款总额除以减去**暂列金额**的**合同协议书**中规定的**合同价格**得出的比率进行计算。

雇主在收到(ⅰ)(根据**第 14.3 款[期中付款的申请]**规定的)报表，(ⅱ)按照**第 4.2 款[履约担保]**的规定，递交的**履约担保**，和(ⅲ)由**雇主**批准的国家(或其他司法管辖区)的实体按**专用条件**所附格式或**雇主**批准的其他格式签发的，金额与币种等同于预付款的保函后，应支付首次分期付款。除非并直到**雇主**收到此保函，本**款**应不适用。

在还清预付款前，**承包商**应确保该保函一直有效并可执行；但其总额可根据**承包商**付还的金额逐渐减少。如果该保函条款中规定了期满日期，而在期满日期前 28 天预付款尚未还清时，**承包商**应将保函有效期延至预付款还清为止。

预付款应通过在期中付款中按比例扣减的方式付还。扣减应按照**专用条件**中规定的分期摊还比率(或，如无此规定，则如上述(d)项中所述比率）计算，这种扣减方法应用于其他应付款项(不包括预付款、扣减额和保留金的付还)，直到预付款还清时为止。

如果在颁发**工程移交证书**前，或根据**第 15 条[由雇主终止]**、**第 16 条[由承包商暂停和终止]**、或**第 19 条[不可抗力]**(视情况而定)的规定终止前，预付款尚未还清，则全部余额应立即成为**承包商**对**雇主**的到期应付款。

14.3

期中付款的申请

承包商应在**合同**规定的支付期限末(如无规定，则在每月月末)后，按**雇主**批准的格式，向**雇主**提交一式六份**报表**，详细说明**承包商**自己认为有权得到的款额，同时提交包括按**第 4.21 款[进度报告]**的规定编制的相关进度报告在内的证明文件。

适用时，该**报表**应包括下列项目，以**合同价格**应付的各种货币表示，并按下列顺序排列：

(a) 截至月末已实施的**工程**和已提出的**承包商文件**的估算合同价值(包括各项**变更**，但不包括以下(b)至(f)项所列项目）；

(b) 按照**第 13.7 款[因法律改变的调整]**和**第 13.8 款[因成本改变的调整]**的规定，由于法律改变和成本改变，应增减的任何款额；

(c) 至**雇主**提取的保留金额达到**专用条件**中规定的保留金限额(如果有)

above amounts, until the amount so retained by the Employer reaches the limit of Retention Money (if any) stated in the Particular Conditions;

(d) any amounts to be added and deducted for the advance payment and repayments in accordance with Sub-Clause 14.2 [*Advance Payment*];

(e) any other additions or deductions which may have become due under the Contract or otherwise, including those under Clause 20 [*Claims, Disputes and Arbitration*]; and

(f) the deduction of amounts included in previous Statements.

14.4

Schedule of Payments

If the Contract includes a Schedule of Payments specifying the instalments in which the Contract Price will be paid, then unless otherwise stated in this Schedule:

(a) the instalments quoted in the Schedule of Payments shall be the estimated contract values for the purposes of sub-paragraph (a) of Sub-Clause 14.3 [*Application for Interim Payments*], subject to Sub-Clause 14.5 [*Plant and Materials intended for the Works*]; and

(b) if these instalments are not defined by reference to the actual progress achieved in executing the Works, and if actual progress is found to be less than that on which the Schedule of Payments was based, then the Employer may proceed in accordance with Sub-Clause 3.5 [*Determinations*] to agree or determine revised instalments, which shall take account of the extent to which progress is less than that on which the instalments were previously based.

If the Contract does not include a Schedule of Payments, the Contractor shall submit non-binding estimates of the payments which he expects to become due during each quarterly period. The first estimate shall be submitted within 42 days after the Commencement Date. Revised estimates shall be submitted at quarterly intervals, until the Taking-Over Certificate has been issued for the Works.

14.5

Plant and Materials intended for the Works

If the Contractor is entitled, under the Contract, to an interim payment for Plant and Materials which are not yet on the Site, the Contractor shall nevertheless not be entitled to such payment unless:

(a) the relevant Plant and Materials are in the Country and have been marked as the Employer's property in accordance with the Employer's instructions; or

(b) the Contractor has delivered, to the Employer, evidence of insurance and a bank guarantee in a form and issued by an entity approved by the Employer in amounts and currencies equal to such payment. This guarantee may be in a similar form to the form referred to in Sub-Clause 14.2 [*Advance Payment*] and shall be valid until the Plant and Materials are properly stored on Site and protected against loss, damage or deterioration.

14.6

Interim Payments

No amount will be paid until the Employer has received and approved the Performance Security. Thereafter, the Employer shall within 28 days after receiving a Statement and supporting documents, give to the Contractor notice of any items in the Statement with which the Employer disagrees, with supporting particulars. Payments due shall not be withheld, except that:

(a) if any thing supplied or work done by the Contractor is not in accordance with the Contract, the cost of rectification or replacement may be withheld until rectification or replacement has been completed; and/or

(b) if the Contractor was or is failing to perform any work or obligation in accordance with the Contract, and had been so notified by the Employer, the

前，用**专用条件**中规定的保留金百分比乘以对上述款项总额计算的应扣减的任何保留金额；

(d) 按照**第 14.2 款**[**预付款**]的规定，因预付款的支付和付还，应增加和扣减的任何款额；

(e) 根据**合同**或包括**第 20 条**[**索赔、争端和仲裁**]规定等其他理由，应付的任何其他增加额或扣减额；

(f) 所有以前**报表**中包括的扣减额。

14.4

付款计划表

如果**合同**包括对**合同价格**的支付规定了分期支付的**付款计划表**，除非该表中另有规定，否则：

(a) 该**付款计划表**所列分期付款额，应是为了应对**第 14.3 款**[**期中付款的申请**]中(a)项，并依照**第 14.5 款**[**拟用于工程的生产设备和材料**]的规定估算的合同价值；

(b) 如果分期付款额不是参照**工程**实施达到的实际进度确定，且发现实际进度比**付款计划表**依据的进度落后时，**雇主**可按照**第 3.5 款**[**确定**]的要求进行商定或确定，修改该分期付款额。这种修改应考虑实际进度落后于该分期付款额原依据的进度的程度。

如果**合同**未包括**付款计划表**，**承包商**应在每个季度，提交他预计应付的无约束性估算付款额。第一次估算应在**开工日期**后 42 天内提交。直到颁发**工程接收证书**前，应按季度提交修正的估算。

14.5

拟用于工程的生产设备和材料

如果根据**合同**规定，**承包商**有权获得尚未运到**现场**的**生产设备**和**材料**的期中付款，**承包商**必须具备下列条件才有权得到：

(a) 相关**生产设备**和**材料**在**工程所在国**，并已按**雇主**的指示，标明是**雇主**的财产；或

(b) **承包商**已向**雇主**提交保险的证据和经**雇主**批准的实体按批准的格式签发的、数额和币种与该项付款相同的银行保函。该保函可以用与**第 14.2 款**[**预付款**]中提到的格式相似的格式，并应做到在**生产设备**和**材料**在**现场**妥善储存并做好防止损失、损害或变质的保护以前一直有效。

14.6

期中付款

在**雇主**收到并认可**履约担保**前，不办理付款。其后，**雇主**应在收到有关**报表**和证明文件后 28 天内，向**承包商**发出关于报表中**雇主**不同意的任何项目的通知，并附细节证明。除下列情况外，对应付款项不应予以扣发：

(a) 如果**承包商**供应的任何物品或完成的工作不符合**合同**要求，在修正或更换完成前，可以扣发该修正或更换所需费用；和(或)

(b) 如果**承包商**未能按照**合同**要求履行任何工作或义务，且**雇主**已曾为

value of this work or obligation may be withheld until the work or obligation has been performed.

The Employer may, by any payment, make any correction or modification that should properly be made to any amount previously considered due. Payment shall not be deemed to indicate the Employer's acceptance, approval, consent or satisfaction.

14.7

Timing of Payments

Except as otherwise stated in Sub-Clause 2.5 [*Employer's Claims*], the Employer shall pay to the Contractor:

(a) the first instalment of the advance payment within 42 days after the date on which the Contract came into full force and effect or within 21 days after the Employer receives the documents in accordance with Sub-Clause 4.2 [*Performance Security*] and Sub-Clause 14.2 [*Advance Payment*], whichever is later;
(b) the amount which is due in respect of each Statement, other than the Final Statement, within 56 days after receiving the Statement and supporting documents; and
(c) the final amount due, within 42 days after receiving the Final Statement and written discharge in accordance with Sub-Clause 14.11 [*Application for Final Payment*] and Sub-Clause 14.12 [*Discharge*].

Payment of the amount due in each currency shall be made into the bank account, nominated by the Contractor, in the payment country (for this currency) specified in the Contract.

14.8

Delayed Payment

If the Contractor does not receive payment in accordance with Sub-Clause 14.7 [*Timing of Payments*], the Contractor shall be entitled to receive financing charges compounded monthly on the amount unpaid during the period of delay.

Unless otherwise stated in the Particular Conditions, these financing charges shall be calculated at the annual rate of three percentage points above the discount rate of the central bank in the country of the currency of payment, and shall be paid in such currency.

The Contractor shall be entitled to this payment without formal notice, and without prejudice to any other right or remedy.

14.9

Payment of Retention Money

When the Taking-Over Certificate has been issued for the Works, and the Works have passed all specified tests (including the Tests after Completion, if any), the first half of the Retention Money shall be paid to the Contractor. If a Taking-Over Certificate is issued for a Section, the relevant percentage of the first half of the Retention Money shall be paid when the Section passes all tests.

Promptly after the latest of the expiry dates of the Defects Notification Periods, the outstanding balance of the Retention Money shall be paid to the Contractor. If a Taking-Over Certificate was issued for a Section, the relevant percentage of the second half of the Retention Money shall be paid promptly after the expiry date of the Defects Notification Period for the Section.

However, if any work remains to be executed under Clause 11 [*Defects Liability*] or Clause 12 [*Tests after Completion*], the Employer shall be entitled to withhold the estimated cost of this work until it has been executed.

此发出通知时，可以在该项工作或义务完成前，扣发该工作或义务的价值。

雇主可以在任一次付款时，对以前曾被认为应付的任何款额做出应有的任何正当的改正或修正。付款不应被认为，表明**雇主**的接受、批准、同意或满意。

14.7

付款的时间安排

除**第2.5款**[**雇主的索赔**]另有规定以外，**雇主**应在以下时间向**承包商**支付：

(a) 在**合同**开始实施和生效日期后42天，或雇主收到按照**第4.2款**[**履约担保**]和**第14.2款**[**预付款**]规定提出的文件后21天，二者中较晚的日期内，支付首期预付款；

(b) 在收到有关**报表**和证明文件后56天内，**最终报表**除外，支付每期**报表**的应付款额；

(c) 在收到按照**第14.11款**[**最终付款的申请**]和**第14.12款**[**结清证明**]的规定提交的**最终报表**和书面结清证明42天内，支付应付的最终款额。

每种货币的应付款额，应汇入**合同**(为此货币)指定的付款国境内**承包商**指定的银行帐户。

14.8

延误的付款

如果**承包商**没有在按照**第14.7款**[**付款的时间安排**]规定的时间收到付款，**承包商**应有权就未付款额按月计算复利，收取延误期的融资费用。

除非**专用条件**中另有规定，上述融资费用应以高出付款货币所在国中央银行的贴现率三个百分点的年利率进行计算，并应用同种货币支付。

承包商应有权得到上述付款，无需正式通知，且不损害他的任何其他权利或对其补偿。

14.9

保留金的支付

当已颁发**工程接收证书**，且**工程**已通过所有规定的试验(包括**竣工后试验**，如果有)时，应将**保留金**的前一半付给承包商。如果对某**单位工程**颁发了接收证书，当该**单位工程**通过了所有试验时，应付给**保留金**前一半的相关百分比部分。

在各**缺陷通知期限**的最末一个期满日期后，应立即将**保留金**未付的余额付给**承包商**。如对某**单位工程**颁发了**接收证书**，在该**单位工程的缺陷通知期限**期满日期后，应立即支付**保留金**后一半的相关百分比部分。

但如果根据**第11条**[**缺陷责任**]或**第12条**[**竣工后试验**]的规定，还有任何工作要做，**雇主**应有权在该项工作完成前，扣发完成该工作的估算费用。

The relevant percentage for each Section shall be the percentage value of the Section as stated in the Contract. If the percentage value of a Section is not stated in the Contract, no percentage of either half of the Retention Money shall be released under this Sub-Clause in respect of such Section.

14.10

Statement at Completion

Within 84 days after receiving the Taking-Over Certificate for the Works, the Contractor shall submit to the Employer six copies of a Statement at completion with supporting documents, in accordance with Sub-Clause 14.3 [*Application for Interim Payments*], showing:

(a) the value of all work done in accordance with the Contract up to the date stated in the Taking-Over Certificate for the Works,
(b) any further sums which the Contractor considers to be due, and
(c) an estimate of any other amounts which the Contractor considers will become due to him under the Contract. Estimated amounts shall be shown separately in this Statement at completion.

The Employer shall then give notice to the Contractor in accordance with Sub-Clause 14.6 [*Interim Payments*] and make payment in accordance with Sub-Clause 14.7 [*Timing of Payments*].

14.11

Application for Final Payment

Within 56 days after receiving the Performance Certificate, the Contractor shall submit, to the Employer, six copies of a draft final statement with supporting documents showing in detail in a form approved by the Employer:

(a) the value of all work done in accordance with the Contract, and
(b) any further sums which the Contractor considers to be due to him under the Contract or otherwise.

If the Employer disagrees with or cannot verify any part of the draft final statement, the Contractor shall submit such further information as the Employer may reasonably require and shall make such changes in the draft as may be agreed between them. The Contractor shall then prepare and submit to the Employer the final statement as agreed. This agreed statement is referred to in these Conditions as the "Final Statement".

However if, following discussions between the Parties and any changes to the draft final statement which are agreed, it becomes evident that a dispute exists, the Employer shall pay the agreed parts of the draft final statement in accordance with Sub-Clause 14.6 [*Interim Payments*] and Sub-Clause 14.7 [*Timing of Payments*]. Thereafter, if the dispute is finally resolved under Sub-Clause 20.4 [*Obtaining Dispute Adjudication Board's Decision*] or Sub-Clause 20.5 [*Amicable Settlement*], the Contractor shall then prepare and submit to the Employer a Final Statement.

14.12

Discharge

When submitting the Final Statement, the Contractor shall submit a written discharge which confirms that the total of the Final Statement represents full and final settlement of all moneys due to the Contractor under or in connection with the Contract. This discharge may state that it becomes effective when the Contractor has received the Performance Security and the out-standing balance of this total, in which event the discharge shall be effective on such date.

14.13

Final Payment

In accordance with sub-paragraph (c) of Sub-Clause 14.7 [*Timing of Payments*], the Employer shall pay to the Contractor the amount which is finally due, less all amounts

每个**单位工程**的相关百分比应是**合同**中规定的该**单位工程**的价值百分比。如果**合同**中没有规定该**单位工程**的价格百分比，则对该**单位工程**不应根据本**款**对**保留金**任何一半按百分比放还。

14.10

竣工报表

承包商在收到工程**接收证书**后 84 天内，应按照**第 14.3 款**[**期中付款的申请**]的要求，向**雇主**递交竣工**报表**并附证明文件，一式六份，列出：

(a) 截至**工程接收证书**载明的日期，按**合同**要求完成的所有工作的价值；

(b) **承包商**认为应付的任何其他款额；

(c) **承包商**认为根据**合同**规定将应付给他的任何其他款项的估计款额。估计款额在竣工**报表**中应单独列出。

此时**雇主**应按照**第 14.6 款**[**期中付款**]的规定核发支付证书，并按照**第 14.7 款**[**付款的时间安排**]的规定支付。

14.11

最终付款的申请

承包商应在收到**履约证书**后 56 天内，向**雇主**提交按照**雇主**批准的格式编制的最终报表草案，并附证明文件，一式六份，详细列出：

(a) 根据**合同**完成的所有工作的价值，

(b) **承包商**认为根据**合同**或其他规定应支付给他的任何其他款额。

如果**雇主**不同意或无法核实最终报表草案中的任何部分，**承包商**应按**雇主**可能提出的合理要求提交补充资料，并按双方可能商定的意见，对该草案进行修改。然后，**承包商**应按商定的意见编制并向**雇主**提交最终报表。这份经商定的报表在本**条件**中称为“**最终报表**”。

如果在**双方**协商并就协商一致的意见对最终报表草案进行修改过程中，明显存在争端，**雇主**应按照**第 14.6 款**[**期中付款**]和**第 14.7 款**[**付款的时间安排**]的规定，支付最终报表草案中同意的部分。此后，如果争端根据**第 20.4 款**[**取得争端裁决委员会的决定**]、或**第 20.5 款**[**友好解决**]的规定，最终得到解决，**承包商**随后应编制并向**雇主**提交**最终报表**。

14.12

结清证明

承包商在提交**最终报表**时，应提交一份书面结清证明，确认**最终报表**上的总额代表了根据**合同**或与**合同**有关的事项，应付给**承包商**的所有款项的全部和最终的结算总额。该结清证明可注明在**承包商**收到退回的**履约担保**和该总额中尚未付清的余额后生效，在此情况下，结清证明应在该日期生效。

14.13

最终付款

雇主应按照**第14.7款**[**付款的时间安排**](c)项的规定，向**承包商**支付最终

previously paid by the Employer and any deductions in accordance with Sub-Clause 2.5 [*Employer's Claims*].

14.14

Cessation of Employer's Liability

The Employer shall not be liable to the Contractor for any matter or thing under or in connection with the Contract or execution of the Works, except to the extent that the Contractor shall have included an amount expressly for it:

(a) in the Final Statement and also
(b) (except for matters or things arising after the issue of the Taking-Over Certificatefor the Works) in the Statement at completion described in Sub-Clause 14.10 [*Statement at Completion*].

However, this Sub-Clause shall not limit the Employer's liability under his indemnification obligations, or the Employer's liability in any case of fraud, deliberate default or reckless misconduct by the Employer.

14.15

Currencies of Payment

The Contract Price shall be paid in the currency or currencies named in the Contract Agreement. Unless otherwise stated in the Particular Conditions, if more than one currency is so named, payments shall be made as follows:

(a) if the Contract Price was expressed in Local Currency only:

(i) the proportions or amounts of the Local and Foreign Currencies, and the fixed rates of exchange to be used for calculating the payments, shall be as stated in the Contract Agreement, except as otherwise agreed by both Parties;
(ii) payments and deductions under Sub-Clause 13.5 [*Provisional Sums*] and Sub-Clause 13.7 [*Adjustments for Changes in Legislation*] shall be made in the applicable currencies and proportions; and
(iii) other payments and deductions under sub-paragraphs (a) to (d) of Sub-Clause 14.3 [*Application for Interim Payments*] shall be made in the currencies and proportions specified in sub-paragraph (a)(i) above;

(b) payment of the damages specified in the Particular Conditions shall be made in the currencies and proportions specified in the Particular Conditions;
(c) other payments to the Employer by the Contractor shall be made in the currency in which the sum was expended by the Employer, or in such currency as may be agreed by both Parties;
(d) if any amount payable by the Contractor to the Employer in a particular currency exceeds the sum payable by the Employer to the Contractor in that currency, the Employer may recover the balance of this amount from the sums otherwise payable to the Contractor in other currencies; and
(e) if no rates of exchange are stated in the Contract, they shall be those prevailing on the Base Date and determined by the central bank of the Country.

15 Termination by Employer

15.1

Notice to Correct

If the Contractor fails to carry out any obligation under the Contract, the Employer may by notice require the Contractor to make good the failure and to remedy it within a specified reasonable time.

应付款额扣除**雇主**过去已付的全部款额、以及按照**第 2.5 款**[**雇主的索赔**]的规定决定的任何减少额后的款额。

14.14

雇主责任的中止

除**承包商**在下列文件中，为**合同**或**工程**实施引发的或与之有关的任何问题或事项，明确提出款额要求以外，**雇主**应不再为上述问题或事项对**承包商**承担责任：

(a) 在**最终报表**中，
(b) 在**第 14.10 款**[**竣工报表**]所述的竣工**报表**中(颁发**工程接收证书**后发生的问题或事项除外)。

但**本款**不应减少**雇主**因其保障义务，或因其任何欺骗、有意违约、或轻率的不当行为等情况引起的责任。

14.15

支付的货币

合同价格应按**合同协议书**规定的货币或几种货币支付。除非**专用条件**中另有说明，如果规定了一种以上货币，应按以下办法支付：

(a) 如果**合同价格**只是用**当地货币**表示的：

(ⅰ) **当地货币**和**外币**的比例或款额，以及计算付款采用的固定汇率，除**双方**另有商定外，应按**合同协议书**的规定。

(ⅱ) 根据**第 13.5 款**[**暂列款**]和**第 13.7 款**[**因法律改变的调整**]规定的付款和扣减，应按适用货币和比例。

(ⅲ) 根据**第 14.3 款**[**期中付款的申请**](a)至(d)项做出的其他支付和扣减，应按上述(a)(ⅰ)项规定的货币和比例。

(b) **专用条件**中规定的对损害赔偿费的支付，应按**专用条件**中规定的货币和比例；
(c) 由**承包商**付给**雇主**的其他款应以**雇主**花费该款项实际用的货币，或双方可能商定的货币；

(d) 如果**承包商**应付给**雇主**的某种货币的款额，超过了**雇主**应付给**承包商**的该种货币的款额，**雇主**可以从另应付给**承包商**的其他货币的款额中，收回该项差额；

(e) 如果在**合同**中未说明汇率，应采用**基准日期**当天**工程所在国**中央银行确定的汇率。

15 由雇主终止

15.1

通知改正

如果**承包商**未能根据**合同**履行任何义务，**雇主**可通知**承包商**，要求其在规定的合理时间内，纠正并补救上述未履约。

15.2 Termination by Employer

The Employer shall be entitled to terminate the Contract if the Contractor:

(a) fails to comply with Sub-Clause 4.2 [*Performance Security*] or with a notice under Sub-Clause 15.1 [*Notice to Correct*],
(b) abandons the Works or otherwise plainly demonstrates the intention not to continue performance of his obligations under the Contract,
(c) without reasonable excuse fails to proceed with the Works in accordance with Clause 8 [*Commencement, Delays and Suspension*],
(d) subcontracts the whole of the Works or assigns the Contract without the required agreement,
(e) becomes bankrupt or insolvent, goes into liquidation, has a receiving or administration order made against him, compounds with his creditors, or carries on business under a receiver, trustee or manager for the benefit of his creditors, or if any act is done or event occurs which (under applicable Laws) has a similar effect to any of these acts or events, or
(f) gives or offers to give (directly or indirectly) to any person any bribe, gift, gratuity, commission or other thing of value, as an inducement or reward:

  (i) for doing or forbearing to do any action in relation to the Contract, or
  (ii) for showing or forbearing to show favour or disfavour to any person in relation to the Contract,

  or if any of the Contractor's Personnel, agents or Subcontractors gives or offers to give (directly or indirectly) to any person any such inducement or reward as is described in this sub-paragraph (f). However, lawful inducements and rewards to Contractor's Personnel shall not entitle termination.

In any of these events or circumstances, the Employer may, upon giving 14 days' notice to the Contractor, terminate the Contract and expel the Contractor from the Site. However, in the case of sub-paragraph (e) or (f), the Employer may by notice terminate the Contract immediately.

The Employer's election to terminate the Contract shall not prejudice any other rights of the Employer, under the Contract or otherwise.

The Contractor shall then leave the Site and deliver any required Goods, all Contractor's Documents, and other design documents made by or for him, to the Employer. However, the Contractor shall use his best efforts to comply immediately with any reasonable instructions included in the notice (i) for the assignment of any subcontract, and (ii) for the protection of life or property or for the safety of the Works.

After termination, the Employer may complete the Works and/or arrange for any other entities to do so. The Employer and these entities may then use any Goods, Contractor's Documents and other design documents made by or on behalf of the Contractor.

The Employer shall then give notice that the Contractor's Equipment and Temporary Works will be released to the Contractor at or near the Site. The Contractor shall promptly arrange their removal, at the risk and cost of the Contractor. However, if by this time the Contractor has failed to make a payment due to the Employer, these items may be sold by the Employer in order to recover this payment. Any balance of the proceeds shall then be paid to the Contractor.

15.3 Valuation at Date of Termination

As soon as practicable after a notice of termination under Sub-Clause 15.2 [*Termination by Employer*] has taken effect, the Employer shall proceed in accordance with Sub-Clause 3.5 [*Determinations*] to agree or determine the value of the Works,

15.2
由雇主终止

如果**承包商**有下列行为，**雇主**应有权终止**合同**：

(a) 未能遵守**第 4.2 款**[*履约担保*]的规定，或根据**第 15.1 款**[*通知改正*]的规定发出通知的要求；
(b) 放弃**工程**，或明确表现出不愿继续按照**合同**履行其义务的意向；
(c) 无合理解释，未按照**第 8 条**[*开工、延误和暂停*]的规定进行**工程**；
(d) 未经必要的许可，将整个**工程**分包出去，或将合同转让他人；
(e) 破产或无力偿债，停业清理，已有对其财产的接管令或管理令，与债权人达成和解，或为其债权人的利益在财产接管人、受托人或管理人的监督下营业，或采取了任何行动或发生任何事件(根据有关适用**法律**)具有与前述行动或事件相似的效果；
(f) (直接或间接)向任何人付给或企图付给任何贿赂、礼品、赏金、回扣、或其他贵重物品，以引诱或报偿他人：

(ⅰ) 采取或不采取有关**合同**的任何行动；或
(ⅱ) 对与**合同**有关的任何人做出或不做有利或不利的表示；

或任何**承包商人员**、代理人或**分包商**(直接或间接)向任何人付给或企图付给本**款**(f)项所述的任何此类引诱或报偿。但对给予**承包商人员**的合法鼓励和奖赏无权终止。

在出现任何上述事件或情况时，**雇主**可提前 14 天向**承包商**发出通知，终止**合同**，并要求其离开**现场**。但在(e)或(f)项情况下，**雇主**可发出通知立即终止**合同**。

雇主做出终止**合同**的选择，不应损害其根据**合同**或其他规定所享有的其他任何权利。

此时，**承包商**应撤离**现场**，并将任何需要的**货物**、所有**承包商文件**、以及由或为他做的其他设计文件交给**雇主**。但**承包商**应立即尽最大努力遵从包括通知中关于(ⅰ)转让任何分包合同，及(ⅱ)保护生命或财产、或**工程**的安全的任何合理的指示。

终止后，**雇主**可以继续完成**工程**，和(或)安排其他实体完成。这时**雇主**和这些实体可以使用任何**货物**、**承包商文件**和由**承包商**或以其名义编制的其他设计文件。

其后**雇主**应发出通知，将在**现场**或其附近把**承包商设备**和**临时工程**放还给**承包商**。**承包商**应自行承担风险和费用，迅速安排将它们运走。但如果此时**承包商**还有应付**雇主**的款项没有付清，**雇主**可以出售这些物品，以收回欠款。收益的任何余款应付给**承包商**。

15.3
终止日期时的估价

在根据**第15.2款**[*由雇主终止*]的规定发出的终止通知生效后，**雇主**应立即

Goods and Contractor's Documents, and any other sums due to the Contractor for work executed in accordance with the Contract.

15.4

Payment after Termination

After a notice of termination under Sub-Clause 15.2 [*Termination by Employer*] has taken effect, the Employer may:

(a) proceed in accordance with Sub-Clause 2.5 [*Employer's Claims*],

(b) with-hold further payments to the Contractor until the costs of design, execution, completion and remedying of any defects, damages for delay in completion (if any), and all other costs incurred by the Employer, have been established, and/or

(c) recover from the Contractor any losses and damages incurred by the Employer and any extra costs of completing the Works, after allowing for any sum due to the Contractor under Sub-Clause 15.3 [*Valuation at Date of Termination*]. After recovering any such losses, damages and extra costs, the Employer shall pay any balance to the Contractor.

15.5

Employer's Entitlement to Termination

The Employer shall be entitled to terminate the Contract, at any time for the Employer's convenience, by giving notice of such termination to the Contractor. The termination shall take effect 28 days after the later of the dates on which the Contractor receives this notice or the Employer returns the Performance Security. The Employer shall not terminate the Contract under this Sub-Clause in order to execute the Works himself or to arrange for the Works to be executed by another contractor.

After this termination, the Contractor shall proceed in accordance with Sub-Clause 16.3 [*Cessation of Work and Removal of Contractor's Equipment*] and shall be paid in accordance with Sub-Clause 19.6 [*Optional Termination, Payment and Release*].

16 Suspension and Termination by Contractor

16.1

Contractor's Entitlement to Suspend Work

If the Employer fails to comply with Sub-Clause 2.4 [*Employer's Financial Arrangements*] or Sub-Clause 14.7 [*Timing of Payments*], the Contractor may, after giving not less than 21 days' notice to the Employer, suspend work (or reduce the rate of work) unless and until the Contractor has received the reasonable evidence or payment, as the case may be and as described in the notice.

The Contractor's action shall not prejudice his entitlements to financing charges under Sub-Clause 14.8 [*Delayed Payment*] and to termination under Sub-Clause 16.2 [*Termination by Contractor*].

If the Contractor subsequently receives such evidence or payment (as described in the relevant Sub-Clause and in the above notice) before giving a notice of termination, the Contractor shall resume normal working as soon as is reasonably practicable.

If the Contractor suffers delay and/or incurs Cost as a result of suspending work (or reducing the rate of work) in accordance with this Sub-Clause, the Contractor shall give notice to the Employer and shall be entitled subject to Sub-Clause 20.1 [*Contractor's Claims*] to:

(a) an extension of time for any such delay, if completion is or will be delayed, under Sub-Clause 8.4 [*Extension of Time for Completion*], and

按照**第 3.5 款**[**确定**]的要求，商定或确定**工程**、**货物**和**承包商文件**的价值、以及**承包商**按照**合同**实施的工作应得的任何其他款项。

15.4
终止后的付款

在根据**第 15.2 款**[**由雇主终止**]的规定发出的终止通知生效后，**雇主**可以：

(a) 按照**第 2.5 款**[**雇主的索赔**]的规定进行；
(b) 在确定设计、施工、竣工和修补任何缺陷的费用、因延误竣工(如果有)的损害赔偿费、以及由**雇主**负担的全部其他费用前，暂不向**承包商**支付进一步款额；和(或)
(c) 在根据**第 15.3 款**[**终止日期时的估价**]的规定答应付给**承包商**的任何款额后，先从**承包商**处收回**雇主**蒙受的任何损失和损害赔偿费，以及完成**工程**所需的任何额外费用。在收回任何此类损失、损害赔偿费和额外费用后，**雇主**应将任何余额付给**承包商**。

15.5
雇主终止的权利

雇主应有权在对他方便的任何时候，通过向**承包商**发出终止通知，终止**合同**。此项终止应在**承包商**收到该通知或**雇主**退回的**履约担保**两者中较晚的日期后第 28 日生效。**雇主**不应为了要自己实施或安排另外的承包商实施**工程**，而根据本**款**终止**合同**。

在此项终止后，**承包商**应按照**第 16.3 款**[**停止工作和承包商设备的撤离**]的规定执行，并应按照**第 19.6 款**[**自主选择的终止、付款和解除**]的规定获得付款。

16 由承包商暂停和终止

16.1
承包商暂停工作的权利

如果**雇主**未能遵守**第 2.4 款**[**雇主的资金安排**]或**第 14.7 款**[**付款的时间安排**]的规定，**承包商**可在不少于 21 天前通知**雇主**，暂停工作(或放慢工作速度)，除非并直到**承包商**根据情况和通知中所述，收到**付款证书**、合理的证明或付款为止。

承包商的上述行动不应影响他根据**第 14.8 款**[**延误的付款**]的规定获得融资费用，以及根据**第 16.2 款**[**由承包商终止**]的规定提出终止的权利。

如果在发出终止通知前，**承包商**随后收到了上述证明或付款(如有关条款和上述通知中所述)，**承包商**应在合理可能情况下，尽快恢复正常工作。

如果因按照本**款**暂停工作(或放慢工作速度)，使**承包商**遭受延误和(或)招致**费用**，**承包商**应向**雇主**发出通知，有权根据**第 20.1 款**[**承包商的索赔**]的规定，要求：

(a) 根据**第 8.4 款**[**竣工时间的延长**]的规定，如竣工已或将受到延误，对任何此类延误给予延长期；

(b) payment of any such Cost plus reasonable profit, which shall be added to the Contract Price.

After receiving this notice, the Employer shall proceed in accordance with Sub-Clause 3.5 [*Determinations*] to agree or determine these matters.

16.2

Termination by Contractor

The Contractor shall be entitled to terminate the Contract if:

(a) the Contractor does not receive the reasonable evidence within 42 days after giving notice under Sub-Clause 16.1 [*Contractor's Entitlement to Suspend Work*] in respect of a failure to comply with Sub-Clause 2.4 [*Employer's Financial Arrangements*],
(b) the Contractor does not receive the amount due within 42 days after the expiry of the time stated in Sub-Clause 14.7 [*Timing of Payments*] within which payment is to be made (except for deductions in accordance with Sub-Clause 2.5 [*Employer's Claims*]),
(c) the Employer substantially fails to perform his obligations under the Contract,
(d) the Employer fails to comply with Sub-Clause 1.7 [*Assignment*],
(e) a prolonged suspension affects the whole of the Works as described in Sub-Clause 8.11 [*Prolonged Suspension*], or
(f) the Employer becomes bankrupt or insolvent, goes into liquidation, has a receiving or administration order made against him, compounds with his creditors, or carries on business under a receiver, trustee or manager for the benefit of his creditors, or if any act is done or event occurs which (under applicable Laws) has a similar effect to any of these acts or events.

In any of these events or circumstances, the Contractor may, upon giving 14 days' notice to the Employer, terminate the Contract. However, in the case of sub-paragraph (e) or (f), the Contractor may by notice terminate the Contract immediately.

The Contractor's election to terminate the Contract shall not prejudice any other rights of the Contractor, under the Contract or otherwise.

16.3

Cessation of Work and Removal of Contractor's Equipment

After a notice of termination under Sub-Clause 15.5 [*Employer's Entitlement to Termination*], Sub-Clause 16.2 [*Termination by Contractor*] or Sub-Clause 19.6 [*Optional Termination, Payment and Release*] has taken effect, the Contractor shall promptly:

(a) cease all further work, except for such work as may have been instructed by the Employer for the protection of life or property or for the safety of the Works,
(b) hand over Contractor's Documents, Plant, Materials and other work, for which the Contractor has received payment, and
(c) remove all other Goods from the Site, except as necessary for safety, and leave the Site.

16.4

Payment on Termination

After a notice of termination under Sub-Clause 16.2 [*Termination by Contractor*] has taken effect, the Employer shall promptly:

(a) return the Performance Security to the Contractor,
(b) pay the Contractor in accordance with Sub-Clause 19.6 [*Optional Termination, Payment and Release*], and
(c) pay to the Contractor the amount of any loss of profit or other loss or damage sustained by the Contractor as a result of this termination.

(b) 任何此类**费用**和合理的利润，应加入**合同价格**，给予支付。

雇主收到此通知后，应按照**第3.5款**[**确定**]的规定对这些事项进行商定或确定。

16.2

由承包商终止

如出现下列情况，**承包商**应有权终止**合同**：

(a) **承包商**在根据**第16.1款**[**承包商暂停工作的权利**]的规定，就未能遵守**第2.4款**[**雇主的资金安排**]规定的事项发出通知后42天内，仍未收到合理的证明；
(b) 在**第14.7款**[**付款的时间安排**]规定的付款时间到期后42天内，**承包商**仍未收到该期间的应付款额(按照**第2.5款**[**雇主的索赔**]规定的减少部分除外)；
(c) **雇主**实质上未能根据**合同**规定履行其义务；
(d) **雇主**未遵守**第1.7款**[**权益转让**]的规定；
(e) **第8.11款**[**拖长的暂停**]所述的拖长的停工影响了整个**工程**；或
(f) **雇主**破产或无力偿债，停业清理，已有对其财产的接管令或管理令，与债权人达成和解，或为其债权人的利益在财产接管人、受托人或管理人的监督下营业，或采取了任何行动或发生任何事件(根据有关适用**法律**)具有与前述行动或事件相似的效果。

在上述任何事件或情况下，**承包商**可通知雇主14天后终止**合同**。但在(e)或(f)项情况下，**承包商**可发出通知立即终止**合同**。

承包商做出终止**合同**的选择，不应影响其根据**合同**或其他规定所享有的其他任何权利。

16.3

停止工作和承包商设备的撤离

在根据**第15.5款**[**雇主终止合同的权利**]、**第16.2款**[**由承包商终止**]、或**第19.6款**[**自主选择的终止、付款和解除**]的规定发出的终止通知生效后，**承包商**应迅速：

(a) 停止所有进一步的工作，**雇主**为保护生命或财产或**工程**的安全可能指示的工作除外；
(b) 移交**承包商**已得到付款的**承包商文件**、**生产设备**、**材料**和其他工作；
(c) 从**现场**运走除为了安全需要以外的所有其他**货物**，并撤离**现场**。

16.4

终止时的付款

在根据**第16.2款**[**由承包商终止**]的规定发出的终止通知生效后，**雇主**应迅速：

(a) 将**履约担保**退还**承包商**；
(b) 按照**19.6款**[**自主选择的终止、付款和解除**]的规定，向**承包商**付款；
(c) 付给**承包商**因此项终止而蒙受的任何利润损失或其他损失或损害的款额。

17 Risk and Responsibility

17.1
Indemnities

The Contractor shall indemnify and hold harmless the Employer, the Employer's Personnel, and their respective agents, against and from all claims, damages, losses and expenses (including legal fees and expenses) in respect of:

(a) bodily injury, sickness, disease or death, of any person whatsoever arising out of or in the course of or by reason of the design, execution and completion of the Works and the remedying of any defects, unless attributable to any negligence, wilful act or breach of the Contract by the Employer, the Employer's Personnel, or any of their respective agents, and

(b) damage to or loss of any property, real or personal (other than the Works), to the extent that such damage or loss:

(i) arises out of or in the course of or by reason of the design, execution and completion of the Works and the remedying of any defects, and

(ii) is not attributable to any negligence, wilful act or breach of the Contract by the Employer, the Employer's Personnel, their respective agents, or anyone directly or indirectly employed by any of them.

The Employer shall indemnify and hold harmless the Contractor, the Contractor's Personnel, and their respective agents, against and from all claims, damages, losses and expenses (including legal fees and expenses) in respect of (1) bodily injury, sickness, disease or death, which is attributable to any negligence, wilful act or breach of the Contract by the Employer, the Employer's Personnel, or any of their respective agents, and (2) the matters for which liability may be excluded from insurance cover, as described in sub-paragraphs (d)(i), (ii) and (iii) of Sub-Clause 18.3 [*Insurance Against Injury to Persons and Damage to Property*].

17.2
Contractor's Care of the Works

The Contractor shall take full responsibility for the care of the Works and Goods from the Commencement Date until the Taking-Over Certificate is issued (or is deemed to be issued under Sub-Clause 10.1 [*Taking Over of the Works and Sections*]) for the Works, when responsibility for the care of the Works shall pass to the Employer. If a Taking-Over Certificate is issued (or is so deemed to be issued) for any Section of the Works, responsibility for the care of the Section shall then pass to the Employer.

After responsibility has accordingly passed to the Employer, the Contractor shall take responsibility for the care of any work which is outstanding on the date stated in a Taking-Over Certificate, until this outstanding work has been completed.

If any loss or damage happens to the Works, Goods or Contractor's Documents during the period when the Contractor is responsible for their care, from any cause not listed in Sub-Clause 17.3 [*Employer's Risks*], the Contractor shall rectify the loss or damage at the Contractor's risk and cost, so that the Works, Goods and Contractor's Documents conform with the Contract.

The Contractor shall be liable for any loss or damage caused by any actions performed by the Contractor after a Taking-Over Certificate has been issued. The Contractor shall also be liable for any loss or damage which occurs after a Taking-Over Certificate has been issued and which arose from a previous event for which the Contractor was liable.

17 风险与职责

17.1 保障

承包商应保障并保持使**雇主**、**雇主人员**、以及他们各自的代理人免受以下所有索赔、损害赔偿费、损失和开支(包括法律费用和开支)带来的损害:

(a) 由**工程**设计、施工和竣工,以及修补任何缺陷引起、或在其过程中、或因其原因产生的任何人员的人身伤害、患病、疾病或死亡,除非是由于**雇主**、**雇主人员**或他们各自的任何代理人的任何疏忽、故意行为或违反**合同**造成的;

(b) 由下列情况造成的对任何财产,不动产或动产(**工程**除外)的损害或损失:

(ⅰ) 由于**工程**设计、施工和竣工、以及修补任何缺陷引起,或在其其过程中,或因其原因产生的;

(ⅱ) 不是由于**雇主**、**雇主人员**、他们各自的代理人、或他们中任何人直接或间接雇用的任何人员的疏忽、故意行为或违反**合同**造成的。

雇主应保障并保持使**承包商**、**承包商人员**及他们各自的代理人,免受以下方面所有索赔、损害赔偿费、损失和开支(包括法律费用和开支)带来的损害:(1)由**雇主**、**雇主人员**或他们各自的代理人的任何疏忽、故意行为、或违反**合同**造成的人身伤害、患病、疾病或死亡;以及(2)如**第 18.3 款**[**人身伤害和财产损失险**](d)项(ⅰ)、(ⅱ)和(ⅲ)目中所述的其责任可以不包括在保险范围的各类事项。

17.2 承包商对工程的照管

承包商应从开工**日期**起承担照管**工程**和**货物**的全部职责,直到颁发**工程接收证书**(或根据**第 10.1 款**[**工程和单位工程的接收**]的规定应视为已颁发)之日止,这时**工程**照管职责应移交给**雇主**。如果对某**单位工程**颁发了(或照上述应视为已颁发)**接受证书**,则对该**单位工程**的照管职责应移交给**雇主**。

在照管职责按上述规定移交给**雇主**后,**承包商**仍应对在**接收证书**上注明日期时的任何扫尾工作承担照管职责,直到该扫尾工作完成为止。

如果在**承包商**负责照管期间,由于**第 17.3 款**[**雇主的风险**]中所列风险以外的原因,致使**工程**、**货物**、或**承包商文件**发生任何损失或损害,**承包商**应自行承担风险和费用,修正该项损失或损害,使**工程**、**货物**和**承包商文件**符合**合同**要求。

承包商应对颁发**接收证书**后由其采取的任何行动造成的任何损失或损害负责。**承包商**还应对颁发**接收证书**后发生的,由**承包商**负责的以前的事件引起的任何损失或损害负责。

GENERAL CONDITIONS

GUIDANCE

FORMS

17.3
Employer's Risks

The risks referred to in Sub-Clause 17.4 below are:

(a) war, hostilities (whether war be declared or not), invasion, act of foreign enemies,
(b) rebellion, terrorism, revolution, insurrection, military or usurped power, or civil war, within the Country,
(c) riot, commotion or disorder within the Country by persons other than the Contractor's Personnel and other employees of the Contractor and Subcontractors,
(d) munitions of war, explosive materials, ionising radiation or contamination by radio-activity, within the Country, except as may be attributable to the Contractor's use of such munitions, explosives, radiation or radio-activity, and
(e) pressure waves caused by aircraft or other aerial devices travelling at sonic or supersonic speeds.

17.4

Consequences of Employer's Risks

If and to the extent that any of the risks listed in Sub-Clause 17.3 above results in loss or damage to the Works, Goods or Contractor's Documents, the Contractor shall promptly give notice to the Employer and shall rectify this loss or damage to the extent required by the Employer.

If the Contractor suffers delay and/or incurs Cost from rectifying this loss or damage, the Contractor shall give a further notice to the Employer and shall be entitled subject to Sub-Clause 20.1 [*Contractor's Claims*] to:

(a) an extension of time for any such delay, if completion is or will be delayed, under Sub-Clause 8.4 [*Extension of Time for Completion*], and
(b) payment of any such Cost, which shall be added to the Contract Price.

After receiving this further notice, the Employer shall proceed in accordance with Sub Clause 3.5 [*Determinations*] to agree or determine these matters.

17.5

Intellectual and Industrial Property Rights

In this Sub-Clause, "infringement" means an infringement (or alleged infringement) of any patent, registered design, copyright, trade mark, trade name, trade secret or other intellectual or industrial property right relating to the Works; and "claim" means a claim (or proceedings pursuing a claim) alleging an infringement.

Whenever a Party does not give notice to the other Party of any claim within 28 days of receiving the claim, the first Party shall be deemed to have waived any right to indemnity under this Sub-Clause.

The Employer shall indemnify and hold the Contractor harmless against and from any claim alleging an infringement which is or was:

(a) an unavoidable result of the Contractor's compliance with the Employer's Requirements, or
(b) a result of any Works being used by the Employer:

    (i) for a purpose other than that indicated by, or reasonably to be inferred from, the Contract, or
    (ii) in conjunction with any thing not supplied by the Contractor, unless such use was disclosed to the Contractor prior to the Base Date or is stated in the Contract.

The Contractor shall indemnify and hold the Employer harmless against and from any other claim which arises out of or in relation to (i) the Contractor's design,

17.3
雇主的风险

下述**第 17.4 款**谈到的风险是指：

(a) 战争、敌对行动(不论宣战与否)、入侵、外敌行动；
(b) **工程所在国**内的叛乱、恐怖主义、革命、暴动、军事政变或篡夺政权，或内战；
(c) **承包商人员**及**承包商**和**分包商**的其他雇员以外的人员，在**工程所在国**内的骚动、喧闹、或混乱；

(d) **工程所在国**内的战争军火、爆炸物资、电离辐射或放射性引起的污染，但可能由**承包商**使用此类军火、炸药、幅射或放射性引起的除外；
(e) 由音速或超音速飞行的飞机或飞行装置所产生的压力波。

17.4
雇主风险的后果

如果上述**第 17.3 款**列举的任何风险达到对**工程**、**货物**、或**承包商文件**造成损失或损害的程度，**承包商**应立即通知**雇主**，并应按**雇主**要求，修正此类损失或损害。

如果因修正此类损失或损害使**承包商**遭受延误和(或)招致增加**费用**，**承包商**应进一步通知雇主，有权根据**第 20.1 款**[**承包商的索赔**]的规定，要求：

(a) 根据**第 8.4 款**[**竣工时间的延长**]的规定，如果竣工已或将受到延误，对任何此类延误给予延长期；
(b) 任何此类**费用**，应加入**合同价格**，给予支付。

雇主收到此类进一步通知后，应按照**第 3.5 款**[**确定**]的要求，对这些事项进行商定或确定。

17.5
知识产权和工业产权

在本**款**中，“侵权”是指侵犯(或被指称侵犯)与**工程**有关的任何专利权、已登记的设计、版权、商标、商号商品名称、商业机密、或其他知识产权或工业产权；“索赔”是指对指称一项侵权的索赔(或为索赔进行的诉讼)。

当一**方**未能在收到任何索赔 28 天内，向另一**方**发出关于索赔的通知时，该**方**应被认为已放弃根据本**款**规定的任何受保障的权利。

雇主应保障并保持**承包商**免受因以下情况提出的指称侵权的任何索赔引起的损害：

(a) 因**承包商**遵从**雇主**的要求，而造成的不可避免的结果；

(b) 因**雇主**为以下原因使用任何**工程**的结果：

(ⅰ) 为了**合同**中指明的或根据**合同**可合理推断的事项以外的目的；

(ⅱ) 与非**承包商**提供的任何物品联合使用，除非此项使用已在**基准日期**前向**承包商**透露，或在**合同**中有规定。

承包商应保障并保持**雇主**免受由以下事项产生或与之有关的任何其他索赔

manufacture, construction or execution of the Works, (ii) the use of Contractor's Equipment, or (iii) the proper use of the Works.

If a Party is entitled to be indemnified under this Sub-Clause, the indemnifying Party may (at its cost) conduct negotiations for the settlement of the claim, and any litigation or arbitration which may arise from it. The other Party shall, at the request and cost of the indemnifying Party, assist in contesting the claim. This other Party (and its Personnel) shall not make any admission which might be prejudicial to the indemnifying Party, unless the indemnifying Party failed to take over the conduct of any negotiations, litigation or arbitration upon being requested to do so by such other Party.

17.6
Limitation of Liability

Neither Party shall be liable to the other Party for loss of use of any Works, loss of profit, loss of any contract or for any indirect or consequential loss or damage which may be suffered by the other Party in connection with the Contract, other than under Sub-Clause 16.4 [*Payment on Termination*] and Sub-Clause 17.1 [*Indemnities*].

The total liability of the Contractor to the Employer, under or in connection with the Contract other than under Sub-Clause 4.19 [*Electricity, Water and Gas*], Sub-Clause 4.20 [*Employer's Equipment and Free-Issue Material*], Sub-Clause 17.1 [*Indemnities*] and Sub-Clause 17.5 [*Intellectual and Industrial Property Rights*], shall not exceed the sum stated in the Particular Conditions or (if a sum is not so stated) the Contract Price stated in the Contract Agreement.

This Sub-Clause shall not limit liability in any case of fraud, deliberate default or reckless misconduct by the defaulting Party.

18 Insurance

18.1
General Requirements for Insurances

In this Clause, "insuring Party" means, for each type of insurance, the Party responsible for effecting and maintaining the insurance specified in the relevant Sub-Clause.

Wherever the Contractor is the insuring Party, each insurance shall be effected with insurers and in terms approved by the Employer. These terms shall be consistent with any terms agreed by both Parties before they signed the Contract Agreement. This agreement of terms shall take precedence over the provisions of this Clause.

Wherever the Employer is the insuring Party, each insurance shall be effected with insurers and in terms consistent with the details annexed to the Particular Conditions.

If a policy is required to indemnify joint insured, the cover shall apply separately to each insured as though a separate policy had been issued for each of the joint insured. If a policy indemnifies additional joint insured, namely in addition to the insured specified in this Clause, (i) the Contractor shall act under the policy on behalf of these additional joint insured except that the Employer shall act for Employer's Personnel, (ii) additional joint insured shall not be entitled to receive payments directly from the insurer or to have any other direct dealings with the insurer, and (iii) the insuring Party shall require all additional joint insured to comply with the conditions stipulated in the policy.

Each policy insuring against loss or damage shall provide for payments to be made in the currencies required to rectify the loss or damage. Payments received from insurers shall be used for the rectification of the loss or damage.

引起的损害：(i)**承包商**的**工程**设计、制造、施工或实施；(ii)**承包商设备**的使用；或(iii)**工程**的正确使用。

如果**一方**根据本**款**规定有权受保障，保障**方**可(由其承担费用)组织解决索赔的谈判，以及可能由其引起的任何诉讼或仲裁。在保障方请求并承担费用的情况下，另**一方**应协助争辩该索赔。此另一**方**(及其人员)不应做出可能损害保障**方**的任何承认，除非保障**方**未能在该另一**方**请求下，接办组织任何谈判、诉讼或仲裁事宜。

17.6

责任限度

除根据**第 16.4 款**[*终止时的支付*]和**第 17.1 款**[*保障*]的规定外，任何一**方**不应对另一**方**使用任何**工程**中的损失、利润损失、任何合同的损失，或对另一**方**可能遭受的与**合同**有关的任何间接的或引发的损失或损害负责。

除根据**第 4.19 款**[*电、水和燃气*]、**第 4.20 款**[*雇主的设备和免费供应的材料*]、**第 17.1 款**[*保障*]和**第 17.5 款**[*知识产权和工业产权*]的规定外，**承包商**根据或有关**合同**对**雇主**的全部责任不应超过**专用条件**中规定的总额，或(如果没有规定该总额)**合同协议书**中规定的**合同价格**。

本**款**不应限制违约**方**的欺骗、有意违约、或轻率的不当行为等任何情况的责任。

18 保险

18.1

有关保险的一般要求

在**本条**中，对于每种类型的保险，“应投保方”是指对办理并保持相关**条款**中规定的保险负有责任的一**方**。

当**承包商**是应投保**方**时，应按照**雇主**批准的条件向保险人办理每项保险。这些条件应与**双方**在签订**合同协议书**前协商同意的任何条件相一致。这一条件协议的地位应优先于**本条**各项规定。

当**雇主**是应投保**方**时，应按照与**专用条件**所附的详细内容相一致的条件，向保险人办理每项保险。

如果保险单需要对联合被保人提供保障，保险赔偿应如同已向联合被保人的每一方发出单独保险单一样，对每个被保人分别施用。如果保险单对附加联合被保人提供保障，即在**本条**规定的被保人之外附加，则(i)除**雇主**应代表**雇主人员**行动外，**承包商**应代表这些附加联合被保人根据保险单行动；(ii)附加联合被保人无权从保险人处直接获得付款，或与保险人有其他直接往来；以及(iii)应投保**方**应要求所有附加联合被保人遵守保险单规定的条件。

每份承保损失或损害的保险单应以修正损失或损害需要的货币进行赔偿。从保险人处收到的付款应用于修正损失或损害。

The relevant insuring Party shall, within the respective periods stated in the Particular Conditions (calculated from the Commencement Date), submit to the other Party:

(a) evidence that the insurances described in this Clause have been effected, and
(b) copies of the policies for the insurances described in Sub-Clause 18.2 [*Insurance of Works and Contractor's Equipment*] and Sub-Clause 18.3 [*Insurance against Injury to Persons and Damage to Property*].

When each premium is paid, the insuring Party shall submit evidence of payment to the other Party.

Each Party shall comply with the conditions stipulated in each of the insurance policies. The insuring Party shall keep the insurers informed of any relevant changes to the execution of the Works and ensure that insurance is maintained in accordance with this Clause.

Neither Party shall make any material alteration to the terms of any insurance without the prior approval of the other Party. If an insurer makes (or attempts to make) any alteration, the Party first notified by the insurer shall promptly give notice to the other Party.

If the insuring Party fails to effect and keep in force any of the insurances it is required to effect and maintain under the Contract, or fails to provide satisfactory evidence and copies of policies in accordance with this Sub-Clause, the other Party may (at its option and without prejudice to any other right or remedy) effect insurance for the relevant coverage and pay the premiums due. The insuring Party shall pay the amount of these premiums to the other Party, and the Contract Price shall be adjusted accordingly.

Nothing in this Clause limits the obligations, liabilities or responsibilities of the Contractor or the Employer, under the other terms of the Contract or otherwise. Any amounts not insured or not recovered from the insurers shall be borne by the Contractor and/or the Employer in accordance with these obligations, liabilities or responsibilities. However, if the insuring Party fails to effect and keep in force an insurance which is available and which it is required to effect and maintain under the Contract, and the other Party neither approves the omission nor effects insurance for the coverage relevant to this default, any moneys which should have been recoverable under this insurance shall be paid by the insuring Party.

Payments by one Party to the other Party shall be subject to Sub-Clause 2.5 [*Employer's Claims*] or Sub-Clause 20.1 [*Contractor's Claims*], as applicable.

18.2

Insurance for Works and Contractor's Equipment

The insuring Party shall insure the Works, Plant, Materials and Contractor's Documents for not less than the full reinstatement cost including the costs of demolition, removal of debris and professional fees and profit. This insurance shall be effective from the date by which the evidence is to be submitted under sub-paragraph (a) of Sub-Clause 18.1 [*General Requirements for Insurances*], until the date of issue of the Taking-Over Certificate for the Works.

The insuring Party shall maintain this insurance to provide cover until the date of issue of the Performance Certificate, for loss or damage for which the Contractor is liable arising from a cause occurring prior to the issue of the Taking-Over Certificate, and for loss or damage caused by the Contractor or Subcontractors in the course of any other operations (including those under Clause 11 [*Defects Liability*] and Clause 12 [*Tests after Completion*]).

有关应投保**方**应在**专业条件**中规定的各自期限内(从**开工日期**算起)，向另**一方**提交：

(a) **本条**中所述保险已经生效的证据；
(b) **第 18.2 款**[**工程和承包商设备的保险**]、及**第 18.3 款**[**人员伤害和财产损害险**]所述保险的保险单副本。

当每笔保险费已付时，应投保**方**应向另**一方**提供支付证据。

每方应遵守每份保险单规定的条件。应投保**方**应保持使保险人随时了解**工程**实施中的任何相关变化，并确保按照**本条**要求维持保险。

没有得到另**一方**的事先批准，任**一方**都不应对任何保险的条件做出实质性变动。如果保险人做出(或要做出)任何变动，首先收到保险人通知的**一方**应迅速通知另**一方**。

如果应投保**方**对**合同**要求办理并维持的任何保险未按要求办好并保持有效，或未能按**本款**要求提供满意的证据和保险单的副本，另**一方**可以(由其选择,并在不影响任何其他权利或补偿的情况下)办理该保险范围的保险，并付应交的保险费。应投保**方**应向另**一方**支付这些保险费，并相应调整**合同价格**。

本条规定不限制**合同**其余条款或其他文件所规定的**承包商**或**雇主**的义务、责任、或职责。任何未保险或未能从保险人处收回的款项，应由**承包商**和(或)**雇主**按照这些义务、责任、或职责的规定承担。但是，如果应投保**方**对于能做到的并在**合同**中规定要办理并保持的某项保险，未能按要求办好并保持有效，而另**一方**既没有认可这项省略，又没有办理与此项违约有关的保险范围的保险，则根据此项保险应能收回的任何款额应由应投保**方**支付。

一方向另**一方**的支付，应按适用情况，根据**第 2.5 款**[**雇主的索赔**]或**第 20.1 款**[**承包商的索赔**]的规定办理。

18.2

工程和承包商设备的保险

应投保**方**应为**工程**、**生产设备**、**材料**和**承包商文件**投保，保险额不低于全部复原费用，包括拆除、运走废弃物的费用、以及专业费用和利润。该保险应从**第18.1 款**[**有关保险的一般要求**](a)项规定的提交证据的日期起，至颁发**工程接收证书**的日期止保持有效。

应投保**方**应维持该保险在直到颁发**履约证书**的日期为止的期间继续有效，以便对**承包商**应负责的，由颁发**接收证书**前发生的某项原因引起的损失或损害，以及由**承包商**或**分包商**在任何其他作业(包括根据**第 11 条**[**缺陷责任**]和**第 12 条**[**竣工后试验**]规定的作业) 过程中造成的损失或损害，提供保险。

The insuring Party shall insure the Contractor's Equipment for not less than the full replacement value, including delivery to Site. For each item of Contractor's Equipment, the insurance shall be effective while it is being transported to the Site and until it is no longer required as Contractor's Equipment.

Unless otherwise stated in the Particular Conditions, insurances under this Sub-Clause:

(a) shall be effected and maintained by the Contractor as insuring Party,
(b) shall be in the joint names of the Parties, who shall be jointly entitled to receive payments from the insurers, payments being held or allocated between the Parties for the sole purpose of rectifying the loss or damage,
(c) shall cover all loss and damage from any cause not listed in Sub-Clause 17.3 [*Employer's Risks*],
(d) shall also cover loss or damage from the risks listed in sub-paragraph (c) of Sub-Clause 17.3 [*Employer's Risks*], with deductibles per occurrence of not more than the amount stated in the Particular Conditions (if an amount is not so stated, this sub-paragraph (d) shall not apply), and
(e) may however exclude loss of, damage to, and reinstatement of:

   (i) a part of the Works which is in a defective condition due to a defect in its design, materials or workmanship (but cover shall include any other parts which are lost or damaged as a direct result of this defective condition and not as described in sub-paragraph (ii) below),
   (ii) a part of the Works which is lost or damaged in order to reinstate any other part of the Works if this other part is in a defective condition due to a defect in its design, materials or workmanship,
   (iii) a part of the Works which has been taken over by the Employer, except to the extent that the Contractor is liable for the loss or damage, and
   (iv) Goods while they are not in the Country, subject to Sub-Clause 14.5 [*Plant and Materials intended for the Works*].

If, more than one year after the Base Date, the cover described in sub-paragraph (d) above ceases to be available at commercially reasonable terms, the Contractor shall (as insuring Party) give notice to the Employer, with supporting particulars. The Employer shall then (i) be entitled subject to Sub-Clause 2.5 [*Employer's Claims*] to payment of an amount equivalent to such commercially reasonable terms as the Contractor should have expected to have paid for such cover, and (ii) be deemed, unless he obtains the cover at commercially reasonable terms, to have approved the omission under Sub-Clause 18.1 [*General Requirements for Insurances*].

18.3

Insurance against Injury to Persons and Damage to Property

The insuring Party shall insure against each Party's liability for any loss, damage, death or bodily injury which may occur to any physical property (except things insured under Sub-Clause 18.2 [*Insurance for Works and Contractor's Equipment*]) or to any person (except persons insured under Sub-Clause 18.4 [*Insurance for Contractor's Personnel*]), which may arise out of the Contractor's performance of the Contract and occurring before the issue of the Performance Certificate.

This insurance shall be for a limit per occurrence of not less than the amount stated in the Particular Conditions, with no limit on the number of occurrences. If an amount is not stated in the Contract, this Sub-Clause shall not apply.

Unless otherwise stated in the Particular Conditions, the insurances specified in this Sub-Clause:

应投保方应对**承包商设备**投保，保险金额不低于全部重置价值，包括运至**现场**的费用。对每项**承包商设备**，该保险都应从该设备运往**现场**的过程起，直到其不需再作为**承包商设备**为止的期间保持有效。

除非在**专用条件**中另有规定，**本款**规定的各项保险：

(a) 应由**承包商**作为应投保**方**办理和维持；
(b) 应由共同有权从保险人处得到赔偿的**各方**联名投保，保险赔偿金在**各方**间保有或分配，唯一用于修正损失或损害；
(c) 应对未列入**第 17.3 款**[*雇主的风险*]列举的任何原因造成的所有损失和损害提供保险；
(d) 还应对因**第 17.3 款**[*雇主的风险*](c)项中列举的风险造成的损失或损害提供保险，每次事件的免赔额不应超过**专用条件**中规定的数额(如果没有规定此数额,**本**(d)项应不适用)；
(e) 但可以不包括下列部分的损失、损害、及复原：

(ⅰ) 由于其本身的设计、材料或工艺缺陷造成的处于有缺陷状况的**工程**部分(但保险应包括不属于下述第(ⅱ)项情况的，由上述有缺陷状况直接造成损失或损害的任何其他部分)；

(ⅱ) 为复原因设计、材料、或工艺缺陷造成的其他处于有缺陷状况的**工程**部分，而遭受损失或损害的某一**工程**部分；

(ⅲ) **雇主**已经接收的**工程**部分，但**承包商**对其损失或损害应负责任的除外；

(ⅳ) 根据**第 14.5 款**[*拟用于工程的生产设备和材料*]的规定，不在**工程所在国**的**货物**。

如果在**基准日期**后一年以上，上述(d)项所述保险不能在合理的商务条件下继续投保，**承包商**(作为应投保**方**)应通知**雇主**，并附详细说明。这时，**雇主**应(ⅰ)有权根据**第 2.5 款**[*雇主的索赔*]的规定，获得等同于**承包商**在该合理商务条件下，为该类保险预期要支付的款额，及(ⅱ)除非他在商务合理条件下获得该保险，被认为已根据**第 18.1 款**[*有关保险的一般要求*]的规定，批准了此项省略。

18.3 人身伤害和财产损害险

应投保**方**应为可能由**承包商**履行**合同**引起、并在**履约证书**颁发前发生的，任何物质财产(根据**第 18.2 款**[*工程和承包商设备的保险*]规定被保的物品除外) 的任何损失或损害，或任何人员(根据**第 18.4 款**[*承包商人员的保险*]规定被保的人员除外) 的任何死亡或伤害，办理每**方**责任险。

此类保险，对发生每次事件的保险金限额应不低于**专用条件**中规定的数额，事件发生次数不限。如果**合同**没有规定数额，**本款**应不适用。

除非在**专用条件**中另有规定，**本款**规定的各项保险：

(a) shall be effected and maintained by the Contractor as insuring Party,
(b) shall be in the joint names of the Parties,
(c) shall be extended to cover liability for all loss and damage to the Employer's property (except things insured under Sub-Clause 18.2) arising out of the Contractor's performance of the Contract, and
(d) may however exclude liability to the extent that it arises from:

  (i) the Employer's right to have the Permanent Works executed on, over, under, in or through any land, and to occupy this land for the Permanent Works,
  (ii) damage which is an unavoidable result of the Contractor's obligations to execute the Works and remedy any defects, and
  (iii) a cause listed in Sub-Clause 17.3 [*Employer's Risks*], except to the extent that cover is available at commercially reasonable terms.

18.4

Insurance for Contractor's Personnel

The Contractor shall effect and maintain insurance against liability for claims, damages, losses and expenses (including legal fees and expenses) arising from injury, sickness, disease or death of any person employed by the Contractor or any other of the Contractor's Personnel.

The Employer shall also be indemnified under the policy of insurance, except that this insurance may exclude losses and claims to the extent that they arise from any act or neglect of the Employer or of the Employer's Personnel.

The insurance shall be maintained in full force and effect during the whole time that these personnel are assisting in the execution of the Works. For a Subcontractor's employees, the insurance may be effected by the Subcontractor, but the Contractor shall be responsible for compliance with this Clause.

19 Force Majeure

19.1

Definition of Force Majeure

In this Clause, "Force Majeure" means an exceptional event or circumstance:

(a) which is beyond a Party's control,
(b) which such Party could not reasonably have provided against before entering into the Contract,
(c) which, having arisen, such Party could not reasonably have avoided or overcome, and
(d) which is not substantially attributable to the other Party.

Force Majeure may include, but is not limited to, exceptional events or circumstances of the kind listed below, so long as conditions (a) to (d) above are satisfied:

  (i) war, hostilities (whether war be declared or not), invasion, act of foreign enemies,
  (ii) rebellion, terrorism, revolution, insurrection, military or usurped power, or civil war,
  (iii) riot, commotion, disorder, strike or lockout by persons other than the Contractor's Personnel and other employees of the Contractor and Subcontractors,
  (iv) munitions of war, explosive materials, ionising radiation or contamination

(a) 应由**承包商**作为应投保**方**办理和维持；
(b) 应以**各方**联合名义投保；
(c) 保险范围应扩展到因**承包商**履行**合同**引起的对**雇主**财产(根据**第 18.2 款**规定被保的物品除外)的所有损失或损害的责任；

(d) 但可以不包括由以下事项引起的责任：

(i) **雇主**在任何土地上面、上方、下面、范围内，或穿过它实施**永久工程**，以及为了**永久工程**占用该土地的权利；

(ii) 由**承包商**实施**工程**和修补任何缺陷的义务造成的不可避免的损害；
(iii) **第 17.3 款**[*雇主的风险*]列举的某项原因，但可以按合理商务条件得到保险的范围除外。

18.4

承包商人员的保险

承包商应对**承包商**雇用的任何人员或任何其他**承包商人员**的伤害、患病、疾病或死亡引起的索赔、损害赔偿费、损失或开支(包括法律费用和开支)的责任办理并维持保险。

除该保险可不包括由**雇主**或**雇主人员**的任何行为或疏忽引起的损失和索赔的情况以外，**雇主**也应由该项保险单得到保障。

此类保险应在这些人员参加**工程**实施的整个期间保持全面实施和有效。对于**分包商**的雇员，此类保险可以由**分包商**投保，但**承包商**应对其符合**本条**规定负责。

19 不可抗力

19.1

不可抗力的定义

在**本条**中，"**不可抗力**"系指某种特殊的事件或情况：

(a) 一**方**无法控制的；
(b) **该方**在签订**合同**前，不能对之进行合理防备的；

(c) 发生后，**该方**不能合理避免或克服的；

(d) 不主要归因于**他方**的。

只要满足上述(a)至(d)项条件，**不可抗力**可包括但不限于下列各种特殊事件或情况：

(i) 战争、敌对行动(不论宣战与否)、入侵、外敌行为；

(ii) 叛乱、恐怖主义、革命、暴动、军事政变或篡夺政权、或内战；
(iii) **承包商人员**和**承包商**及其**分包商**的其他雇员以外的人员的骚动、喧闹、混乱、罢工或停工；

(iv)战争军火、爆炸物资、电离幅射或放射性污染，但可能因承

by radio-activity, except as may be attributable to the Contractor's use of such munitions, explosives, radiation or radio-activity, and

(v) natural catastrophes such as earthquake, hurricane, typhoon or volcanic activity.

19.2

Notice of Force Majeure

If a Party is or will be prevented from performing any of its obligations under the Contract by Force Majeure, then it shall give notice to the other Party of the event or circumstances constituting the Force Majeure and shall specify the obligations, the performance of which is or will be prevented. The notice shall be given within 14 days after the Party became aware, or should have become aware, of the relevant event or circumstance constituting Force Majeure.

The Party shall, having given notice, be excused performance of such obligations for so long as such Force Majeure prevents it from performing them.

Notwithstanding any other provision of this Clause, Force Majeure shall not apply to obligations of either Party to make payments to the other Party under the Contract.

19.3

Duty to Minimise Delay

Each Party shall at all times use all reasonable endeavours to minimise any delay in the performance of the Contract as a result of Force Majeure.

A Party shall give notice to the other Party when it ceases to be affected by the Force Majeure.

19.4

Consequences of Force Majeure

If the Contractor is prevented from performing any of his obligations under the Contract by Force Majeure of which notice has been given under Sub-Clause 19.2 [*Notice of Force Majeure*], and suffers delay and/or incurs Cost by reason of such Force Majeure, the Contractor shall be entitled subject to Sub-Clause 20.1 [*Contractor's Claims*] to:

(a) an extension of time for any such delay, if completion is or will be delayed, under Sub-Clause 8.4 [*Extension of Time for Completion*], and

(b) if the event or circumstance is of the kind described in sub-paragraphs (i) to (iv) of Sub-Clause 19.1 [*Definition of Force Majeure*] and, in the case of sub-paragraphs (ii) to (iv), occurs in the Country, payment of any such Cost.

After receiving this notice, the Employer shall proceed in accordance with Sub-Clause 3.5 [*Determinations*] to agree or determine these matters.

19.5

Force Majeure Affecting Subcontractor

If any Subcontractor is entitled under any contract or agreement relating to the Works to relief from force majeure on terms additional to or broader than those specified in this Clause, such additional or broader force majeure events or circumstances shall not excuse the Contractor's non-performance or entitle him to relief under this Clause.

19.6

Optional Termination, Payment and Release

If the execution of substantially all the Works in progress is prevented for a continuous period of 84 days by reason of Force Majeure of which notice has been given under Sub-Clause 19.2 [*Notice of Force Majeure*], or for multiple periods which total more than 140 days due to the same notified Force Majeure, then either Party may give to the other Party a notice of termination of the Contract. In this event, the termination shall take effect 7 days after the notice is given, and the Contractor shall proceed in accordance with Sub-Clause 16.3 [*Cessation of Work and Removal of Contractor's Equipment*].

包商使用此类军火、炸药、幅射或放射性引起的除外；

（ⅴ）自然灾害，如地震、飓风、台风、或火山活动。

19.2

不可抗力的通知

如果一**方**因**不可抗力**使其履行**合同**规定的任何义务已或将受到阻碍，应向**他方**发出关于构成**不可抗力**的事件或情况的通知，并应明确说明履行已或将受到阻碍的各项义务。此项通知应在**该方**察觉或应已察觉到构成**不可抗力**的有关事件或情况后 14 天内发出。

发出通知后，该**方**应在该**不可抗力**阻碍其履行义务期内免于履行该义务。

不管**本条**的其他任何规定，**不可抗力**的规定不应施用于任一**方**根据**合同**向另一**方**支付的义务。

19.3

将延误减至最小的义务

每方都应始终尽所有合理的努力，使**不可抗力**对履行**合同**造成的任何延误减至最小。

当一**方**不再受**不可抗力**影响时，应向另一**方**发出通知。

19.4

不可抗力的后果

如果**承包商**因已根据**第 19.2 款**[**不可抗力的通知**]的规定发出通知的**不可抗力**，妨碍其履行**合同**规定的任何义务，使其遭受延误和（或）招致增加**费用**，**承包商**应有权根据**第 20.1 款**[**承包商的索赔**]的规定，要求：

(a) 根据**第 8.4 款**[**竣工时间的延长**]的规定，如果竣工已或将受到延误，对任何此类延误给予延长期；

(b) 如果是**第 19.1 款**[**不可抗力的定义**]中第（ⅰ）至（ⅳ）目所述的事件或情况，且第（ⅱ）至（ⅵ）目所述事件或情况发生在**工程所在国**，对任何此类**费用**给予支付。

雇主收到此通知后，应按照**第 3.5 款**[**确定**]的规定，对这些事项进行商定或确定。

19.5

不可抗力影响分包商

如果任何**分包商**根据有关**工程**的任何合同或协议，有权因较**本条**规定更多或更广范围的不可抗力免除其某些义务，此类更多或更广的不可抗力事件或情况，不应成为**承包商**不履约的借口，或有权根据**本条**规定免除其义务。

19.6

自主选择终止、付款和解除

如果因已根据**第 19.2 款**[**不可抗力的通知**]的规定发出通知的**不可抗力**，使基本上全部进展中的**工程**实施受到阻碍已连续 84 天，或由于同一通知的**不可抗力**断续阻碍几个期间累计超过 140 天，任一**方**可向**他方**发出终止**合同**的通知。在此情况下，终止应在该通知发出 7 天后生效，**承包商**应按照**第 16.3 款**[**停止工作和承包商设备的撤离**]的规定进行。

Upon such termination, the Employer shall pay to the Contractor:

(a) the amounts payable for any work carried out for which a price is stated in the Contract;
(b) the Cost of Plant and Materials ordered for the Works which have been delivered to the Contractor, or of which the Contractor is liable to accept delivery: this Plant and Materials shall become the property of (and be at the risk of) the Employer when paid for by the Employer, and the Contractor shall place the same at the Employer's disposal;
(c) any other Cost or liability which in the circumstances was reasonably incurred by the Contractor in the expectation of completing the Works;
(d) the Cost of removal of Temporary Works and Contractor's Equipment from the Site and the return of these items to the Contractor's works in his country (or to any other destination at no greater cost); and
(e) the Cost of repatriation of the Contractor's staff and labour employed wholly in connection with the Works at the date of termination.

19.7

Release from Performance under the Law

Notwithstanding any other provision of this Clause, if any event or circumstance outside the control of the Parties (including, but not limited to, Force Majeure) arises which makes it impossible or unlawful for either or both Parties to fulfil its or their contractual obligations or which, under the law governing the Contract, entitles the Parties to be released from further performance of the Contract, then upon notice by either Party to the other Party of such event or circumstance:

(a) the Parties shall be discharged from further performance, without prejudice to the rights of either Party in respect of any previous breach of the Contract, and
(b) the sum payable by the Employer to the Contractor shall be the same as would have been payable under Sub-Clause 19.6 [*Optional Termination, Payment and Release*] if the Contract had been terminated under Sub-Clause 19.6.

20 Claims, Disputes and Arbitration

20.1

Contractor's Claims

If the Contractor considers himself to be entitled to any extension of the Time for Completion and/or any additional payment, under any Clause of these Conditions or otherwise in connection with the Contract, the Contractor shall give notice to the Employer, describing the event or circumstance giving rise to the claim. The notice shall be given as soon as practicable, and not later than 28 days after the Contractor became aware, or should have become aware, of the event or circumstance.

If the Contractor fails to give notice of a claim within such period of 28 days, the Time for Completion shall not be extended, the Contractor shall not be entitled to additional payment, and the Employer shall be discharged from all liability in connection with the claim. Otherwise, the following provisions of this Sub-Clause shall apply.

The Contractor shall also submit any other notices which are required by the Contract, and supporting particulars for the claim, all as relevant to such event or circumstance.

The Contractor shall keep such contemporary records as may be necessary to substantiate any claim, either on the Site or at another location acceptable to the Employer. Without admitting liability, the Employer may, after receiving any notice under this Sub-Clause, monitor the record-keeping and/or instruct the Contractor to

在此类终止的情况下，**雇主**应向**承包商**支付：

(a) 已完成的、**合同**中有价格规定的任何工作的应付款额；

(b) 为**工程**订购的、已交付给**承包商**或**承包商**有责任接受交付的**生产设备**和**材料**的**费用**；当**雇主**支付上述费用后，此项**生产设备**与**材料**应成为**雇主**的财产(风险也由其承担)，**承包商**应将其交由**雇主**处理；

(c) 在**承包商**原预期要完成**工程**的情况下，合理导致的任何其他**费用**或债务；

(d) 将**临时工程**和**承包商设备**撤离**现场**、并运回**承包商**本国工作地点的**费用**，(或运往任何其他目的地,但其费用不得超过)；

(e) 将终止日期时完全为**工程**雇用的**承包商**的员工遣返回国的**费用**。

19.7

根据法律解除履约

不管**本条**的任何其他规定，如果发生**各方**不能控制的任何事件或情况(包括但不限于**不可抗力**)，使任**一方**或**双方**完成他或他们的**合同**义务成为不可能或非法，或根据管理**合同**的法律规定，**各方**有权解除进一步履行**合同**的义务，则根据任**一方**向**他方**发出此类事件或情况的通知：

(a) **双方**应解除进一步履约的义务，并不影响任**一方**对过去任何违反**合同**事项的权利；

(b) **雇主**应支付给**承包商**的款额，应等于如已根据**第 19.6 款**[**自主选择终止、付款和解除**]的规定终止**合同**，按该**款**规定应予支付的款额。

20 索赔、争端和仲裁

20.1

承包商的索赔

如果**承包商**认为，根据**本条件**任何条款或与**合同**有关的其他文件，他有权得到**竣工时间**的任何延长期和(或)任何追加付款，**承包商**应向**雇主**发出通知，说明引起索赔的事件或情况。该通知应尽快在**承包商**察觉或应已察觉该事件或情况后 28 天内发出。

如果**承包商**未能在上述 28 天期限内发出索赔通知，则**竣工时间**不得延长，**承包商**应无权获得追加付款，而**雇主**应免除有关该索赔的全部责任。否则，应适用**本款**以下规定。

承包商还应提交所有有关该事件或情况的、**合同**要求的任何其他通知，以及支持索赔的详细资料。

承包商应在**现场**或**雇主**认可的其他地点，保持用以证明任何索赔可能需要的此类同期记录。**雇主**收到根据**本款**发出的任何通知后，未承认责任前，可检查记录保持情况，并可指示**承包商**保持进一步的同期记录。**承包商**应

keep further contemporary records. The Contractor shall permit the Employer to inspect all these records, and shall (if instructed) submit copies to the Employer.

Within 42 days after the Contractor became aware (or should have become aware) of the event or circumstance giving rise to the claim, or within such other period as may be proposed by the Contractor and approved by the Employer, the Contractor shall send to the Employer a fully detailed claim which includes full supporting particulars of the basis of the claim and of the extension of time and/or additional payment claimed. If the event or circumstance giving rise to the claim has a continuing effect:

(a) this fully detailed claim shall be considered as interim;
(b) the Contractor shall send further interim claims at monthly intervals, giving the accumulated delay and/or amount claimed, and such further particulars as the Employer may reasonably require; and
(c) the Contractor shall send a final claim within 28 days after the end of the effects resulting from the event or circumstance, or within such other period as may be proposed by the Contractor and approved by the Employer.

Within 42 days after receiving a claim or any further particulars supporting a previous claim, or within such other period as may be proposed by the Employer and approved by the Contractor, the Employer shall respond with approval, or with disapproval and detailed comments. He may also request any necessary further particulars, but shall nevertheless give his response on the principles of the claim within such time.

Each interim payment shall include such amounts for any claim as have been reasonably substantiated as due under the relevant provision of the Contract. Unless and until the particulars supplied are sufficient to substantiate the whole of the claim, the Contractor shall only be entitled to payment for such part of the claim as he has been able to substantiate.

The Employer shall proceed in accordance with Sub-Clause 3.5 [*Determinations*] to agree or determine (i) the extension (if any) of the Time for Completion (before or after its expiry) in accordance with Sub-Clause 8.4 [*Extension of Time for Completion*], and/or (ii) the additional payment (if any) to which the Contractor is entitled under the Contract.

The requirements of this Sub-Clause are in addition to those of any other Sub-Clause which may apply to a claim. If the Contractor fails to comply with this or another Sub-Clause in relation to any claim, any extension of time and/or additional payment shall take account of the extent (if any) to which the failure has prevented or prejudiced proper investigation of the claim, unless the claim is excluded under the second paragraph of this Sub-Clause.

20.2 Appointment of the Dispute Adjudication Board

Disputes shall be adjudicated by a DAB in accordance with Sub-Clause 20.4 [*Obtaining Dispute Adjudication Board's Decision*]. The Parties shall jointly appoint a DAB by the date 28 days after a Party gives notice to the other Party of its intention to refer a dispute to a DAB in accordance with Sub-Clause 20.4.

The DAB shall comprise, as stated in the Particular Conditions, either one or three suitably qualified persons ("the members"). If the number is not so stated and the Parties do not agree otherwise, the DAB shall comprise three persons.

If the DAB is to comprise three persons, each Party shall nominate one member for the approval of the other Party. The Parties shall consult both these members and shall agree upon the third member, who shall be appointed to act as chairman.

允许**雇主**检查所有这些记录，并应向**雇主**(若有指示要求)提供复印件。

在**承包商**觉察(或应已觉察)引起索赔的事件或情况后42天内，或在**承包商**可能建议并经**雇主**认可的其他期限内，**承包商**应向**雇主**递交一份充分详细的索赔报告，包括索赔的依据、要求延长的时间和(或)追加的付款的全部详细资料。如果引起索赔的事件或情况具有连续影响，则：

(a) 上述充分详细的索赔报告应被视为是中间的；
(b) **承包商**应按月递交进一步的中间索赔报告，说明累计索赔的延误时间和(或)款额，以及**雇主**可能合理要求的此类进一步详细资料；

(c) **承包商**应在引起索赔的事件或情况产生的影响结束后28天内，或在**承包商**可能建议并经**雇主**认可的此类其他期限内，递交一份最终索赔报告。

雇主在收到索赔报告或对过去索赔的任何进一步证明资料后42天内，或在**雇主**可能建议并经**承包商**认可的其他期限内，做出回应，表示批准，或不批准并附具体意见。他还可以要求任何必要的进一步的资料，但他仍要在上述时间内对索赔的原则做出回应。

每次期中付款应包括已根据**合同**有关规定，合理证明是有依据的、对任何索赔的应付款额。除非并直到提供的详细资料足以证明索赔的全部要求是有依据的以前，**承包商**只有权得到索赔中他已能证明有依据部分的付款。

雇主应按照**第3.5款**[*确定*]的要求，就以下事项商定或确定：(ⅰ)根据**第8.4款**[*竣工时间的延长*]的规定，应给予的**竣工时间**(其期满前或后)的延长期(如果有)；和(或)(ⅱ)根据**合同**，**承包商**有权得到的追加付款(如果有)。

本款各项要求是对适用于索赔的任何其他条款的追加要求。如果**承包商**未能达到**本款**或有关任何索赔的其他条款的要求，除非该索赔根据本**款**第二段的规定被拒绝，对给予任何延长期和(或)追加付款，应考虑**承包商**此项未达到要求对索赔的彻底调查造成阻碍或影响(如果有)的程度。

20.2 争端裁决委员会的任命

争端应按照**第20.4款**[*取得争端裁决委员会的决定*]的规定，由争端裁决委员会(简称DAB——译注*)裁决。双方应在**一方**向另**一方**发出通知，提出按**第20.4款**将争端提交DAB的意向后28天内，联合任命一个DAB。

DAB应按**专用条件**中的规定，由具有适当资格的一名或三名人员(“成员”)组成。如果对委员人数没有规定，且双方没有另外协议，DAB应由三人组成。

如果DAB由三人组成，**各方**均应推荐一人，报**他方**认可，**双方**应与这些成员协商，并商定第三名成员，此人应任命为主席。

* 译注：下文中争端裁决委员会用全称或简称都按原文本。

However, if a list of potential members is included in the Contract, the members shall be selected from those on the list, other than anyone who is unable or unwilling to accept appointment to the DAB.

The agreement between the Parties and either the sole member ("adjudicator") or each of the three members shall incorporate by reference the General Conditions of Dispute Adjudication Agreement contained in the Appendix to these General Conditions, with such amendments as are agreed between them.

The terms of the remuneration of either the sole member or each of the three members shall be mutually agreed upon by the Parties when agreeing the terms of appointment. Each Party shall be responsible for paying one-half of this remuneration.

If at any time the Parties so agree, they may appoint a suitably qualified person or persons to replace any one or more members of the DAB. Unless the Parties agree otherwise, the appointment will come into effect if a member declines to act or is unable to act as a result of death, disability, resignation or termination of appointment. The replacement shall be appointed in the same manner as the replaced person was required to have been nominated or agreed upon, as described in this Sub-Clause.

The appointment of any member may be terminated by mutual agreement of both Parties, but not by the Employer or the Contractor acting alone. Unless otherwise agreed by both Parties, the appointment of the DAB (including each member) shall expire when the DAB has given its decision on the dispute referred to it under Sub-Clause 20.4, unless other disputes have been referred to the DAB by that time under Sub-Clause 20.4, in which event the relevant date shall be when the DAB has also given decisions on those disputes.

20.3 Failure to Agree Dispute Adjudication Board

If any of the following conditions apply, namely:

(a) the Parties fail to agree upon the appointment of the sole member of the DAB by the date stated in the first paragraph of Sub-Clause 20.2.

(b) either Party fails to nominate a member (for approval by the other Party) of a DAB of three persons by such date,

(c) the Parties fail to agree upon the appointment of the third member (to act as chairman) of the DAB by such date, or

(d) the Parties fail to agree upon the appointment of a replacement person within 42 days after the date on which the sole member or one of the three members declines to act or is unable to act as a result of death, disability, resignation or termination of appointment,

then the appointing entity or official named in the Particular Conditions shall, upon the request of either or both of the Parties and after due consultation with both Parties, appoint this member of the DAB. This appointment shall be final and conclusive. Each Party shall be responsible for paying one-half of the remuneration of the appointing entity or official.

20.4 Obtaining Dispute Adjudication Board's Decision

If a dispute (of any kind whatsoever) arises between the Parties in connection with, or arising out of, the Contract or the execution of the Works, including any dispute as to any certificate, determination, instruction, opinion or valuation of the Employer, then after a DAB has been apponted pursuant to Sub-Clauses 20.2 [*Appointment of the DAB*] and 20.3 [*Failure to Agree DAB*], either Party may refer the dispute in writing to the DAB for its decision, with a copy to the other Party. Such reference shall state that it is given under this Sub-Clause.

但如果**合同**中包括有备选成员名单，除有人不能或不愿接受DAB的任命外，成员应从名单上的人员中选择。

双方与该唯一成员(裁决人)、或该三人成员中的每个人间的协议书，应参考本**通用条件**附录的**争端裁决协议书一般条件**，结合他们间商定的此类修订意见拟定。

该唯一成员或三人成员中的每个人的报酬条件，应由**双方**在协商任命条件时共同商定。**每方**应负担上述报酬的一半。

如果经**双方**同意，他们可以在任何时候任命一位或几位有适当资格的人员，替代DAB的任何一位或几位成员。除非**双方**另有协议，在某一成员拒绝履行职责，或因其死亡、无行为能力、辞职、或任命期满而不能履行职责时，上述替代任命即告生效。替代任命应按本**款**所述对被替代人员在提名或商定时所需的同样方式进行。

对任何成员的任命，可以经过**双方**相互协议终止，但**雇主**或**承包商**都不能单独采取行动。除非**双方**另有协议，对DAB(包括每位成员)的任命应在DAB已就根据**第20.4款**提交给它的争端做出决定时期满，除非这时又有其他争端根据第20.4款提交给DAB，在此情况下，相应的期满日期应是DAB也对这些争端做出决定时。

20.3

对争端裁决委员会未能取得一致

如果下列任一情况适用，即：

(a) 到**第20.2款**第一段规定的日期，**双方**未能就DAB唯一成员的任命达成一致意见；
(b) 到该日期，任一**方**未能提名DAB三人成员中的一人(供另一**方**认可)；
(c) 到该日期，**双方**未能就DAB第3位成员(将担任主席)的任命达成一致意见；或
(d) 在唯一成员或三人成员中的一人拒绝履行职责，或因其死亡、无行为能力、辞职、或任命期满而不能履行职责后42天内，**双方**未能就任命一位替代人员达成一致意见；

这时，在**专用条件**中指名的任命实体或官员，应在任一**方**或**双方**请求下，并经与**双方**做应有的协商后，任命DAB该成员。此项任命应是最终的，决定性的。**每方**应负责支付给该任命实体或官员报酬的一半。

20.4

取得争端裁决委员会的决定

如果**双方**间发生了有关或起因于**合同**或**工程**实施的争端(不论任何种类)，包括对**雇主**的任何证明、确定、指示、意见或估价的任何争端，在已依照**第20.2款**[**争端裁决委员会的任命**]和**第20.3款**[**对争端裁决委员会未能取得一致**]的规定任命DAB后，任一**方**可将该争端事项以书面形式提交DAB，供其裁定，并抄送另一方。此项委托应说明是根据**本款**规定做出的。

For a DAB of three persons, the DAB shall be deemed to have received such reference on the date when it is received by the chairman of the DAB.

Both Parties shall promptly make available to the DAB all information, access to the Site, and appropriate facilities, as the DAB may require for the purposes of making a decision on such dispute. The DAB shall be deemed to be not acting as arbitrator(s).

Within 84 days after receiving such reference, or the advance payment referred to in Clause 6 of the Appendix - General Conditions of the Dispute Adjudication Agreement, whichever date is later, or within such other period as may be proposed by the DAB and approved by both Parties, the DAB shall give its decision, which shall be reasoned and shall state that it is given under this Sub-Clause. However, if neither of the Parties has paid in full the invoices submitted by each Member pursuant to Clause 6 of the Appendix, the DAB shall not be obliged to give its decision until such invoices have been paid in full. The decision shall be binding on both Parties, who shall promptly give effect to it unless and until it shall be revised in an amicable settlement or an arbitral award as described below. Unless the Contract has already been abandoned, repudiated or terminated, the Contractor shall continue to proceed with the Works in accordance with the Contract.

If either Party is dissatisfied with the DAB's decision, then either Party may, within 28 days after receiving the decision, give notice to the other Party of its dissatisfaction. If the DAB fails to give its decision within the period of 84 days (or as otherwise approved) after receiving such reference or such payment, then either Party may, within 28 days after this period has expired, give notice to the other Party of its dissatisfaction.

In either event, this notice of dissatisfaction shall state that it is given under this Sub-Clause, and shall set out the matter in dispute and the reason(s) for dissatisfaction. Except as stated in Sub-Clause 20.7 [*Failure to Comply with Dispute Adjudication Board's Decision*] and Sub-Clause 20.8 [*Expiry of Dispute Adjudication Board's Appointment*], neither Party shall be entitled to commence arbitration of a dispute unless a notice of dissatisfaction has been given in accordance with this Sub-Clause.

If the DAB has given its decision as to a matter in dispute to both Parties, and no notice of dissatisfaction has been given by either Party within 28 days after it received the DAB's decision, then the decision shall become final and binding upon both Parties.

20.5

Amicable Settlement

Where notice of dissatisfaction has been given under Sub-Clause 20.4 above, both Parties shall attempt to settle the dispute amicably before the commencement of arbitration. However, unless both Parties agree otherwise, arbitration may be commenced on or after the fifty-sixth day after the day on which notice of dissatisfaction was given, even if no attempt at amicable settlement has been made.

20.6

Arbitration

Unless settled amicably, any dispute in respect of which the DAB's decision (if any) has not become final and binding shall be finally settled by international arbitration. Unless otherwise agreed by both Parties:

(a) the dispute shall be finally settled under the Rules of Arbitration of the International Chamber of Commerce,

(b) the dispute shall be settled by three arbitrators appointed in accordance with these Rules, and

(c) the arbitration shall be conducted in the language for communications defined in Sub-Clause 1.4 [*Law and Language*].

对于 3 人**DAB**，该**DAB**应被认为，在其主席收到委托的日期已收到该项委托。

双方应迅速向 DAB 提供，DAB 为对此类争端做出决定可能需要的所有资料、**现场**进入权及相应设施。DAB 应被认为不是在进行仲裁人的工作。

DAB 应在收到此项委托、或**附录—争端裁决协议书一般条件第 6 条**中提到的预付款额，二者中较晚的日期后 84 天内，或在可能由DAB 建议并经**双方**认可的此类其他期限内，提出它的决定，决定应是有理由的，并说明是根据本**款**规定提出的。但是，如果任一方未能对每位**成员**按照**附录第 6 条**的规定提交的发票全部付清，在直到该发票全部被付清前，DAB 应有权不提交它的决定。决定应对**双方**具有约束力，**双方**都应迅速遵照实行，除非并直到如下文所述，决定在友好解决或仲裁裁决中应做出修改。除非**合同**已被放弃、拒绝或终止，**承包商**应继续按照**合同**进行**工程**。

如果任一**方**对DAB 的决定不满意，可在收到该决定通知后 28 天内，将其不不满向另一**方**发出通知。如果DAB 未能在收到此项委托或此项付款后 84 天(或经认可的其他)期限内，提出其决定，则任一**方**可以在该期限期满后 28 天内，向另一**方**发出其不满的通知。

在上述任一情况下，表示不满的通知应说明是根据本**款**规定发出的，并应说明争端的事项和不满的理由。除**第 20.7 款**[**未能遵守争端裁决委员会的决定**]和**第 20.8 款**[**争端裁决委员会任命期满**]所述情况外，除非已按本**款**规定发出表示不满的通知，任一方都无权着手争端的仲裁。

如果DAB 已就争端事项向**双方**提交了它的决定，而任一**方**在收到DAB 决定后 28 天内，均未发出表示不满的通知，则该决定应成为最终的、对**双方**均具有约束力。

20.5

友好解决

如果已按上述**第 20.4 款**发出了表示不满的通知，**双方**应在着手仲裁前，努力以友好方式来解决争端。但是，除非**双方**另有协议，仲裁可在表示不满的通知发出后第 56 天或其后着手进行，即使未曾做过友好解决的努力。

20.6

仲裁

经DAB 对之做出的决定(如果有)未能成为最终的和有约束力的任何争端，除非已获得友好解决，应通过国际仲裁对其作出最终解决。除非**双方**另有协议：

(a) 争端应根据**国际商会仲裁规则**最终解决；

(b) 争端应由按上述**规则**任命的 3 位仲裁人员负责解决；

(c) 仲裁应以**第 1.4 款**[**法律和语言**]规定的交流语言进行。

The arbitrator(s) shall have full power to open up, review and revise any certificate, determination, instruction, opinion or valuation of (or on behalf of) the Employer, and any decision of the DAB, relevant to the dispute.

Neither Party shall be limited in the proceedings before the arbitrator(s) to the evidence or arguments previously put before the DAB to obtain its decision, or to the reasons for dissatisfaction given in its notice of dissatisfaction. Any decision of the DAB shall be admissible in evidence in the arbitration.

Arbitration may be commenced prior to or after completion of the Works. The obligations of the Parties and the DAB shall not be altered by reason of any arbitration being conducted during the progress of the Works.

20.7 Failure to Comply with Dispute Adjudication Board's Decision

In the event that:

(a) neither Party has given notice of dissatisfaction within the period stated in Sub-Clause 20.4 [*Obtaining Dispute Adjudication Board's Decision*],
(b) the DAB's related decision (if any) has become final and binding, and
(c) a Party fails to comply with this decision,

then the other Party may, without prejudice to any other rights it may have, refer the failure itself to arbitration under Sub-Clause 20.6 [*Arbitration*]. Sub-Clause 20.4 [*Obtaining Dispute Adjudication Board's Decision*] and Sub-Clause 20.5 [*Amicable Settlement*] shall not apply to this reference.

20.8 Expiry of Dispute Adjudication Board's Appointment

If a dispute arises between the Parties in connection with, or arising out of, the Contract or the execution of the Works and there is no DAB in place, whether by reason of the expiry of the DAB's appointment or otherwise:

(a) Sub-Clause 20.4 [*Obtaining Dispute Adjudication Board's Decision*] and Sub-Clause 20.5 [Amicable Settlement] shall not apply, and
(b) the dispute may be referred directly to arbitration under Sub-Clause 20.6 [*Arbitration*].

仲裁员应有全权公开、审查和修改与该争端有关的**雇主**(或其代表)发出的任何证明、确定、指示、意见、或估价，以及DAB的任何决定。

任一**方**在仲裁员面前的诉讼中，应不受以前为获得DAB的决定而向其提供的证据或论据、或在其表示不满的通知中提出的不满意理由的限制。DAB的任何决定都应可以作为仲裁中的证据。

仲裁在**工程**竣工前或竣工后，都可以着手进行。**双方**与DAB的义务，不得因为在**工程**进行过程中正在进行任何仲裁而改变。

20.7

未能遵守争端裁决委员会的决定

在以下情况下：

(a) 任一**方**在**第20.4款**[**取得争端裁决委员会的决定**]规定的期限内均未发出表示不满的通知；
(b) DAB的有关决定(如果有)已成为最终的并有约束力的；
(c) 有一**方**未遵守上述决定。

这时，另一**方**可以在不损害其可能拥有的其他权利的情况下，根据**第20.6款**[**仲裁**]的规定，将上述未遵守决定的事项提交仲裁。在此情况下，**第20.4款**[**取得争端裁决委员会的决定**]和**第20.5款**[**友好解决**]的规定应不适用。

20.8

争端裁决委员会任命期满

如果**双方**间因与**合同**或**工程**实施相关或由其引起的问题产生争端，且又因DAB任命期满或其他原因，没有DAB进行工作，则：

(a) **第20.4款**[**取得争端裁决委员会的决定**]和**第20.5款**[**友好解决**]的规定应不适用；
(b) 此项争端可根据**第20.6款**[**仲裁**]的规定，直接提交仲裁。

APPENDIX

General Conditions of Dispute Adjudication Agreement

1

Definitions

Each "Dispute Adjudication Agreement" is a tripartite agreement by and between:

(a) the "Employer";

(b) the "Contractor"; and

(c) the "Member" who is defined in the Dispute Adjudication Agreement as being:

(i) the sole member of the "DAB" (or "adjudicator") and, where this is the case, all references to the "Other Members" do not apply,

or

(ii) one of the three persons who are jointly called the "DAB" (or "dispute adjudication board") and, where this is the case, the other two persons are called the "Other Members".

The Employer and the Contractor have entered (or intend to enter) into a contract, which is called the "Contract" and is defined in the Dispute Adjudication Agreement, which incorporates this Appendix. In the Dispute Adjudication Agreement, words and expressions which are not otherwise defined shall have the meanings assigned to them in the Contract.

2

General Provisions

The Dispute Adjudication Agreement shall take effect when the Employer, the Contractor and each of the Members (or Member) have respectively each signed a dispute adjudication agreement.

When the Dispute Adjudication Agreement has taken effect, the Employer and the Contractor shall each give notice to the Member accordingly. If the Member does not receive either notice within six months after entering into the Dispute Adjudication Agreement, it shall be void and ineffective.

This employment of the Member is a personal appointment. No assignment or subcontracting of the Dispute Adjudication Agreement is permitted without the prior written agreement of all the parties to it and of the Other Members (if any).

3

Warranties

The Member warrants and agrees that he/she is and shall be impartial and independent of the Employer, the Contractor and the Employer's Representative. The Member shall promptly disclose, to each of them and to the Other Members (if any), any fact or circumstance which might appear inconsistent with his/her warranty and agreement of impartiality and independence.

When appointing the Member, the Employer and the Contractor relied upon the Member's representations that he/she is:

(a) experienced in the work which the Contractor is to carry out under the Contract,

(b) experienced in the interpretation of contract documentation, and

(c) fluent in the the language for communications defined in the Contract.

4

General Obligations of the Member

The Member shall:

(a) have no interest financial or otherwise in the Employer or the Contractor, nor any financial interest in the Contract except for payment under the Dispute Adjudication Agreement;

附录

争端裁决协议书一般条件

1
定义

每份“**争端裁决协议书**”是由下列三方间签订的三方协议书，
(a)“**雇主**”；
(b)“**承包商**”；
(c)“**成员**”，在**争端裁决协议书**中定义为：
(ⅰ)“DAB”的唯一成员(或“裁决员”)，在此情况下，所有“**其他成员**”的说法都不适用；或

(ⅱ)联合称为“**DAB**”(“争端裁决委员会”)的三人中的一人，在此情况下，另外两人称为“**其他成员**”。

雇主和**承包商**已(或将)签一份合同，在**争端裁决协议书**中称为“**合同**”，其含义是确定的，该合同包括**本附录**。**争端裁决协议书**中的词语和措辞，除另有规定的以外，应具有**合同**赋予它们的含义。

2
一般规定

争端裁决协议书应在**雇主**、**承包商**和三人**成员**中的每位**成员**(或唯一**成员**)分别签署争端裁决协议书后生效。

争端裁决协议书生效后，**雇主**和**承包商**各自都应相应向**成员**发出通知。如果在签订**争端裁决协议书**6个月内，**成员**没有收到任一份通知，该协议书应作废和无效。

这种对**成员**的聘任属对个人的任命，事先未经涉及各方和**其他成员**(如果有)的书面同意，**争端裁决协议书**不得转让或分包。

3
保证

成员保证并同意，他(或她)对**雇主**、**承包商**和**雇主代表**保持和应保持公正和独立。**成员**应将看来可能与其公正和独立的保证和同意不相符的任何事实或情况，迅速告知他们各人及**其他成员**(如果有)。

当任命**成员**时，**雇主**和**承包商**依据**成员**他(或她)的下列表现：

(a) 具有**承包商**根据**合同**要进行的工作的经验；
(b) 具有解释合同文件的经验；
(c) 能流利地使用**合同**规定的交流语言。

4
成员的一般义务

成员应：
(a) 除根据**争端裁决协议书**的付款外，与**雇主**或**承包商**没有财务或其他利益关系；在**合同**中没有任何财务利益；

(b) not previously have been employed as a consultant or otherwise by the Employer or the Contractor, except in such circumstances as were disclosed in writing to the Employer and the Contractor before they signed the Dispute Adjudication Agreement;
(c) have disclosed in writing to the Employer, the Contractor and the Other Members (if any), before entering into the Dispute Adjudication Agreement and to his/her best knowledge and recollection, any professional or personal relationships with any director, officer or employee of the Employer or the Contractor, and any previous involvement in the overall project of which the Contract forms part;
(d) not, for the duration of the Dispute Adjudication Agreement, be employed as a consultant or otherwise by the Employer or the Contractor, except as may be agreed in writing by the Employer, the Contractor and the Other Members (if any);
(e) comply with the annexed procedural rules and with Sub-Clause 20.4 of the Conditions of Contract;
(f) not give advice to the Employer, the Contractor, the Employer's Personnel or the Contractor's Personnel concerning the conduct of the Contract, other than in accordance with the annexed procedural rules;
(g) not while a Member enter into discussions or make any agreement with the Employer or the Contractor regarding employment by any of them, whether as a consultant or otherwise, after ceasing to act under the Dispute Adjudication Agreement;
(h) ensure his/her availability for any site visit and hearings as are necessary; and
(i) treat the details of the Contract and all the DAB's activities and hearings as private and confidential, and not publish or disclose them without the prior written consent of the Employer, the Contractor and the Other Members (if any).

5

General Obligations of the Employer and the Contractor

The Employer, the Contractor, the Employer's Personnel and the Contractor's Personnel shall not request advice from or consultation with the Member regarding the Contract, otherwise than in the normal course of the DAB's activities under the Contract and the Dispute Adjudication Agreement, and except to the extent that prior agreement is given by the Employer, the Contractor and the Other Members (if any). The Employer and the Contractor shall be responsible for compliance with this provision, by the Employer's Personnel and the Contractor's Personnel respectively.

The Employer and the Contractor undertake to each other and to the Member that the Member shall not, except as otherwise agreed in writing by the Employer, the Contractor, the Member and the Other Members (if any):
(a) be appointed as an arbitrator in any arbitration under the Contract;
(b) be called as a witness to give evidence concerning any dispute before arbitrator(s) appointed for any arbitration under the Contract; or
(c) be liable for any claims for anything done or omitted in the discharge or purported discharge of the Member's functions, unless the act or omission is shown to have been in bad faith.

The Employer and the Contractor hereby jointly and severally indemnify and hold the Member harmless against and from claims from which he/she is relieved from liability under the preceding paragraph.

6

Payment

The Member shall be paid as follows, in the currency named in the Dispute Adjudication Agreement:
(a) a daily fee which shall be considered as payment in full for:

(b) 以前未曾被**雇主**或**承包商**聘任咨询顾问或其他职务，在签订争**端裁决协议书**前，已书面告知**雇主**和**承包商**的情况除外；

(c) 在签订**争端裁决协议书**前，已就他(或她)的了解和记忆所及，将其与**雇主**或**承包商**的董事、职员或雇员间的任何业务或个人关系，以及此前在本**合同**为其组成部分的全面**工程**中的任何参与情况，书面告知**雇主**、**承包商**和**其他成员**(如果有)；

(d) 在执行**争端裁决协议书**期间，除经**雇主**、**承包商**和**其他成员**(如果有)的书面同意外，不接受**雇主**或**承包商**的聘任，担任咨询顾问或其他职位；

(e) 依从所附程序规则和**合同条件第 20.4 款**规定；

(f) 除按照所附程序规则办事外，不向**雇主**、**承包商**、**雇主人员**、或**承包商人员**提供有关执行**合同**的建议；

(g) 在担任**成员**期间，不与**雇主**或**承包商**，就其停止按**争端裁决协议书**任职后就任他们中某一**方**的咨询顾问或其他职位进行洽谈或签订任何协议；

(h) 保证出席任何必要的现场视察和意见听取会；

(i) 将**合同**的所有细节、及DAB的所有活动和意见听取会情况视为私人的和机密的事项，没有**雇主**、**承包商**和**其他成员**(如果有)的事先书面同意，不将前述各事项公开发表或向外泄露。

5

雇主和承包商的一般义务

除事先经**雇主**、**承包商**和**其他成员**(如果有)同意的范围以外，**雇主**、**承包商**、**雇主人员**和**承包商人员**不应在DAB根据**合同**和本**争端裁决协议书**进行活动的正常过程之外，就**合同**有关问题要求**成员**提供建议，或与其协商。**雇主**和**承包商**应分别对**雇主人员**和**承包商人员**遵守此规定负责。

除另经**雇主**、**承包商**、**成员**和**其他成员**(如果有)书面同意外，**雇主**和**承包商**应互相并向**成员**承诺，**成员**不应：

(a) 在根据**合同**进行的任何仲裁中，被任命为仲裁员；

(b) 在根据**合同**进行的任何仲裁中任命的仲裁员面前，被请来作为对任何争端提供证据的证人；或

(c) 对因执行或据称执行**成员**任务中的任何行为或遗漏提出的任何索赔负责，除非该行为或遗漏表明是不诚实的。

雇主和**承包商**在此共同并各自保障和保持**成员**免受因上段中他(或她)已被解除的责任引起的索赔带来的损害。

6

报酬

成员应按**争端裁决协议书**中规定的货币，得到以下付款：

(a) 日酬金，此项费用应被视为对下列事项的全部付款：

(i) each working day spent reading submissions, attending hearings (if any), preparing decisions, or making site visits (if any); and

(ii) each day or part of a day up to maximum of two day's travel time in each direction for the journey (if any) between the Member's home and site or an other location of a meeting with Other Members (if any) and/or the Employer and the Contractor;

(b) all reasonable expenses incurred in connection with the Member's duties, including the cost of secretarial services, telephone calls, courier charges, faxes and telexes, travel expenses, hotel and subsistence costs; a receipt shall be required for each item in excess of five percent of the daily fee referred to in sub-paragraph (a) of this Clause; and

(c) any taxes properly levied in the Country on payments made to the Member (unless a national or permanent resident of the Country) under this Clause 6.

The daily fee shall be as specified in the Dispute Adjudication Agreement.

Immediately after the Dispute Adjudication Agreement takes effect, the Member shall, before engaging in any activities under the Dispute Adjudication Agreement, submit to the Contractor, with a copy to the Employer, an invoice for (a) an advance of twenty-five (25) percent of the estimated total amount of daily fees to which he/she will be entitled and (b) an advance equal to the estimated total expenses that he/she shall incur in connection with his/her duties. Payment of such invoice shall be made by the Contractor upon his receipt of the invoice. The Member shall not be obliged to engage in activities under the Dispute Adjudication Agreement until each Member has been paid in full for invoices submitted under this paragraph.

Thereafter the Member shall submit to the Contractor, with a copy to the Employer, invoices for the balance of his/her daily fees and expenses, less the amounts advanced. The DAB shall not be obliged to render its decision until invoices for all daily fees and expenses of each Member for making a decision shall have paid in full.

Unless paid earlier in accordance with the above, the Contractor shall pay each of the Member's invoices in full within 28 calendar days after receiving each invoice and shall apply to the Employer (in the Statements under the Contract) for reimbursement of one-half of the amounts of these invoices. The Employer shall then pay the Contractor in accordance with the Contract.

If the Contractor fails to pay to the Member the amount to which he/she is entitled under the Dispute Adjudication Agreement, the Employer shall pay the amount due to the Member and any other amount which may be required to maintain the operation of the DAB; and without prejudice to the Employer's rights or remedies. In addition to all other rights arising from this default, the Employer shall be entitled to reimbursement of all sums paid in excess of one-half of these payments, plus all costs of recovering these sums and financing charges calculated at the rate specified in Sub-Clause 14.8 of the Conditions of Contract.

If the Member does not receive payment of the amount due within 28 days after submitting a valid invoice, the Member may (i) suspend his/her services (without notice) until the payment is received, and/or (ii) resign his/her appointment by giving notice to the Employer and the Contractor. The notice shall take effect when received by them both. Any such notice, shall be final and binding on the Employer, the Contractor and the Member.

7

Default of the Member

If the Member fails to comply with any obligation under Clause 4, he/she shall not be entitled to any fees or expenses hereunder and shall, without prejudice to their other

（ⅰ）用于阅读提交的资料、参加意见听取会（如果有）、准备决定意见、或进行现场视察（如果有）的每个工作日；

（ⅱ）在**成员**住所与现场，或与**其他成员**（如果有）和（或）**雇主**和**承包商**开会的其他地点之间，单向一天或不足一天，最多至两天时间的旅程；

(b) 因履行**成员**义务而发生的所有合理开支，包括秘书服务费、电话费、信差等服务费、传真和电传费、旅差费、旅馆和生活补助费。当每项费用超过本**条**(a)项所述日酬金的百分之五时，应提交费用的收据；

(c) 在**工程所在国**对**成员**（如果不是**工程所在国**的国民或永久性居民）根据本**第6条**取得的付款，合理征收的任何税款。

日酬金应按**争端裁决协议书**的规定执行。

在**争端裁决协议书**生效后，**成员**应在根据**争端裁决协议书**进行任何活动前，立即向**承包商**提交一份下列内容的发票，并送**雇主**一份复印件，(a)他（或她）有权得到的日酬金估算总额的25%的预付款额，及(b)等于他（或她）为其义务将发生的全部开支估算额的预付款额。**承包商**应在收到发票后，按该发票付款。在每位**成员**收到根据本段规定提交的发票的全部付款前，**成员**没有义务根据**争端裁决协议书**的规定开展活动。

其后，**成员**应向**承包商**提交他（或她）的日酬金和各项开支扣除预付款额后的余额的发票，并送**雇主**一份复印件。在每位**成员**为做出决定意见的全部日酬金和各项开支都按发票全部收到付款前，DAB没有义务提交其决定意见。

除非按照上述程序提前进行了支付，**承包商**应在收到每份发票后28个日历日内，按每位**成员**的发票全部付清，同时向**雇主**（在根据**合同**提交的报表中）申请付还这些发票款额的一半。这时，**雇主**应按照**合同**付给**承包商**。

如果**承包商**未能向**成员**支付他（或她）根据**争端裁决协议书**的规定应得的款额，**雇主**应向**成员**支付其应得款额和维持DAB运作可能需要的任何其他款额；此项支付不损害**雇主**的权利或应得补偿。除由此项违约引起的所有其他权利外，**雇主**对他支付的超过这些付款一半的所有款额应有权获得偿还，还应加上回收这些款项的全部费用和按**合同条件第14.8款**规定的利率计算的融资费用。

如果**成员**在提交有效发票后28天内，没有收到应付款额的支付，成员可以（ⅰ）暂停他（或她）的服务（不需通知），直到收到付款为止，和（或）（ⅱ）通过向**雇主**和**承包商**发出通知，辞去他（或她）的职务。通知应在**双方**收到后生效。任何此类通知应是最终的，对**雇主**、**承包商**和**成员**都有约束力的。

7

成员的违约

如果**成员**未能遵守**第4条**规定的任何义务，他（或她）应无权得到在此所述的任何酬金和开支；并应在不损害**雇主**和**承包商**其他权利的条件下，将该

rights, reimburse each of the Employer and the Contractor for any fees and expenses received by the Member and the Other Members (if any), for proceedings or decisions (if any) of the DAB which are rendered void or ineffective.

8

Disputes

Any dispute or claim arising out of or in connection with this Dispute Adjudication Agreement, or the breach, termination or invalidity thereof, shall be finally settled under the Rules of Arbitration of the International Chamber of Commerce by one arbitrator appointed in accordance with these Rules of Arbitration.

成员及**其他成员**(如果有)为已导致作废或无效的**DAB**的工作和决定(如果有)收到的任何费用和开支，分别付还**雇主**和**承包商**。

8

争端

因本**争端裁决协议书**或与之有关的、或因对其违反或其终止或失效而引起的任何争端或索赔，应根据**国际商会仲裁规则**，由一位按这些**仲裁规则**任命的仲裁员最终解决。

Annex PROCEDURAL RULES

1 The Employer and the Contractor shall furnish to the DAB one copy of all documents which the DAB may request, including Contract documents, progress reports, variation instructions, certificates and other documents pertinent to the matter in dispute. All communications between the DAB and the Employer or the Contractor shall be copied to the other Party. If the DAB comprises three persons, the Employer and the Contractor shall send copies of these requested documents and these communications to each of these persons.

2 The DAB shall proceed in accordance with Sub-Clause 20.4 and these Rules. Subject to the time allowed to give notice of a decision and other relevant factors, the DAB shall:

(a) act fairly and impartially as between the Employer and the Contractor, giving each of them a reasonable opportunity of putting his case and responding to the other's case, and
(b) adopt procedures suitable to the dispute, avoiding unnecessary delay or expense.

3 The DAB may conduct a hearing on the dispute, in which event it will decide on the date and place for the hearing and may request that written documentation and arguments from the Employer and the Contractor be presented to it prior to or at the hearing.

4 Except as otherwise agreed in writing by the Employer and the Contractor, the DAB shall have power to adopt an inquisitorial procedure, to refuse admission to hearings or audience at hearings to any persons other than representatives of the Employer and the Contractor, and to proceed in the absence of any party who the DAB is satisfied received notice of the hearing; but shall have discretion to decide whether and to what extent this power may be exercised.

5 The Employer and the Contractor empower the DAB, among other things, to:

(a) establish the procedure to be applied in deciding a dispute,
(b) decide upon the DAB's own jurisdiction, and as to the scope of any dispute referred to it,
(c) conduct any hearing as it thinks fit, not being bound by any rules or procedures other than those contained in the Contract and these Rules,
(d) take the initiative in ascertaining the facts and matters required for a decision,
(e) make use of its own specialist knowledge, if any,
(f) decide upon the payment of financing charges in accordance with the Contract,
(g) decide upon any provisional relief such as interim or conservatory measures, and
(h) open up, review and revise any certificate, decision, determination, instruction, opinion or valuation of the Employer, relevant to the dispute.

6 The DAB shall not express any opinions during any hearing concerning the merits of any arguments advanced by the Parties. Thereafter, the DAB shall make and give notice to its decision in accordance with Sub-Clause 20.4, or as otherwise agreed by the Employer and the Contractor in writing. If the DAB comprises three persons:

附件 程序规则

1 **雇主**和**承包商**应向DAB提供一份其可能要求的所有文件，包括**合同**文件、进度报告、变更指示、证明和有关争端事项的其他文件。DAB和**雇主**或**承包商**间的所有函件，都应抄送其他**当事方**。如果DAB由三人组成，**雇主**和**承包商**应将这些要求的文件和这些信函的复印件提供给三人中的每位成员。

2 DAB应按照**合同条件第20.4款**和本**规则**进行工作。根据发出决定和其他有关因素的通知所允许的时间，DAB应：

(a) 公平、公正地对待**雇主**和**承包商**，对每方都给予合理的机会陈述己方的论据，回应他方的论据；

(b) 采取对争端事项适宜的程序，避免不必要的延误或开支。

3 DAB可以就争端事项召开意见听取会，在此情况下，它将决定意见听取会的时间和地点，并可要求**雇主**和**承包商**在意见听取会前或开会时递交书面文件和论据。

4 除另经**雇主**和**承包商**书面同意外，DAB应有权采取讯问调查程序，拒绝除**雇主**、**承包商**的代表以外的任何人参加或旁听意见听取会；并有权在任一方缺席，且DAB确信其已收到意见听取会通知的情况下，进行会议；但对是否实施这一权利或可能实施的范围，应有权自主做出决定。

5 在其他方面，**雇主**和**承包商**给予DAB以下权力：

(a) 确定在决定争端中应用的程序；
(b) 决定DAB自身的权限，及委托其处理的任何争端涉及的范围；

(c) 召开其认为适宜的任何意见听取会，除包括在**合同**和本**规则**中的规定外，不受任何规则或程序的约束；
(d) 主动确定为做出决定所需的事实和情况；
(e) 利用其自身的专家知识，如果有；
(f) 按照**合同**规定，决定融资费用的支付；

(g) 决定任何暂时补救办法，如暂时的或保护性的措施；

(h) 公开、审查和修正**雇主**发出的与争端有关的任何证明、决定、确定、指示、意见、或估价。

6 DAB在任何意见听取会期间，不应就**各方**提出的任何论据的是非表示任何意见。其后，DAB应按照**合同条件第20.4款**，或经**雇主**和**承包商**书面同意的其他规定，做出决定，并发出通知。如果DAB由3人组成，则：

(a) it shall convene in private after a hearing, if any, in order to have discussions and prepare its decision;

(b) it shall endeavour to reach a unanimous decision: if this proves impossible, the applicable decision shall be made by a majority of the Members, who may require the minority Member to prepare a written report for submission to the Employer and the Contractor; and

(c) if a Member fails to attend a meeting or hearing, or to fulfil any required function, the other two Members may nevertheless proceed to make a decision, unless:

   (i) either the Employer or Contractor does nor agree that they do so, or

   (ii) the absent Member is the chairman, and he/she instructs the other Members to not make a decision.

(a) 为讨论和做出其决定，应在意见听取会(如果有)后，召开秘密会议，

(b) 应努力作出一致决定。如果不可能，应由多数**成员**作出合适的决定，并要求该少数**成员**编写一份书面报告，提交给**雇主**和**承包商**；

(c) 如果某一**成员**未参加会议或意见听取会，或未履行其应尽的职责，另外两名**成员**仍可继做出决定，除非：

(ⅰ) **雇主**或**承包商**不同意他们这样做，或
(ⅱ) 该缺席**成员**是主席，并且他(或她)通知其他**成员**不要做出决定。

INDEX OF SUB-CLAUSES

条款索引

（原文按英文字母顺序排列，中译文按汉语拼音字母顺序排列）

通用条件
GENERAL CONDITIONS

专用条件编写指南
GUIDANCE FOR THE PREPARATION OF PARTICULAR CONDITIONS

投标函、合同协议书和争端裁决协议书格式
FORMS OF LETTER OF TENDER, CONTRACT AGREEMENT AND DISPUTE ADJUDICATION AGREEMENT

设计采购施工(EPC)/交钥匙工程合同条件

Conditions of Contract for **EPC/Turnkey Projects**

专用条件编写指南

Guidance for the Preparation of Particular Conditions

国际咨询工程师联合会

FEDERATION INTERNATIONALE DES INGENIEURS-CONSEILS
INTERNATIONAL FEDERATION OF CONSULTING ENGINEERS
INTERNATIONALE VEREINIGUNG BERATENDER INGENIEURE
FEDERACION INTERNACIONAL DE INGENIEROS CONSOLTORES

Guidance
for the Preparation of Particular Conditions

CONTENTS

专用条件编写指南

目　　录

Guidance for the Preparation of Particular Conditions

INTRODUCTION

The terms of the Conditions of Contract for EPC/Turnkey Projects have been prepared by the Fédération Internationale des Ingénieurs-Conseils (FIDIC) and are recommended where one entity takes total responsibility for an engineering project, including design, manufacture, delivery and installation of plant, and the design and execution of building or engineering works, tenders having been invited on an international basis. Modifications to the Conditions may be required in some legal jurisdictions, particularly if they are to be used on domestic contracts.

Major turnkey projects may require some negotiation between the parties. Having studied the variety of options offered by tenderers, the Employer may consider it essential to meet and discuss with them the technical options which the Employer considers preferable. Under the usual arrangements for this type of contract, the Contractor carries out the Engineering, Procurement and Construction, and provides a fully-equipped facility, ready for operation (at the "turn of the key").

The guidance hereafter is intended to assist writers of the Particular Conditions by giving options for various sub-clauses where appropriate. As far as possible, example wording is included, between lines. In some cases, however, only an aide-memoire is given.

Before incorporating any example wording, it must be checked to ensure that it is wholly suitable for the particular circumstances. Unless it is considered suitable, example wording should be amended before use.

Where example wording is amended, and in all cases where other amendments or additions are made, care must be taken to ensure that no ambiguity is created, either with the General Conditions or between the clauses in the Particular Conditions.

In the preparation of the Conditions of Contract to be included in the tender documents for a contract, the following text can be used:

> The Conditions of Contract comprise the "General Conditions", which form part of the "Conditions of Contract for EPC/Turnkey Projects" First Edition 1999 published by the Fédération Internationale des Ingénieurs-Conseils (FIDIC), and the following "Particular Conditions", which include amendments and additions to such General Conditions.

The following Sub-Clauses of the General Conditions require data to be included in the Particular Conditions:

1.1.3.3 & 8.2	Time for Completion
1.1.3.7 & 11.1	Defects Notification Period
1.1.5.6	Definition of each Section, if any
1.3	Electronic systems for communications
1.4	Laws and languages
2.1	Time for possession of the Site
4.2	Performance Security

专用条件编写指南

引　言

国际咨询工程师联合会(**FIDIC 即菲迪克**)已编制了《**EPC**(**设计采购施工**)/**交钥匙工程合同条件**》，推荐用于进行国际招标，由一个实体承担工程项目的全部职责，包括生产设备设计、制造、交付和安装，以及建筑或工程的设计和施工。在某些法律管辖地区，特别是用于国内合同时，可能需要对**条件**做些修改。

一些较大的交钥匙项目，各方之间可能需要进行一些协商。**雇主**在研究投标人提交的各种可选方案后，可能认为有必要会见他们，并就**雇主**认为可取的技术方案进行讨论。根据这类合同的通常安排，**承包商**将承担**设计**、**采购**和**施工**，提交一个配备完整，做好运行准备(处于"交钥匙"状态)的设施。

下述指南旨在通过在适当处给出各类备选条款，为**专用条件**的编写人提供帮助。尽可能包括一些文字间的范例措辞，但在有些情况下只给出备忘要点。

在使用任何范例措辞前，必须核实以确保完全适用于特定的情况。除非认为是适宜的，使用前对范例措辞应进行修改。

当对范例措辞进行修改时，以及在所有其他修改和补充的情况下，必须注意确保不与**通用条件**产生歧义，或在**专用条件**条款间产生歧义。

在编写包括在一项合同的招标文件中的**合同条件**时，可以使用下列文字：

> **合同条件**包括"**通用条件**"和"**专用条件**"。**通用条件**是**国际咨询工程师联合会**(FIDIC)1999年出版的"**EPC**(**设计采购施工**)**交钥匙工程合同条件**"第一版的组成部分；其后的"**专用条件**"包括对上述**通用条件**的修改和补充。

通用条件中的下列条款需要在**专用条件**中补充具体内容：

1.1.3.3 和 8.2	**竣工时间**
1.1.3.7 和 11.1	**缺陷通知期限**
1.1.5.6	各**单位工程**的定义，如果有
1.3	电子通讯系统
1.4	法律和语言
2.1	给予**现场**占用权的时间
4.2	**履约担保**

4.4	Notice of Subcontractors
8.7/12.4 & 14.15(b)	Delay/performance damages
13.8	Adjustments for changes in Cost
14.2	Advance payment(s)
14.3(c)	Retention
17.6	Limitation of liability
18.1	Employer's insurance (if any). Evidence of insurances
18.2(d)	Insurance of Employer's risks
18.3	Insurance against injury to persons and damage to property
20.2	Number of members of the dispute adjudication board
20.3	Appointing entity for the dispute adjudication board

Notes on the Preparation of Tender Documents

The tender documents should be prepared by suitably-qualified engineers who are familiar with the technical aspects of the required works, and a review by suitably-qualified lawyers may be advisable. The tender documents issued to tenderers will consist of the Conditions of Contract and the Employer's Requirements, and (possibly) the preferred form for the Letter of Tender. In addition, each of the Tenderers should receive the data referred to in Sub-Clause 4.10, and the Instructions to Tenderers to advise them of any matters which the Employer wishes them to include in their Tender but which do not form part of the Employer's Requirements for the Works.

When the Contract Agreement is signed by the Employer and the Contractor, the Contract (which then comes into full force and effect) includes the Tender and any memoranda annexed to the Contract Agreement.

The Employer's Requirements should specify the particular requirements for the completed Works on a functional basis, including detailed requirements on quality and scope, and may require the Contractor to supply items such as consumables. The matters referred to in some or all of the following Sub-Clauses might be included:

1.8	Number of copies of Contractor's Documents
1.13	Permissions obtained by the Employer
2.1	Phased possession of foundations, structures, plant or means of access
4.1	Intended purposes for which the Works are required
4.6	Other contractors (and others) on the Site
4.7	Setting-out points, lines and levels of reference
4.18	Environmental constraints
4.19	Electricity, water, gas and other services available on the Site
4.20	Employer's Equipment and free-issue material
5.1	Requirements, data and information for which the Employer is responsible
5.2	Contractor's Documents required for review
5.4	Technical standards and building regulations
5.5	Operational training for the Employer's Personnel
5.6	As-built drawings and other records of the Works
5.7	Operation and maintenance manuals
6.6	Facilities for Personnel
7.2	Samples
7.3	Off-Site inspection requirements
7.4	Testing during manufacture and/or construction
9.1	Tests on Completion
9.4	Damages for failure to pass Tests on Completion
12.1	Tests after Completion
12.4	Damages for failure to pass Tests after Completion

4.4	关于**分包商**的通知
8.7/12.4 和 14.15 (b)	延误/履约损害赔偿费
13.8	因**成本**改变的调整
14.2	预付款
14.3 (c)	保留金
17.6	责任限度
18.1	雇主的保险(如果有)，保险的证据
18.2 (d)	雇主的风险的保险
18.3	人员伤害和财产损害险
20.2	争端裁决委员会成员人数
20.3	任命争端裁决委员会的指名实体

编写招标文件注意事项

招标文件应由具有适当资质、熟悉要建工程技术情况的工程师编写，并请有适当资质的律师进行审核可能是明智的。发给投标人的招标文件将包括**合同条件**和**雇主要求**，以及(可能)选用的**投标函**格式。此外，每位投标人都应收到在**第 4.10 款**中提到的资料，以及**投标人须知**，以告诉他们**雇主**希望他们在**投标书**中包括，但不列为关于工程的**雇主要求**一部分的任何事项。

当**雇主**和**承包商**签署**合同协议书**后，**合同**(这时全面实施和生效)包括**投标书**和**合同协议书**所附任何备忘录。

雇主要求中应规定竣工**工程**在功能方面的特定要求，包括质量和范围的详细要求，还可以包括要求**承包商**供应的物品如消耗品等。可能包括下列部分或全部**条款**中提出的事项：

1.8	**承包商文件**的份数
1.13	**雇主**取得的许可
2.1	基础、结构、生产设备分阶段的占用权或进入的方法
4.1	要求达到的**工程**预期目的
4.6	在**现场**的其他承包商(和其他人员)
4.7	放线的基准点、线和标高
4.18	环境约束
4.19	**现场**可供的电、水、燃气和其他服务
4.20	**雇主设备**和免费供应的材料
5.1	**雇主**应负责的要求内容、数据和资料
5.2	要求送审的**承包商文件**
5.4	技术标准和建筑法规
5.5	对**雇主人员**的操作培训
5.6	竣工图和**工程**的其他记录
5.7	操作和维修手册
6.6	为**人员**提供设施
7.2	样品
7.3	**场外**检验要求
7.4	制造和(或)施工期间的试验
9.1	**竣工试验**
9.4	未通过**竣工试验**的损害赔偿费
12.1	**竣工后试验**
12.4	未通过**竣工后试验**的损害赔偿费

Many Sub-Clauses in the General Conditions make reference to the Particular Conditions for such data as would typically be specified by the Employer, or to the Tender for such data as would typically be specified by the tenderer.

The Instructions to Tenderers may need to specify any constraints on the data proposed in the Tender, and/or specify the extent of other information which each Tenderer is to include with his Tender. If each Tenderer is to produce a parent company guarantee and/or a tender security, these requirements (which apply prior to the Contract becoming effective) should be included in the Instructions to Tenderers: example forms are annexed to this document as Annexes A and B. The Instructions may include matters referred to in some or all of the following Sub-Clauses:

4.3 Contractor's Representative (name and curriculum vitae)
4.9 Quality Assurance system
9.1 Tests on Completion
12.1 Tests after Completion
18 Insurances
20 Resolution of disputes

Turnkey contracts typically include design, construction, fixtures, fittings and equipment (f.f.e.), the scope of which should be defined in the Employer's Requirements. Full consideration should be given to detailed requirements, such as the extent to which the Works are to be fully equipped, ready for operation, with spare parts and consumables provided for operation for a specified period. In addition, the Contractor may be required to operate the Works, either for a few months' trial operation period under Sub-Clause 9.1(c), or for some years' operation.

Understandably, tenderers are often reluctant, in the face of intense competition, to incur great expense in the preparation of tender designs. When preparing the Instructions to Tenderers, thought should be given as to the extent of detail which tenderers can realistically be expected to prepare and include in their Tenders. The extent of detail required should be described in the Instructions to Tenderers. Note that there can be no description in the documents which will constitute the Contract, which only comes into full force and effect when the Agreement is signed.

Consideration may be given to offering some remuneration to tenderers if, in order to provide a responsive Tender, they have to undertake studies or carry out design work of a conceptual nature.

通用条件中的许多**条款**提到**专用条件**中由**雇主**特别做出规定的一些数据，或谈到**投标书**中由投标人特别提出的一些数据。

在**投标人须知**中可能需要对**投标书**中的建议数据规定任何约束，和(或)对每位**投标人**在其**投标书**中包括的其他资料规定范围。如果要每位**投标人**取得母公司保函和(或)投标保函，这些要求(将在**合同**生效前应用)应包括在**投标人须知**内。本文件**附件 A 和 B** 给出了范例格式。**须知**中可包括下列部分或全部**条款**中提出的事项：

4.3　**承包商代表**(姓名和简历)
4.9　**质量保证**体系
9.1　**竣工试验**
12.1　**竣工后试验**
18　保险
20　争端的解决

交钥匙合同一般包括设计、施工、固定件(fixtures)、配件(fittings)和设备(equipment)(f.f.e)，其范围应在**雇主要求**中明确规定。应充分考虑具体的要求，如达到**工程**全部配齐、做好运行准备、为某规定期间的运行提供备用部件和消耗品的范围。此外，可要求**承包商**按**第 9.1 款**(c)项的要求，对**工程**进行几个月的试运行，或负责几年的运行。

可以理解，面对激烈竞争，**投标人**往往不愿为编制投标设计方案投入大量开支。在编写**投标人须知**时，应考虑对**投标人**在**投标书**中编写和包含的详细程度可以预期的现实要求。要求的详细程度应在**投标人须知**中说明。要注意，在组成**合同**的文件中可能对此没有描述，而只在签署**合同协议书**后就进入全面实施和生效。

如果投标人为了提出回应**投标书**，必须进行研究或概念性设计工作，可以考虑给他们适当报酬。

GENERAL CONDITIONS
GUIDANCE
FORMS

Clause 1 General Provisions

Sub-Clause 1.1 Definitions

The Particular Conditions should specify the Time for Completion for the Works, and the Defects Notification Period.

If the Works are to be taken-over in stages, which is unusual under a turnkey contract, the Particular Conditions should specify each stage as a Section, and should define its scope, geographical extent and Time for Completion.

It may be necessary to amend some of the definitions. For example:

1.1.3.1 the Base Date could be defined as a particular calendar date
1.1.4.4 one particular Foreign Currency may be required by the financing institution
1.1.4.5 a different currency may be required to be the contract Local Currency
1.1.6.2 the references to "Country" may be inappropriate for a cross-border Site

Sub-Clause 1.2 Interpretation

If the references to "profit" are to be more precisely specified, this Sub-Clause may be varied:

EXAMPLE At the end of Sub-Clause 1.2, insert:

In these Conditions, provisions including the expression "Cost plus reasonable profit" require this profit to be one-twentieth (5%) of this Cost.

Sub-Clause 1.3 Communications

The Particular Conditions should specify the systems of electronic communications (if any), and may also specify the address for the Contractor's notices to the Employer.

Sub-Clause 1.4 Laws and Language

The Particular Conditions should specify:

(a) the law which will govern the Contract,

(b) (if any part of the Contract has been written in one language and then translated) the ruling language, and

(c) (if communications are not to be written in the same language as that in which the Contract is written) the language for communications.

Sub-Clause 1.5 Priority of Documents

An order of precedence is usually necessary, in case a conflict is subsequently found among the contract documents. If no order of precedence is to be prescribed, this Sub-Clause may be varied:

EXAMPLE Delete Sub-Clause 1.5 and substitute:

The documents forming the Contract are to be taken as mutually explanatory of one another. If an ambiguity or discrepancy is found, the priority shall be such as may be accorded by the governing law.

第 1 条　　一般规定

第 1.1 款　　定义

专用条件中应规定**工程**的**竣工时间**和**缺陷通知期限**。

如果**工程**要分阶段接收，这在交钥匙合同是不多见的，**专用条件**应明确每个作为**分项工程**的阶段，并规定它们的范围、地理区域和**竣工时间**。

可能需要对一些定义进行修改，例如：

1.1.3.1　**基准日期**可规定为某一特定日历日期
1.1.4.4　融资机构可能要求某种特定**外币**
1.1.4.5　合同**当地货币**可能要求另一种货币
1.1.6.2　对于跨边界的**现场**，“**工程所在国**”的提法可能不适宜

第 1.2 款　　解释

如果“利润”的提法要更明确地规定，本**款**可改为：

范例　　在**第 1.2 款**末尾插入：

在本**条件**中，包括“费用加合理利润”词语的规定，要求该利润为该费用的二十分之一(5%)。

第 1.3 款　　通信交流

专用条件应规定电子通信系统(如果有)，还可规定**承包商**发给**雇主**的通知的地址。

第 1.4 款　　法律和语言

专用条件应规定：

(a)　管辖**合同**的法律；

(b)　(如果**合同**任何部分用一种语言书写，又给出译文时)主导语言；

(c)　(如果通讯与**合同**不是用同一语言书写时)通信用语言。

第 1.5 款　　文件优先次序

由于随后合同文件间可能发现矛盾，优先次序通常是需要的。如果不准备规定优先次序，本**款**可改为：

范例　　删除**第 1.5 款**，代之以：

组成**合同**的各项文件将被认为是互作说明的。如出现歧义或矛盾时，应按管辖的法律确定先后次序。

GENERAL CONDITIONS

GUIDANCE

FORMS

Sub-Clause 1.6 Contract Agreement

The Contract Agreement is the document which brings the Contract into effect, and is usually preceded by negotiation. The Contract Agreement should therefore be drawn up with care. The form of Agreement should be included in the tender documents as an annex to the Particular Conditions: an example form is included at the end of this publication.

The Contract Agreement must state the name of each Party, the Contract Price, the currencies of payment, the amount due in each currency, and any pre-conditions which are to be satisfied before the Contract comes into full force and effect: all as agreed by the Parties. If lengthy tender negotiations were necessary, it may be considered advisable for the Contract Agreement to record the Base Date and/or Commencement Date also.

If the Employer wished to anticipate the possibility of issuing a letter of acceptance, the Sub-Clause may be amended by deleting the first sentence, which states that the Contract comes into full force and effect when the Parties sign the Contract Agreement. The Letter of Tender should then include the following paragraph:

> "Unless and until a formal Agreement is prepared and executed this Letter of Tender, together with your written acceptance thereof, shall constitute a binding contract between us."

Sub-Clause 1.10 Employer's Use of Contractor's Document

Additional provisions may be required, if all rights to particular items of computer software (for example) are to be assigned to the Employer. The provisions should take account of the applicable Laws.

Sub-Clause 1.13 Compliance with Laws

If the Employer is to arrange import permits and the like, alternative provisions may be appropriate:

EXAMPLE SUB-CLAUSE FOR A PLANT CONTRACT

Insert at the end of Sub-Clause 1.13:

However, the Contractor shall submit, in good time, the details of Goods to the Employer, who shall then promptly obtain all import permits or licences required for these Goods

The Employer shall also obtain or grant all consents including permits-to-work, wayleaves and approvals required for the Works.

Sub-Clause 1.14 Joint and Several Liability

For a major contract, detailed requirements for the joint venture may need to be specified. For example, it may be desirable for each member to produce a parent company guarantee: an example form is annexed to this document as Annex A.

These requirements, which apply prior to the Contract becoming effective, should be included in the Instructions to Tenderers. The Employer will wish the leader of the joint venture to be appointed at an early stage, providing a single point of contact thereafter, and will not wish to be involved in a dispute between the members of a joint venture. The Employer should scrutinise the joint venture agreement carefully, and it may have to be approved by the project's financing institutions.

第 1.6 款　　　　　　**合同协议书**

合同协议书是使**合同**生效的文件，一般要先进行谈判。因此**合同协议书**应小心拟定。**协议书**格式应作为**专用条件**的附件包括在招标文件中：本文本末尾包括有范例格式。

合同协议书须说明每**方**的名称、**合同价格**、付款货币、每种货币的应付款额，以及在**合同**全面实施和生效前要满足的任何前提条件：均按**双方**协商一致的意见。如果需要进行长时间的招标谈判，**合同协议书**最好也写明**基准日期**和(或)**开工日期**。

如果**雇主**希望有预先发一封认可函的机会，可以将**本款**第一句说明**合同**自**双方**签署**合同协议书**起全面实施和生效的内容删除。这时**投标函**应包括以下段落：

“除非并直到正式**协议书**已拟订并生效，本**投标函**连用你方对此的书面认可，将构成你我双方间的有约束力的合同”。

第 1.10 款　　　　　　**雇主使用承包商文件**

如果某些特定内容(例如)计算机软件的全部权利要转让给**雇主**，可能需要增加一些规定。拟定这类规定应考虑适用的**法律**。

第 1.13 款　　　　　　**遵守法律**

如果**雇主**要安排取得进口和类似许可，一些替代规定可能是适宜的：

对生产设备合同的范例条款

在**第 1.13 款**末尾插入：

但**承包商**应在适宜的时间向**雇主**提交**货物**的详细资料，**雇主**应迅速取得这些**货物**所需的所有进口许可或特许；

雇主还应取得或给予**工程**所需要的包括工作许可、道路通行权和认可等所有同意。

第 1.14 款　　　　　　**共同的和各自的责任**

对于大型合同，可能需要对联营体规定一些具体要求。如可能希望每个成员提交一份母公司保函：本文件附范例格式，见**附件 A** 。

这些在**合同**生效前适用的要求，应包括在**投标人须知**中。**雇主**希望早期指定联营体的负责方，以便此后有一个单独的联系方，并避免卷入联营体成员间的争端。**雇主**应仔细审查联营体的协议书，此类协议书可能需经项目的融资机构批准。

Clause 2 The Employer

Sub-Clause 2.1 Right of Access to the Site

The Particular Conditions should specify the time(s) by which the Employer will give the Contractor right of access to the Site, if after the Commencement Date. It may be essential for the Contractor to have early access to the Site for the purposes of survey and sub-surface investigations. If the Employer is arranging for work to be carried out on the Site before right of access is granted, details should be given in the Employer's Requirements.

Sub-Clause 2.3 Employer's Personnel

These provisions should be reflected in the Employer's contracts with any other contractors on the Site.

Clause 3 The Employer's Administration

Sub-Clause 3.1 The Employer's Representative

Although the Employer is not required to appoint a representative, such an appointment may assist the Employer's administration. If the Employer wishes to appoint an independent consulting engineer as the Employer's Representative, he may be named in the Particular Conditions.

Clause 4 The Contractor

Sub-Clause 4.2 Performance Security

The Particular Conditions should specify the amount and currencies of the Performance Security, unless it is not required.

EXAMPLE

The amount of the Performance Security shall be ten percent (10%) of the Contract Price stated in the Contract Agreement, and shall be expressed in the currencies and proportions in which the Contract Price is payable.

The acceptable form(s) of Performance Security should be included in the tender documents, annexed to the Particular Conditions. Example forms are annexed to this document as Annex C and Annex D. They incorporate two sets of Uniform Rules published by the International Chamber of Commerce (the "ICC", which is based at 38 Cours Albert 1er, 75008 Paris, France), which also publishes guides to these Uniform Rules. These example forms and the wording of the Sub-Clause may have to be amended to comply with applicable law.

EXAMPLE

At the end of the second paragraph of Sub-Clause 4.2, insert:

If the Performance Security is in the form of a bank guarantee, it shall be issued either (a) by a bank located in the Country, or (b) directly by a foreign bank acceptable to the Employer. If the Performance Security is not in the form of a bank guarantee, it shall be furnished by a financial entity registered, or licensed to do business, in the Country.

Sub-Clause 4.3 Contractor's Representative

If the Representative is known at the time of submission of the Tender, the Tenderer may propose

第 2 条　　雇主

第 2.1 款　　现场进入权

专用条件中应规定**雇主**给予**承包商**在**开工日期**后**现场**进入权的时间。及早进入**现场**以便进行测量和地下勘探，对**承包商**可能很重要。如果**雇主**要在批准**现场**进入权以前，安排在**现场**开展工作，在**雇主要求**中应给出详细说明。

第 2.3 款　　雇主人员

这些规定应反映在**雇主**与**现场**任何其他承包商间的合同中。

第 3 条　　雇主的管理

第 3.1 款　　雇主代表

虽然没有要求**雇主**一定要指派一名代表，但此类任命可以协助**雇主**的管理。如果**雇主**希望任命一名独立的咨询工程师作**雇主代表**，可以在**专用条件**中提出。

第 4 条　　承包商

第 4.2 款　　履约担保

除非不要求**履约担保**，**专用条件**中应规定**履约担保**的金额和币种。

范例

履约担保的金额应为**合同协议书**中写明的**合同价格**的百分之十(10%)；并应按**合同价格**应付的货币和比例表示。

认可的**履约担保**格式应包括在招标文件中，附在**专用条件**后面。范例格式见本文件**附件 C** 和**附件 D**。它们体现**国际商会**(“ICC”，总部位于法国巴黎，38 Cours Albert 1er,75008 Paris,France)出版的两套**统一规则**，**国际商会**还出版了这些**统一规则**的指南。这些范例格式和条款措词可能需要修改，以符合适用法律。

范例

在**第 4.2 款**第 2 段末尾插入：

如果**履约担保**采用银行担保函的形式，它应(a)由**工程所在国**内的银行，或(b)直接由**雇主**认可的外国银行出具。如果**履约担保**不采用银行担保函形式，应由在**工程所在国**注册或取得营业执照的金融实体提。

第 4.3 款　　承包商代表

如果在递交**投标书**时已确定**代表**人选，**投标人**可提出**代表**人选的建议。**投标人**可能希望提

GENERAL CONDITIONS

GUIDANCE

FORMS

the Representative. The Tenderer may wish to propose alternatives, especially if the contract award seems likely to be delayed. If the ruling language is not the same as the language for day to day communications (under Sub-Clause 1.4), or if for any other reason it is necessary to stipulate that the Contractor's Representative shall be fluent in a particular language, one of the following sentences may be added.

EXAMPLE

At the end of Sub-Clause 4.3, add:

The Contractor's Representative and all these persons shall also be fluent in .... (*insert name of language*)

EXAMPLE

At the end of Sub-Clause 4.3, add:

If the Contractor's Representative, or these persons, is not fluent in .... (*insert name of language*), the Contractor shall make a competent interpreter available during all working hours.

Sub-Clause 4.4 Subcontractor

If the Employer wishes to receive the notices under this Sub-Clause, his requirements should be specified in the Particular Conditions:

EXAMPLE

The Contractor shall give the notices described in sub-paragraphs (a), (b) and (c) of Sub-Clauses 4.4 in respect of the following Subcontractors:

(list the relevant activities and/or parts of the Works)

Sub-Clause 4.12 Unforeseeable Difficulties

If the Works include tunnelling or other substantial sub-surface construction, it is usually preferable for the risk of unforeseen ground conditions to be allocated to the Employer. Responsible contractors will be reluctant to take the risks of unknown ground conditions which are difficult or impossible to estimate in advance. The Conditions of Contract for Plant and Design-Build should be used in these circumstances for works designed by (or on behalf of) the Contract or.

Sub-Clause 4.19 Electricity, Water and Gas

If services are to be available for the Contractor to use, the Employer's Requirements should give details, including locations and prices.

Sub-Clause 4.20 Employer's Equipment and Free-Issue Material

For this Sub-Clause to apply, the Employer's Requirements should describe each item which the Employer will provide and/or operate and should specify all necessary details. With some types of facilities, further provisions may be necessary, in order to clarify aspects such as liability and insurance.

Sub-Clause 4.22 Security of the Site

If the Contractor is sharing occupation of the Site with others, Sub-Clauses 4.8 and/or 4.22 may require amendment, and the Employer's obligations should be specified.

出更换人选，特别是看来可能要推迟授与合同时。如果主导语言不是日常交流语言(根据**第 1.4 款**)，或由于其他任何原因，需要规定**承包商代表**能流利使用某种语言时，可增加下列句子之一：

范例 在**第 4.3 款**末尾增加：

承包商代表及所有此类人员还应能流利地使用＿＿＿＿＿(填入语言名称)

范例 在**第 4.3 款**末尾增加：

如果**承包商代表**或此类人员不能流利地使用＿＿＿＿＿(填入语言名称)，**承包商**应派一名胜任的译员在所有工作时间随时在场。

第 4.4 款 **分包商**

如果**雇主**希望得到根据本**款**提出的通知，其要求可在**专用条件**中做出规定：

范例

承包商应就下列**分包商**给出按**第 4.4 款**(a)、(b)和(c)项所述内容的通知：

(列举相关的活动和(或)某部分**工程**)

第 4.12 款 **不可预见的困难**

如果**工程**包括隧道开挖或其他大量地下施工时，通常较好作法是将场地条件的不可预见的风险分给**雇主**承担。在难以或不能预先估计的情况下，负有责任的承包商是不愿承担未知场地条件的风险的。在此类情况下，对于由(或代表)**承包商**设计的工程，应使用**生产设备和设计-施工合同条件**。

第 4.19 款 **电、水和燃气**

如果这些服务可供**承包商**使用，应在**雇主要求**中给出细节，包括供应地点和价格。

第 4.20 款 **雇主设备和免费供应的材料**

如要适用本**款**，在**雇主要求**中应描述**雇主**将提供和(或)操作的每项内容，并应规定所有必要的细节。对有些类型的设施，可能需要做出进一步规定，以明确责任和保险等方面的事项。

第 4.22 款 **现场保安**

如果**承包商**与其他人员共同占用**现场**，**第 4.8** 和(或)**第 4.22 款**可能需要修改，应对**雇主**的义务做出规定。

Clause 5 Design

Sub-Clause 5.1 General Design Obligations

If the Employer's Requirements include an outline design, in order (for example) to establish the feasibility of the project, tenderers should be advised of the extent to which the outline design is a suggestion or a requirement. If this Sub-Clause is considered inappropriate, the provisions in FIDIC's Conditions of Contract for Plant and Design-Build may be preferred.

Sub-Clause 5.2 Contractor's Documents

The "Contractor's Documents" are defined as the documents which the Contractor must submit to the Employer, as specified elsewhere in the Contract, which typically may not include all the technical documents which the Contractor's Personnel will need in order to execute the Works. For example, it may be appropriate for the Employer's Requirements for a plant contract to specify that the Contractor's Documents shall include drawings showing how the Plant is to be affixed and any other information required for:

(a) preparing suitable foundations or other means of support,

(b) providing suitable access on the Site, for the Plant and any necessary equipment, to the place where the Plant is to be erected, and/or

(c) making necessary connections to the Plant.

Different "review periods" may be specified, taking account of the time necessary to review the different types of drawing, and/or of the possibility of substantial submissions at particular stages of the design process.

Clause 6 Staff and Labour

Sub-Clause 6.6 Facilities for Staff and Labour

If the Employer will make some accommodation available, his obligations to do so should be specified.

Sub-Clause 6.8 Contractor's Superintendence

If the ruling language is not the same as the language for day to day communications (under Sub-Clause 1.4), or if for any other reason it is necessary to stipulate that the Contractor's superintending staff shall be fluent in a particular language, the following sentence may be added.

EXAMPLE

Insert at the end of Sub-Clause 6.8:

A reasonable proportion of the Contractor's superintending staff shall have a working knowledge of

(*insert name of language*)

or the Contractor shall have a sufficient number of competent interpreters available on Site during all working hours.

Additional Sub-Clauses

It may be necessary to add a few sub-clauses to take account of the circumstances and locality of the Site:

第 5 条　　设计

第 5.1 款　　设计义务一般要求

如果为了(比如)确定项目的可行性，**雇主要求**中有一项设计纲要，应告知投标人该设计纲要的作用，是作为一项建议还是作为一项要求。如果认为本**款**规定不适合，采用**菲迪克(FIDIC)生产设备和设计－施工合同条件**可能较好。

第 5.2 款　　承包商文件

“**承包商文件**”是指**承包商**按**合同**其他处规定需要提交给**雇主**的文件，它一般可不包括**承包商人员**为了实施**工程**所需要的全部技术性文件。例如，对于一项生产设备合同，**雇主要求**中规定**承包商文件**应包括表示**生产设备**如何固定的图纸，以及为以下事项所需的任何其他资料，可能是适当的：

(a)　准备适当的基础或其他支撑方法；

(b)　为**生产设备**和任何需要的装备运至**生产设备**安装地点提供合适的**现场**进入方法；

(c)　做好**生产设备**的必要的连结。

考虑到审核各种不同类型图纸所需的时间，和(或)在设计过程某些特定阶段会提交大量的图纸的可能，可以规定不同的“审核期限”。

第 6 条　　员工

第 6.6 款　　为员工提供设施

如果**雇主**将提供某些膳宿设施，其此类义务应予以规定。

第 6.8 款　　承包商的监督

如果主导语言不同于日常交流语言(根据**第 1.4 款**规定)，或由于任何其他原因，有必要规定**承包商**的监督职员应能流利使用某种语言，可增加下列句子：

范例　　在**第 6.8 款**末尾插入：

承包商监督职员中应有合理比例的人员能使用 ________ (填入语言名称)作工作语言；

或**承包商**应有足够数量的能胜任的译员在所有工作时间随时在**现场**。

附加条款

可能需要增加一些条款，以考虑现场的环境与位置的需要。

GENERAL CONDITIONS | GUIDANCE | FORMS

EXAMPLE SUB-CLAUSE

Foreign Staff and Labour

The Contractor may import any personnel who are necessary for the execution of the Works. The Contractor must ensure that these personnel are provided with the required residence visas and work permits. The Contractor shall be responsible for the return to the place where they were recruited or to their domicile of imported Contractor's Personnel. In the event of the death in the Country of any of these personnel or members of their families, the Contractor shall similarly be responsible for making the appropriate arrangements for their return or burial.

EXAMPLE SUB-CLAUSE

Alcoholic Liquor or Drugs

The Contractor shall not, otherwise than in accordance with the Laws of the Country, import, sell, give, barter or otherwise dispose of any alcoholic liquor or drugs, or permit or allow importation, sale, gift, barter or disposal by Contractor's Personnel.

EXAMPLE SUB-CLAUSE

Arms and Ammunition

The Contractor shall not give, barter or otherwise dispose of to any person, any arms or ammunition of any kind, or allow Contractor's Personnel to do so.

EXAMPLE SUB-CLAUSE

Festivals and Religious Customs

The Contractor shall respect the Country's recognised festivals, days of rest and religious or other customs.

Clause 7 Plant, Materials and Workmanship

Additional Sub-Clause

If the Contract is being financed by an institution whose rules or policies require a restriction on the use of its funds, a further sub-clause may be added:

EXAMPLE SUB-CLAUSE

All Goods shall have their origin in eligible source countries as defined in

(insert name of published guidelines for procurement).

Goods shall be transported by carriers from these eligible source countries, unless exempted by the Employer in writing on the basis of potential excessive costs or delays. Surety, insurance and banking services shall be provided by insurers and bankers from the eligible source countries.

范例条款

外国员工

承包商可以引进实施**工程**所需要的任何人员。**承包商**必须确保此类人员所需的居住签证和工作许可。**承包商**应负责引进的**承包商人员**返回他们招聘地点或户籍所在地。在任何此类人员或他们的家属在**工程所在国**死亡的情况下，**承包商**同样应负责对他们的送回或安葬作出适当的安排。

范例条款

酒精饮料或毒品

承包商除遵照**工程所在国**法律外，不得进口、销售、给予、易货交换或以其他方式处理任何酒精饮料或毒品；或许可或容许**承包商人员**进口、销售、馈赠、易货交换或处理上述物品。

范例条款

武器和弹药

承包商不得向任何人给予、易货交换或以其他方式处理任何种类的任何武器或弹药；或容许**承包商人员**这样做。

范例条款

节日和宗教习惯

承包商应尊重**工程所在国**公认的节日、休息日、以及宗教或其他习惯。

第7条　生产设备、材料和工艺

附加条款

如果**合同**由某一机构提供资金，其规则或政策要求对资金的使用加以限制，可增加进一步条款：

范例条款

所有**货物**应产自..........（填写公布的采购指南的名称）中规定的合格来源国。

除非是**雇主**基于可能造成过高费用或延误的考虑，书面通知的免例，**货物**应由这些合格来源国的承运人运输。担保、保险和银行服务应由合格来源国的保险人和银行提供。

GENERAL CONDITIONS

GUIDANCE

FORMS

Clause 8 Commencement, Delays and Suspension

Sub-Clause 8.7 Delay Damages

Under many legal systems, the amount of these pre-defined damages must represent a reasonable pre-estimate of the Employer's probable loss in the event of delay. The Particular Conditions should specify the daily sum, for the Works and for each Section, expressed either as an amount or as a percentage: see also Sub-Clause 14.15(b).

EXAMPLE

In Sub-Clause 8.7, the sum referred to in the second sentence shall be 0.02% of the Contract Price as delay damages in respect of the Works, payable (per day) in the proportions of currencies in which the Contract Price is payable. For each Section, such daily sum shall be 0.02% of the final contract value of such Section, payable (per day) in such currencies. The maximum amount of delay damages shall be ten percent (10%) of the Contract Price stated in the Contract Agreement.

Additional Sub-Clause

Incentives for early completion may be included in the tender documents (although Sub-Clause 13.2 refers to accelerated completion):

EXAMPLE SUB-CLAUSE

Sections are required to be completed by the dates given in the Employer's Requirements in order that these Sections may be occupied and used by the Employer in advance of the completion of the whole of the Works. Details of the work required to be executed to entitle the Contractor to bonus payments and the amount of the bonuses are stated in the Employer's Requirements.

For the purposes of calculating bonus payments, these dates for completion of Sections are fixed. No adjustments of the dates by reason of granting an extension of the Time for Completion will be allowed.

Clause 9 Tests on Completion

Sub-Clause 9.1 Contractor's Obligations

The Employer's Requirements should describe the tests which the Contractor is to carry out before being entitled to a Taking-Over Certificate. It may also be appropriate for the Tender to include detailed arrangements, instrumentation, etc. If the Works are to be tested and taken-over in stages, the tests requirements may have to take account of the effect of some parts of the Works being incomplete.

The wording in the sub-paragraphs includes the conditions which are typically applicable for a plant contract, but otherwise may require amendment. In particular, sub-paragraph (c) refers to trial operation, during which any product produced by the Works becomes the property of the Employer. He thus becomes responsible for disposing of it, and entitled to retain the proceeds from selling it. If the product is to be retained by the Contractor, the Sub-Clause should be amended accordingly.

Sub-Clause 9.4 Failure to Pass Tests on Completion

If the reduction referred to in the final paragraph, based on the extent of the failure, is to be defined in the Particular Conditions or in the Employer's Requirements, minimum acceptable performance criteria should also be specified.

第 8 条 开工、延误和暂停

第 8.7 款 误期损害赔偿费

根据许多法律体系，此类预先规定的损害赔偿费款额，必须是在延误情况下**雇主**可能遭受损失的合理预估额。**专用条件**中应对**工程**和每个**单位工程**规定每日赔偿额，或用金额表示，或用一个百分率表示：还应参见**第 14.15 款**(b)项。

范例

在**第 8.7 款**第 2 句话提出的作为对**工程**的误期损害赔偿费的每日应付金额应为**合同价格**的 0.02%，按照**合同价格**中各种货币的比例支付。对各**单位工程**，每日应付金额为该**分项工程**最终合同价值的 0.02%，按上述货币比例支付。误期损害赔偿费的最高限额应为**合同协议书**规定的**合同价格**的百分之十(10%)。

附加条款

在招标文件中可包括对提前竣工的鼓励(虽然**第 13.2 款**提到加快竣工)：

范例条款

为了在整个**工程**竣工前雇主能提前占有和使用某些**单位工程**，**雇主要求**中给出了这些**单位工程**要求完工的日期。承包商有权获得奖金所需要完成的工作细节及奖金数额都在**雇主要求**中说明。

为了计算奖金数额，这些**单位工程**的完工日期固定不变。不允许以**竣工时间**获准延长为理由，对这些日期进行调整。

第 9 条 竣工试验

第 9.1 款 承包商的义务

雇主要求中应说明**承包商**在有权得到**接收证书**前要进行的试验。要求**投标书**中包括详细安排、测试仪器等也许是适宜的。如果**工程**要分阶段试验和接收，试验的要求可能需要考虑**工程**的某些部分尚未完成的影响。

本款各项中的措词包括了一般适用于生产设备合同的条件，在另外情况下可能需要修改。特别是，(c)项谈到试运行期间**工程**生产出的任何产品均属于**雇主**的财产，因而由他负责处理，并有权得到产品销售后的收益。如果产品归**承包商**所得，本**款**应做相应修改。

第 9.4 款 未能通过竣工试验

如果在**专用条件**或**雇主要求**中，要规定本**款**最后一项中提出的要根据未通过试验的影响程度确定减少额，则对可接受的最低性能标准也应做出规定。

GENERAL CONDITIONS

GUIDANCE

FORMS

Clause 10 Employer's Taking Over

Sub-Clause 10.1 Taking-Over Certificate

If the Works are to be taken-over in stages, which is unusual under a turnkey contract, these stages should to be defined as Sections, in Clause 1 of the Particular Conditions. Precise geographical definitions are advisable.

Clause 11 Defects Liability

Sub-Clause 11.10 Unfulfilled Obligations

It may be necessary to review this Sub-Clause in relation to the period of liability under the applicable law.

Clause 12 Tests after Completion

Sub-Clause 12.1 Procedure for Tests after Completion

In an EPC turnkey project, the Contractor is typically required to prove the reliability and performance of the Plant during the Tests on Completion, and the Works are only taken over after successful completion of these tests. Exceptionally, it may be considered necessary for Tests after Completion to be carried out, after the Employer has taken over and operated the Works, so that the guaranteed performance can be demonstrated under normal operating conditions: for example, after operational fouling of the plant.

The Employer's Requirements should describe the tests he requires, after taking-over, to verify that the Works fulfil the Performance Guarantees promised in the Tender. For some types of Works, these Tests may be the most difficult to specify well, although they are critical to a successful outcome. It may be appropriate for the Tender to include detailed arrangements, and/or to define any instrumentation required, in addition to that included in the Plant.

The provisions in the General Conditions are based upon the Tests after Completion being carried out by the Contractor, with the assistance of the Employer as regards personnel, consumables, etc. These details may need to be specified in the Employer's Requirements. If other arrangements are envisaged, they should be specified in the Employer's Requirements, and the Sub-Clause should be amended accordingly. For example, the provisions in FIDIC's Conditions of Contract for Plant and Design-Build are based upon these Tests being carried out by the Employer and his operating personnel, with guidance from the Contractor's staff.

Sub-Clause 12.4 Failure to Pass Tests after Completion

If the first part of this Sub-Clause is to apply, the method of calculating the non-performance damages (based on the extent of the failure) should be defined in the Particular Conditions or in the Employer's Requirements, and the minimum acceptable performance criteria should also be specified.

Clause 13 Variations and Adjustments

Variations can be initiated by any of three ways:

(a) the Employer may instruct the variation under Sub-Clause 13.1, without prior agreement as to feasibility or price;

第 10 条　　雇主的接收

第 10.1 款　　接收证书

如果**工程**要分阶段接收，这在交钥匙工程是不多见的，这些阶段应确定为**单位工程**，在**专用条件**第 1 条中，最好规定它们的精确的地理定界。

第 11 条　　缺陷责任

第 11.10 款　　未履行的义务

可能需要根据合同适用法律关于责任期限的要求，审核本**款**的规定。

第 12 条　　竣工后试验

第 12.1 款　　竣工后试验的程序

在 EPC（设计采购施工）交钥匙工程中，一般要求**承包商**通过**竣工试验**来证明**生产设备**的可靠性和性能。**工程**只在这些试验顺利完成后进行接收。有时例外地，在**工程**接收和开始运行后，**雇主**可能认为需要进行一些**竣工后试验**，以便证明在通常运行条件下：例如发生设备违规操作后，能够达到保证的性能。

雇主要求中应当说明，为证实**工程**是否达到**投标书**中承诺的**履约保证**的要求，要在接收后进行的各项试验。对于有些类型的**工程**，尽管这些**试验**对于最终结果的成功至关重要，但可能很难做出完善的规定。要求**投标书**中包括一些详细的安排，和(或)在**生产设备**包括的以外规定任何需的测试仪器，可能是适宜的。

通用条件中的规定是根据**竣工后试验**由**承包商**进行，**雇主**在人员、消耗物资等方面给予协助的条件拟定的。这些具体要求可能需要在**雇主要求**中做出规定。如果设想其他的安排，应在**雇主要求**中规定，并相应对本**款**进行修改。例如，**菲迪克**(FIDIC)的《**生产设备和设计－施工合同条件**》，是根据这些试验由**雇主**和其操作人员，在**承包商**职员的指导下进行的条件拟定的。

第 12.4 款　　未能通过竣工后试验

如果本**款**第一部分适用，在**专用条件**或**雇主要求**中，应规定未履约损害赔偿费(根据未通过试验的影响程度)的计算方法，还应规定可接受的最低性能标准。

第 13 条　　变更和调整

变更可通过以下三种中任一种方式提出：

(a)　**雇主**可根据**第 13.1 款**的规定指示进行变更，对变更的可行性和价格无需事先协议；

(b) the Contractor may initiate his own proposals under Sub-Clause 13.2, which are intended to benefit both Parties; or

(c) the Employer may request a proposal under Sub-Clause 13.3, seeking prior agreement so as to minimise dispute.

Sub-Clause 13.5 Provisional Sums

Although generally inappropriate for this type of contract, a Provisional Sum may be required for parts of the Works which are not required to be priced at the risk of the Contractor. For example, a Provisional Sum may be necessary to cover goods which the Employer wants to select. It is essential to define the scope of each Provisional Sum, since the defined scope will then be excluded from the other elements of the Contract Price. If a Provisional Sum is to be valued under Sub-Clause 13.5(b), the percentage should be quoted in the Tender.

Sub-Clause 13.8 Adjustments for Changes in Cost

Provisions for adjustments may be required if it would be unreasonable for the Contractor to bear the risk of escalating costs due to inflation. Wording for provisions based on cost indices have been published in FIDIC's Conditions of Contract for Plant and Design-Build, which may be considered appropriate. Particular care should be taken in the calculation of weightings/coefficients ("a", "b", "c", ..., the total of which must not exceed unity) and in the selection and verification of cost indices. Expert advice may be appropriate.

Clause 14 Contract Price and Payment

Sub-Clause 14.1 The Contract Price

When writing the Particular Conditions, consideration should be given to the amount and timing of payment(s) to the Contractor. A positive cash flow is clearly of benefit to the Contractor, and tenderers will take account of the interim payment procedures when preparing their tenders.

Normally, this type of contract is based on a lump sum price. The Contractor thus takes the risk of changes in cost arising from his design. The lump sum price may consist of two or more amounts, quoted in the currencies of payment (which may, but need not, include the Local Currency).

In order to value Variations, Tenders may be required to be accompanied by detailed price breakdowns, including quantities, unit rates and other pricing information. This information can also be useful for the assessment of interim payments. However, the information may not have been priced competitively. When the tender documents are being prepared, the Employer must therefore decide whether he will accept being bound by the tenderer's breakdowns. If not, he should have ensured that his representative has the necessary expertise to value any Variations which may be required.

Additional Sub-Clauses may be required to cover any exceptions to the options set out in Sub-Clause 14.1, and any other matters relating to payment.

If Sub-Clause 14.1(b) is not to apply, additional Sub-Clause(s) should be added.

EXAMPLE SUB-CLAUSE ON EXEMPTION FROM DUTIES

All Goods imported by the Contractor into the Country shall be exempt from customs and other import duties, if the Employer's prior written approval is obtained for import. The Employer shall endorse the necessary exemption documents prepared by the Contractor for presentation in order to clear the Goods through Customs, and shall also provide the following exemption documents:

(b) **承包商**可根据**第 13.2 款**的规定，提出他自己认为有利于**双方**的建议；

(c) 为尽量减少争端，寻求事先协议，**雇主**可根据**第 13.3 款**的规定，要求提出一份建议书。

第 13.5 款　　暂列金额

虽然对于此类合同一般是不适用的，但对于一些不要求**承包商**承担价格风险的**工程**部分，**暂列金额**可能是需要的。例如，对于一些**雇主**希望选择的货物，可能就需要**暂列金额**。重要的是对每笔**暂列金额**要规定它的使用范围，因为规定的**暂列金额**范围将从**合同价格**的其他成份中单独列出。有的**暂列金额**要根据**第 13.5 款**(b)项规定进行计算，其计算百分率应在**投标书**中提出报价。

第 13.8 款　　因成本改变的调整

如果考虑要**承包商**承担因通货膨胀的成本上升的风险是不合理的，可能需要这些调整的规定。**菲迪克(FIDIC)**在**《生产设备和设计 - 施工合同条件》**中提出的按成本指数规定的措词，可认为是适宜的。但在权重/系数("a"、"b"、"c"……,其总和不应超过 1)的计算中，及对成本指数的选择和核实中应特别予以注意。吸取专家的建议可能是适宜的。

第 14 条　　合同价格和付款

第 14.1 款　　合同价格

在编写**专用条件**时，应考虑向**承包商**支付的款额和时间安排。一个正的现金流量是明显有利于**承包商**的，投标人在编制其投标书时，将会考虑到期中付款的程序。

通常此类合同是按一个总额价格支付的。**承包商**需承担由于他的设计引起的成本改变的风险。总额价格可以包括，用支付货币(可以,但不一定必须包括**当地货币**)表示的两笔或多笔款额的报价。

为了对**变更**进行估价，可要求**投标书**随附详细的价格细目表，包括工程量、单价和其他估价资料。此类资料也可用于期中付款的估价。但此类资料可能不是竞争性的报价。因此**雇主**在编制招标文件时，应决定是否接受投标人的报价细目的约束。如不是，他应确保其代表具有对可能要求的任何**变更**进行估价的必要专业知识。

为了包含**第 14.1 款**提出的可选内容以外的任何其他内容，以及有关付款的其他任何事项，可能需要一些附加**条款**。

如果**第 14.1 款**(b)项不适用，应增加一(或几)款附加条款。

免除关税范例条款

如果事先取得**雇主**对进口的书面批准，**承包商**进口到**工程所在国**的所有**货物**都应免关税和其他进口税。**雇主**应签署支持**承包商**编制的为**货物**结关出示的必要的免税文件，还应提供下列免税文件：

(describe the necessary documents, which the Contractor will be unable to prepare)

If exemption is not then granted, the customs duties payable and paid shall be reimbursed by the Employer.

All imported Goods, which are not incorporated in or expended in connection with the Works, shall be exported on completion of the Contract. If not exported, the Goods will be assessed for duties as applicable to the Goods involved in accordance with the Laws of the Country.

However, exemption may not available for:

(a) Goods which are similar to those locally produced, unless they are not available in sufficient quantities or are of a different standard to that which is necessary for the Works; and

(b) any element of duty or tax inherent in the price of goods or services procured in the Country, which shall be deemed to be included in the Contract Price.

Port dues, quay dues and, except as set out above, any element of tax or duty inherent in the price of goods or services shall be deemed to be included in the Contract Price.

EXAMPLE SUB-CLAUSE ON EXEMPTION FROM TAXES

Expatriate (foreign) personnel shall not be liable for income tax levied in the Country on earnings paid in any foreign currency, or for income tax levied on subsistence, rentals and similar services directly furnished by the Contractor to Contractor's Personnel, or for allowances in lieu. If any Contractor's Personnel have part of their earnings paid in the Country in a foreign currency, they may export (after the conclusion of their term of service on the Works) any balance remaining of their earnings paid in foreign currencies.

The Employer shall seek exemption for the purposes of this Sub-Clause. If it is not granted, the relevant taxes paid shall be reimbursed by the Employer.

Sub-Clause 14.2 Advance Payment

When writing the Particular Conditions, consideration should be given to the benefits of advance payment(s). Unless this Sub-Clause is not to apply, the matters described in sub-paragraphs (a) to (d) of this Sub-Clause should be specified in the Particular Conditions, and the acceptable form(s) of guarantee should be included in the tender documents, annexed to the Particular Conditions: an example form is annexed to this document, as Annex E.

If the Contractor is to provide major items of Plant, consideration should be given to the benefits of stage payments during manufacture. The Employer may consider it advisable to have some form of security, since these payments would not relate to anything in his possession. If the Contractor is to be entitled to stage payments prior to shipment, the tender documents may include:

(a) provisions in the Particular Conditions linking the timing of advance payment instalments (under this Sub-Clause) to the stages of manufacture; or

(描述**承包商**不能编制的必需的文件)

如果未能获准免税，应付和已付的关税应由**雇主**补偿。

所有未用在**工程**上或消耗在有关**工程**方面的进口**货物**，在**合同**完成时应予出口。如不出口，该**货物**应按**工程所在国**的**法律**就涉及**货物**的适用税种估价纳税。

但对下列情况，免税规定可能不适用：

(a) 与当地产品相类似的**货物**，除非因数量不足或标准不同不能满足**工程**需要；

(b) 在**工程所在国**采购的货物或服务的价格中，原本含有的任何关税或其他税收因素，应被视为已包括在**合同价格**中。

港口税、码头税 及上述情况以外的任何原本含在货物或服务价格中的关税或其他税收因素，应被视为已包括在**合同价格**中。

免除税收范例条款

外侨(外籍)人员不应负担**工程所在国**对其任何外币收入征收的所得税，或对由**承包商**直接向其人员提供的生活费、租金和类似服务费、或替代上述费用的津贴征收的所得税。如果任何**承包商人员**在**工程所在国**的部分收入是用外币支付的，他们(在**工程**的服务期结束后)可以将以外币支付的收入的剩余部分汇出或带出境。

雇主应为实现本**款**目标争取免税。如未能获准，支付的相关税费应由**雇主**补偿。

第 14.2 款 **预付款**

在编写**专用条件**时，应考虑预付款的利益。除非本**款**不适用，本**款**(a)至(d)项所述事项都应在**专用条件**中规定。可接受的担保函的格式应包括在招标文件中，附在**专用条件**后：本文件附有范例格式，见**附件E**。

如果**承包商**要提供多项主要**生产设备**，应考虑在制造期间分阶段付款的利益。由于这些付款没有连带使**雇主**得到任何所有权，**雇主**可能认为取得某种形式的担保较好。如果**承包商**将有权在设备装运前得到分阶段付款，招标文件可包括：

(a) 在**专用条件**中关于(根据本**款**规定)预付款分期支付的时间安排与制造阶段的衔接的规定；

(b) in the Schedule of Payments or other document to be used to determine the contract value under Sub-Clause 14.3(a), a price for each of these stages (the Schedule should refer to the Contractor providing the security specified in Sub-Clause 14.5).

Sub-Clause 14.3 Application for Interim Payments

The Particular Conditions should specify the percentage of retention for sub-paragraph (c), and may also specify a limit of Retention Money.

Sub-Clause 14.4 Schedule of Payments

The General Conditions contains provisions for interim payments to the Contractor, which may be based on a Schedule of Payments. If another basis is to be used for determining interim valuations, details should be added in the Particular Conditions. If payments are to be specified in a Schedule of Payments, it could be in one of the following forms:

(a) an amount (or percentage of the estimated final Contract Price) could be entered for each three-month (or other) period during the Time for Completion, which can prove unreasonable if the Contractor's progress differs significantly from the expectation on which the Schedule was based; or

(b) the Schedule could be based on actual progress achieved in executing the Works, which necessitates careful definition of the payment milestones. Disagreements may arise when the work required for a payment milestone is nearly achieved but the balance cannot be completed until some months later.

Sub-Clause 14.7 Timing of Payments

If a different period for payment is to apply, the Sub-Clause may be amended:

EXAMPLE In sub-paragraph (b) of Sub-Clause 14.7, delete "56" and substitute "42".

If the country/countries of payment need to be specified, details may be included in the Tender.

Sub-Clause 14.8 Delayed Payment

If the discount rate of the central bank in the country of the currency of payment is not a reasonable basis for assessing the Contractor's financing costs, a new rate may have to be defined. Alternatively, the actual financing Costs could be paid, taking account of local financing arrangements.

Sub-Clause 14.9 Payment of Retention Money

If part of the Retention Money is to be released and substituted by an appropriate guarantee, an additional Sub-Clause may be added. The acceptable form(s) of guarantee should be included in the tender documents, annexed to the Particular Conditions: an example form is annexed to this document, as Annex F.

EXAMPLE SUB-CLAUSE FOR RELEASE OF RETENTION

When the Retention Money has reached ...., the Employer shall make payment of ....% of the Retention Money to the Contractor if he obtains a guarantee, in a form and provided by an entity approved by the Employer, in amounts and currencies equal to the payment.

(b) 在**付款计划表**或根据**第 14.3 款**(a)项的规定确定合同价值要使用的其他文件中，列出每个阶段的价格(该计划表应参照**承包商**提供**第 14.5 款**规定的担保)。

第 14.3 款　　期中付款的申请

专用条件应规定本**款**(c)项中的提取**保留金**的百分率，还应规定**保留金**的限额。

第 14.4 款　　付款计划表

通用条件包含按**付款计划表**对**承包商**支付期中付款的规定。如果采用其他根据确定期中估价，**专用条件**中应增加详细内容。如果支付用**付款计划表**规定，可采用下列格式之一：

(a) 在**竣工时间**内的每 3 个月(或其他期间)填列一个金额(或估计最终**合同价格**的百分比)，如果**承包商**的进度与**付款计划表**依据的预期进度差别很大，可能发现该金额是 不合理的；

(b) **付款计划表**可以以**工程**实施中达到的实际进度为依据，这需要仔细划定付款里程碑。否则某一付款里程碑所要求的工作虽已接近完成，而剩余的工作直到几月后还不能完成时，可能会产生争执。

第 14.7 款　　付款的时间安排

如果施用不同的付款期间，本**款**可修改如下：

范例　　在**第 14.7 款**(b)项中，删去“56”代之以“42”。

如果需要规定付款的国家(或几个国家)，可在**投标书**中包括具体要求。

第 14.8 款　　延误的付款

如果支付货币国家的中央银行的贴现率不是评定**承包商**融资成本的合理依据，可能需要另定利率，或参照当地融资情况，按实际融资**成本**支付。

第 14.9 款　　保留金的支付

如果要放还部分**保留金**，代之以适当的保函，可增加附加条款。招标文件中应包括认可的担保函格式，附在**专用条件**后：本文件附有范例格式，见**附件F** 。

放还保留金范例条款

当**保留金**达到________时，**雇主**应付给承包商**保留金额**的________%，条件是**承包商**已得到由**雇主**批准的实体，以**雇主**认可的格式出具的金额及货币与下述付给相同的保函。

The Contractor shall ensure that the guarantee is valid and enforceable until the Contractor has executed and completed the Works and remedied any defects, as specified for the Performance Security in Sub-Clause 4.2, and shall be returned to the Contractor accordingly. This release of retention shall be in lieu of the release of the second half of the Retention Money under the second paragraph of Sub-Clause 14.9.

Sub-Clause 14.15 **Currencies of Payment**

If all payments are to be made in Local Currency, it must be named in the Contract Agreement, and only the first sentence of this Sub-Clause will apply. Alternatively, the Sub-Clause may then be replaced:

EXAMPLE SUB-CLAUSE FOR A SINGLE-CURRENCY CONTRACT

The currency of account shall be the Local Currency and all payments made in accordance with the Contract shall be in Local Currency. The Local Currency payments shall be fully convertible, except those for local costs. The percentage attributed to local costs shall be as stated in the Tender.

Financing Arrangements

For major contracts in some markets, there may be a need to secure finance from entities such as aid agencies, development banks, export credit agencies, or other international financing institutions. If financing is to be procured from any of these sources, the Particular Conditions may need to incorporate its special requirements. The exact wording will depend on the relevant institution, so reference will need to be made to them to ascertain their requirements, and to seek approval of the draft tender documents.

These requirements may include tendering procedures which need to be adopted in order to render the eventual contract eligible for financing, and/or special Sub-Clauses which may need to be incorporated into the Particular Conditions. The following examples indicate some of the topics which the institution's requirements may cover:

(a) prohibition from discrimination against the shipping companies of any one country;

(b) ensuring that the Contract is subject to a widely-accepted neutral law;

(c) provision for arbitration under recognised international rules and at a neutral location;

(d) giving the Contractor the right to suspend/terminate in the event of default under the financing arrangements;

(e) restricting the right to reject Plant;

(f) specifying the payments due in the event of termination;

(g) specifying that the Contract does not become effective until certain conditions precedent have been satisfied, including pre-disbursement conditions for the financing arrangements; and

(h) obliging the Employer to make payments from his own resources if, for any reason, the funds under the financing arrangements are insufficient to meet the payments due to the Contractor, whether due to a default under the financing arrangements or otherwise.

承包商应确保该保函如**第 4.2 款**对**履约担保**的规定，直到他完成**工程**的实施、竣工、及修补完任何缺陷时始终有效和可执行，届时保函应相应退还给**承包商**。**保留金**此项放还，应代替根据**第 14.9 款**第 2 段规定的放还**保留金**后一半的要求。

第 14.15 款 **支付的货币**

如果所有付款都用**当地货币**支付，应在**合同协议书**中说明本**款**仅第一句话还适用。代替地本**款**可代之以：

单一货币合同范例条款

结算货币应为**当地货币**，按照**合同**支付的所有款项都应为**当地货币**。除当地开支的费用外，所有**当地货币**的付款应全部可以兑换。当地开支的费用所占百分比应按**投标书**中的规定。

融资安排

对于某些市场上的重要**合同**，可能需要从一些实体，如援助机构、开发银行、出口信贷机构、或其他国际融资组织获取资金。如果从任何这类来源获取资金，**专用条件**可能需要编入这些机构的特定要求。准确的措词要依靠这些相关机构。因此，需征求他们的意见以确定其要求，使招标文件草案得到其批准。

这些要求可能包括，为使最终**合同**具有融资资格要采用的招标程序，和(或)需要编入**专用条件**的某些特定**条款**。下列范例指出了贷款机构的要求可能涉及的一些问题：

(a) 禁止歧视任一国家的航运公司；

(b) 确保**合同**受广泛接受的中立法律管辖；

(c) 在中立地点，按公认的国际规则进行仲裁的规定；

(d) 根据融资安排发生违约时，给予**承包商**暂停或终止的权利；

(e) 对拒收**生产设备**权利的限制；

(f) 终止时应付款项的规定；

(g) 规定直到一些先决条件，包括融资安排中提前支付的条件得到满足后，**合同**才能生效；

(h) 规定如果由于任何原因，不论是根据融资安排发生违约还是其他原因，造成融资安排的资金不能满足应付**承包商**的款项时，**雇主**有义务以其自有资金支付**承包商**。

In addition, the financing institution or bank may wish the Contract to include references to the financing arrangements, especially if funding from more than one source is to be arranged to finance different elements of supply. It is not unusual for the Particular Conditions to include special provisions identifying different categories of Plant and specifying the documents to be presented to the relevant financing institution to obtain payment. If the financing institution's requirements are not met, it may be difficult (or even impossible) to secure suitable financing for the project, and/or the institution may decline to provide finance for part or all of the Contract.

However, where the financing is not tied to the export of goods and services from any particular country but is simply provided by commercial banks lending to the Employer, those banks may be concerned to ensure that the Contractor's rights are very restricted. These banks may wish the Contract to exclude any reference to the financing arrangements, and/or to restrict the Contractor's rights under Clause 16.

FORM OF SUB-CLAUSE WHICH A FINANCING INSTITUTION MAY REQUIRE

The Contract Price is made up as follows:

(breakdown into items and/or into supply/delivery/etc)

and shall be payable by the Employer to the Contractor as set out below.

(a) .... % of the Contract Price shall be payable by a direct payment from the Employer to the Contractor within 28 days of receipt by the Employer of the following documents:

- (i) commercial invoice addressed to the Employer specifying the amount of the payment now due,
- (ii) advance payment security guarantee issued by .... Bank in the form annexed,
- (iii) performance security guarantee issued by .... Bank in the form annexed, and
- (iv) an interim payment certificate confirming the payment due and specifying the amount.

(b) .... % of the contract price for the supply of Plant shall be payable as follows:

- (i) .... % of the estimated contract value of the Plant supplied, by direct payment from the Employer to the Contractor on shipment of each item, against the following documents:
  - (original) commercial invoice,
  - (original) shipping documents,
  - (original) certificate of origin,
  - (original) insurance certificate, and
  - (original) interim payment certificate confirming the payment due and specifying the amount.
- (ii) .... % of the estimated contract value of the Plant supplied, by disbursement from the Loan Agreement to the Contractor on shipment of each item, on presentation of a Qualifying Certificate in the form annexed and copies of the documents listed in sub-paragraph (b)(i) above.

(c) the balance of the Contract Price shall be payable as follows:

此外，融资机构或银行可能希望**合同**中包括融资安排的内容，尤其是对不同部分供货安排一个以上来源提供资金时。通常的情况是，在**专用条件**中包括一些特定的规定，分别不同种类的**生产设备**，规定要向相关融资机构提交申请付款的文件。如果融资机构的要求得不到满足，则可能很难(或甚至不可能)为项目获得适当的资金，和(或)该机构可能拒绝对整个或部分**合同**提供资金。

但如果融资不与从任何特定国家出口货物或服务相联系，只是由商业银行简单地贷款给**雇主**，那些银行关注的可能是要确保严格限制**承包商**的权利。这些银行可能希望**合同**不包括任何融资安排，和(或)希望**合同**限制**承包商**根据**第 16 条**的规定所拥有的权利。

融资机构可能要求的条款格式

合同价格由以下内容构成：

(将**合同价格**内容分解为细目，和(或)分解为供货/交付/等)

将按下列规定由**雇主**向**承包商**支付。

(a) 在**雇主**收到下列文件后 28 天内，应由**雇主**向**承包商**直接支付**合同价格**的 ______ %；

(ⅰ) 致**雇主**的列明现已到期的应付金额的商业发票；

(ⅱ) 由 ______ 银行按附件所列格式出具的预付款担保函；

(ⅲ) 由 ______ 银行按附件所列格式出具的履约担保函；

(ⅳ) 确认到期款项、列明金额的**期中付款证书**。

(b) 用于**生产设备**供货的合同价格的 ______ %应如下支付：

(ⅰ) 在每项设备装船后，**雇主**根据以下文件，向**承包商**直接支付已供**生产设备**估算合同价值的 ______ %；

(原始)商业发票，
(原始)装运单证，
(原始)原产地证书，
(原始)保险证书，
(原始)确认应付款项，列明金额的**期中付款证书**。

(ⅱ) 在每项设备装船后，**雇主**根据提交的按所附格式出具的**资格合格证书**、以及上述(b)项第(ⅰ)目所列文件的复制件，从**贷款协议**中向**承包商**支付已供**生产设备**估算合同价值的 ______ %。

(c) **合同价格**的余额应如下支付：

(i) ____% of the estimated contract value of the services rendered, by direct payment from the Employer to the Contractor on execution of the relevant service, against the following documents:
(original) commercial invoice, and
(original) interim payment certificate confirming the payment due and specifying the amount.

(ii) ____% of the estimated contract value of the services rendered, by disbursement from the Loan Agreement to the Contractor, on presentation of a Qualifying Certificate in the form annexed and copies of the documents listed in sub-paragraph (c)(i) above.

(d) The direct payments by the Employer specified in sub-paragraph (b) shall be made by an irrevocable letter of credit established by the Employer in favour of the Contractor and confirmed by a bank acceptable to the Contractor.

The above arrangements (involving financing institution(s), Employer and Contractor) may be initiated by the Employer; or by the Contractor, before submitting the Tender. Alternatively, the Contractor may be prepared to initiate financing arrangements and retain responsibility for them, although he would probably be unable or unwilling to provide finance from his own resources. His financing bank's requirements would then affect his attitude in contract negotiations. They might well require the Employer to make interim payments, although a large proportion of the Contract Price might be withheld until the Works are complete.

This payment arrangement can be achieved either by a high Percentage of Retention; or by a suitably completed Schedule of Payments, with the Instructions to Tenderers specifying the criteria with which the Tenderer should comply. Since the Contractor would then have to arrange his own financing to cover the shortfall between the payments and his outgoings, he (and his financing bank) would probably require some form of security, guaranteeing payment when due.

It may be appropriate for the Employer, when preparing the tender documents, to anticipate the latter requirement by undertaking to provide a guarantee for the element of payment which the Contractor is to receive when the Works are complete. The acceptable form(s) of guarantee should be included in the tender documents, annexed to the Particular Conditions: an example form is annexed to this document, as Annex G. The following Sub-Clause may be added.

EXAMPLE PROVISIONS FOR CONTRACTOR FINANCE

The Employer shall obtain (at his cost) a payment guarantee in the amount and currencies, and provided by an entity, as stated in ________. The Employer shall deliver the guarantee to the Contractor within 28 days after both Parties have signed the Contract Agreement. The guarantee shall be in the form annexed to these Particular Conditions, or in another form acceptable to the Contractor. Unless and until the Contractor receives the guarantee, the Employer shall not give the notice under Sub-Clause 8.1.

The guarantee shall be returned to the Employer at the earliest of the following dates:

a) when the Contractor has been paid the Contract Price stated in the Contract Agreement;

(ⅰ) 对实施的相关服务，**雇主**根据下列文件，向**承包商**直接支付已提供服务的估算合同价值的＿＿＿%；
(原始)商业发票，
(原始)确认应付款项，列明金额的**期中付款证书**。

(ⅱ) **雇主**根据提交的按所附格式出具的**资格合格证书**，以及上述(c)项第(ⅰ)目所列文件的复制件，从**贷款协议**中向**承包商**支付已提供服务的估算合同价值的＿＿＿%。

(d) 本款(b)项规定的**雇主**直接付款方式应为，由**雇主**开具的经**承包商**认可的银行保兑的、以**承包商**为受益人的不可撤销信用证。

上述安排(涉及融资机构、**雇主**和**承包商**)可以由**雇主**，或由**承包商**在递交**投标书**前提出。另外的作法是，虽然**承包商**可能没能力也不愿自己提供资金，但他可能愿意主动着手融资安排并对之保持责任。因而他的融资银行的要求，会影响他在**合同**谈判中的态度。他们可能尽力要求**雇主**支付期中付款，尽管大部分**合同价格**可能直到**工程**竣工后才能支付。

可以通过采用高**保留金百分比**，或通过适当制定**付款计划表**，并在**投标人须知**中规定**投标人**应遵守的标准等方式，完成此项付款安排。由于**承包商**随后必须自筹资金以弥补其所得付款与其开支间的差额，他(及其融资银行)可能要求某种形式的担保，以保证到期能得到付款。

对于**雇主**来说可能适宜的作法是，在编制**投标人须知**时，就预计到上述后一项要求，承诺为**承包商**在**工程竣工**时应得到的付款提供保函。可接受的保函格式应包括在招标文件中，附在**专用条件**后：本文件附有范例格式，见附件G。这里可增加以下**条款**：

承包商融资范例条款

雇主应(自费)取得一份按＿＿＿＿＿＿＿＿规定的金额和币种，由某实体出具的支付保函。**雇主**应在**双方**签署**合同协议书**后28天内，将该保函提交给**承包商**。保函应采用本**专用条件**所附格式，或**承包商**认可的其他格式。除非并直到**承包商**收到此保函时，**雇主**不应根据**第8.1款**规定发出通知。

保函应在下列日期中的最早日期退回**雇主**：

(a) 已向**承包商**支付**合同协议书**中规定的**合同价格**时；

(b) when obligations under the guarantee expire or have been discharged; or

(c) when the Employer has performed all obligations under the Contract.

Clause 15 Termination by Employer

Sub-Clause 15.2 Termination by Employer

Before inviting tenders, the Employer should verify that the wording of this Sub-Clause, and each anticipated ground for termination, is consistent with the law governing the Contract.

Sub-Clause 15.5 Employer's Entitlement to Termination

Unless inconsistent with the requirements of the Employer and/or financing institutions, a further sentence may be added.

EXAMPLE

Insert at the end of Sub-Clause 15.5:

The Employer shall also pay to the Contractor the amount of any other loss or damage resulting from this termination.

Clause 16 Suspension and Termination by Contractor

Sub-Clause 16.2 Termination by Contractor

Before inviting tenders, the Employer should verify that the wording of this Sub-Clause is consistent with the law governing the Contract. The Contractor should verify that each anticipated ground for termination is consistent with such law.

Clause 17 Risk and Responsibility

Sub-Clause 17.6 Limitation of Liability

EXAMPLE

In Sub-Clause 17.6, the sum referred to in the penultimate sentence shall be ....

Additional Sub-Clause Use of Employer's Accommodation/Facilities

If the Contractor is to occupy the Employer's facilities temporarily, an additional sub-clause may be added:

EXAMPLE SUB-CLAUSE

The Contractor shall take full responsibility for the care of the items detailed below, from the respective dates of use or occupation by the Contractor, up to the respective dates of hand-over or cessation of occupation (where hand-over or cessation of occupation may take place after the date stated in the Taking-Over Certificate for the Works):

(insert details)

(b) 根据保函的义务已期满或已解除时；

(c) **雇主**已根据**合同**履行了其全部义务时。

第 15 条 由雇主终止

第 15.2 款 由雇主终止

招标前，**雇主**应核实本**款**规定的措辞及每项预计终止的依据，符合管辖**合同**的法律。

第 15.5 款 雇主终止的权利

除非与**雇主**和(或)融资机构的要求不符，可增加一句。

范例

在**第 15.5 款**末尾插入：

雇主还应向**承包商**支付由于此项终止产生的任何其他损失或损害的金额。

第 16 条 由承包商暂停和终止

第 16.2 款 由承包商终止

招标前，**雇主**应核实本**款**规定的措辞符合管辖**合同**的法律。**承包商**应核实每项预计终止的依据符合此类法律。

第 17 条 风险与职责

第 17.6 款 责任限度

范例

第 17.6 款中倒数第二句提到的总额应为________。

附加条款 **使用雇主提供的住宿/设施**

如果**承包商**要临时占用**雇主**的设施，可增加附加条款：

范例条款

承包商应自使用或占用下列各项设施的各自日期起，至移交或停止占用(此处移交或停止占用可发生在**工程接收证书**注明的日期之后)的各自日期止，承担对各项设施的全部照管职责。

(填入设施细节)

If any loss or damage happens to any of the above items while the Contractor is responsible for their care, arising from any cause whatsoever other than those for which the Employer is liable, the Contractor shall, at his own cost, rectify the loss or damage to the satisfaction of the Employer.

Clause 18 Insurance

The wording in the General Conditions describes the insurances which are to be arranged by the "insuring Party", who is to be the Contractor unless otherwise stated in the Particular Conditions. Insurances so provided by the Contractor are to be consistent with the general terms agreed with the Employer. The Instructions to Tenderers may therefore require tenderers to provide details of the proposed terms. The Particular Conditions should specify the minimum amount of deductibles for sub-paragraph (d) of Sub-Clause 18.2 and the minimum amount of third party insurance for Sub-Clause 18.3.

If the Employer is to arrange any of the insurances under this Clause, the tender documents should include details as an annex to the Particular Conditions (so that tenderers can estimate what other insurances they wish to have for their own protection), including the conditions, limits, exceptions and deductibles; preferably in the form of a copy of each policy. The Employer may find it difficult to effect the insurances described in the third paragraph of Sub-Clause 18.2 (for Contractor's Equipment, which includes Sub-contractor's equipment), because the Employer may not know the amount or value of these items of equipment. The following sentence may be included in the Particular Conditions:

EXAMPLE

Delete the final paragraph of Sub-Clause 18.2 and substitute:

However, the insurances described in the first two paragraphs of Sub-Clause 18.2 shall be effected and maintained by the Employer as insuring Party, and not by the Contractor.

Clause 19 Force Majeure

Before inviting tenders, the Employer should verify that the wording of this Clause is compatible with the law governing the Contract.

Clause 20 Claims, Disputes and Arbitration

Sub-Clause 20.2 Appointment of the Dispute Adjudication Board

The Contract should include provisions which, whilst not discouraging the Parties from reaching agreement on disputes as the works proceed, allow them to refer contentious matters to an impartial dispute adjudication board ("DAB").

The adjudication procedure depends for its success on, amongst other things, the Parties' confidence in the agreed individual(s) who will serve on the DAB. Therefore, it is essential that candidates for this position are not imposed by either Party on the other Party; and that, if the individual is selected under Sub-Clause 20.3, the selection is made by a wholly impartial entity. FIDIC is prepared to perform this role, if this authority has been delegated in accordance with the example wording suggested below, for Sub-Clause 20.3.

Sub-Clause 20.2 envisages appointment of the DAB after a Party gives notice of its intention to

如果在**承包商**负责照管期间，由于**雇主**应负责的以外的任何原因，使上述设施发生任何损失或损害，**承包商**应自费修正此类损失或损害，达到**雇主**满意。

第 18 条　　保险

通用条件中的措辞描述要由“应投保**方**”办理的保险，该应投保**方**除非在**专用条件**中另有说明，将是**承包商**。**承包商**提供的这些保险都要符合与**雇主**达成一致的一般条件的规定。因此**投标人须知**可要求投标人提供建议条件的细节。**专用条件**应规定**第 18.2 款**(d)项中的免赔额的最低数额，以及**第 18.3 款**中第三方责任险的最低数额。

如果**雇主**要根据本**条**规定办理任何保险，招标文件应包括保险的细节，作为**专用条件**的附件(以使投标人能够判断为保护自己需要的其他保险)，此类细节包括保险条件、限额、除外责任和免赔额，最好采用每份保险单抄件的形式。**雇主**可能感到难以对**第 18.2 款**第 3 段所述保险(对**承包商设备**,包括分包商设备的保险)投保，因为**雇主**可能不知道这些各类设备的数量和价值。在**专用条件**中可以包括下列句子：

范例

删除**第 18.2 款**最后一段，代之以：

但**第 18.2 款**开头两段所述保险，应由**雇主**而不是**承包商**作为应投保**方**办理并保持。

第 19 条　　不可抗力

招标前，**雇主**应核实本**条**措辞与管辖**合同**的法律不相矛盾。

第 20 条　　索赔、争端和仲裁

第 20.2 款　　争端裁决委员会的任命

合同应包括，在不劝阻**双方**在工程进行过程中就争端达成协议的同时，允许他们将争端事项提交公正的争端裁决委员会(“DAB”)的规定。

裁决程序的成功，在许多因素中主要取决于**双方**对商定的将服务于 DAB 的人员的信任。因此重要的是，该职位的候选人不是由某**方**强加于另一**方**；如果是根据**第 20.3 款**的规定选择人员，要由一个完全公正的实体来选择。如果已按照下述对**第 20.3 款**建议的范例措辞委托授权，**菲迪克**(FIDIC)愿承担此任。

第 20.2 款设想在一**方**发出要将争端提交DAB 的意向通知后，任命该 DAB。但对某些类型的项

refer a dispute to a DAB. However, for certain types of project, particularly those involving extensive work on Site, where it would be appropriate for the DAB to visit the Site on a regular basis, it may be decided to retain the services of a permanent DAB. In this case, Sub-Clause 20.2 and 20.4 together with the Appendix and Annex to the General Conditions, and the Dispute Adjudication Agreement, should be amended to comply with the corresponding wording contained in FIDIC's Conditions of Contract for Construction.

Sub-Clause 20.2 provides for two alternative arrangements for the DAB:

(a) one person, who acts as the sole member of the DAB, having entered into a tripartite agreement with both Parties; or

(b) a DAB of three persons, each of whom has entered into a tripartite agreement with both Parties.

The form of this tripartite agreement could be one of the two alternatives shown at the end of this publication, as appropriate to the arrangement adopted. Both of these forms incorporate (by reference) the General Conditions of Dispute Adjudication Agreement, which are included as the Appendix to the General Conditions because they are also referred to in Sub-Clause 20.2. Under either of these alternative forms of Dispute Adjudication Agreement, each individual person is referred to as a Member.

Before the Contract is entered into, consideration should be given as to whether a one-person or three-person DAB is preferable for a particular project, taking account of its size, duration and the fields of expertise which will be involved.

The appointment of the DAB may be facilitated by including an agreed list of potential members in the Contract.

Sub-Clause 20.3 Failure to Agree Dispute Adjudication Board

EXAMPLE

The appointing entity or official shall be the President of FIDIC or a person appointed by its President.

Sub-Clause 20.5 Amicable Settlement

The provisions of this Sub-Clause are intended to encourage the parties to settle a dispute amicably, without the need for arbitration: for example, by direct negotiation, conciliation, mediation or other forms of alternative dispute resolution. Amicable settlement procedures often depend, for their success, on confidentiality and on both Parties' acceptance of the procedure. Therefore, neither Party should seek to impose the procedure on the other Party.

Sub-Clause 20.6 Arbitration

The Contract should include provisions for the resolution by international arbitration of any disputes which are not resolved amicably. In international construction contracts, international commercial arbitration has numerous advantages over litigation in national courts, and may be more acceptable to the Parties.

Careful consideration should be given to ensuring that the international arbitration rules chosen are compatible with the provisions of Clause 20 and with the other elements to be specified in the Contract. The Rules of Arbitration of the International Chamber of Commerce (the "ICC", which is based at 38 Cours Albert 1er, 75008 Paris, France) are frequently included in international contracts. In the absence of specific stipulations as to the number of arbitrators and the place of arbitration, the International Court of Arbitration of the ICC will decide on the number of arbitrators (typically three in any substantial construction dispute) and on the place of arbitration.

目，特别是涉及大量**现场**工作的工程，DAB定期访问**现场**可能较适宜，这时可决定聘请常设DAB的服务。在此情况下，**第20.2**和**20.4款**连同**通用条件**的附录和附件，以及争端裁决协议书，应依照**菲迪克(FIDIC)《施工合同条件》**的相应措词进行修改。

第20.2款对DAB提供了两种备选安排：

(a) 一人，作为DAB的唯一成员，已与**双方**签订三方协议书；

(b) 三人DAB，其中每人都已与**双方**签订三方协议书。

此项三方协议书的格式，根据选用的适宜安排方式，可从本文本最后附的两种备选格式中选择一种。这两种格式体现(参考)了**争端裁决协议书一般条件**，该一般条件因在**第20.2款**规定中谈到，作为附录附在**通用条件**后。在这两种**争端裁决协议书**的备选格式中，每位个人都称为**成员**。

在签订**合同**前，应根据每个具体项目的大小、历时长短和涉及的专业技术领域，考虑选用一人还是三人DAB。

在**合同**中包括一份协商一致的备选成员名单，可能便于DAB的任命。

第20.3款	**对争端裁决委员会未能取得一致**
范例	受托负责任命的实体或职员应为**菲迪克**(FIDIC)主席或其指定的人员。

第20.5款 **友好解决**

本**款**规定的目的是鼓励**双方**友好解决争端，避免对仲裁的需要。例如，通过直接谈判、和解、调解、或其他解决争端的替代作法。友好解决程序的成功，常常取决于程序的保密性和**双方**对程序的认可。因此任何一**方**都不应寻求将程序强加于另一**方**。

第20.6款 **仲裁**

合同中应包括，对未能友好解决的任何争端通过国际仲裁解决的规定。在国际施工**合同**中，国际商事仲裁比国内法庭诉讼具有很多优点，因而可能更易为**双方**接受。

应认真考虑，确保选用的**国际仲裁规则**与**第20条**的规定和合同中规定的其他内容相一致。**国际商会**("ICC",设在法国巴黎75008,38 CoursAlbert 1er)**仲裁规则**常被写入国际**合同**中。在对仲裁员人数、仲裁地点没有具体规定的情况下，**ICC国际仲裁庭**将决定仲裁员人数(在各种重大施工争端中一般为三人)和仲裁地点。

GENERAL CONDITIONS

GUIDANCE

FORMS

If the UNCITRAL (or other non-ICC) arbitration rules are preferred, it may be necessary to designate, in the Particular Conditions, an institution to appoint the arbitrators or to administer the arbitration, unless the institution is named (and their role specified) in the arbitration rules. It may also be necessary to ensure, before so designating an institution, that it is prepared to appoint or administer.

For major projects tendered internationally, it is desirable that the place of arbitration be situated in a country other than that of the Employer or Contractor. This country should have a modern and liberal arbitration law and should have ratified a bilateral or multilateral convention (such as the 1958 New York Convention on the Recognition and Enforcement of Foreign Arbitral Awards), or both, that would facilitate the enforcement of an arbitral award in the states of the Parties.

It may be considered desirable in some cases for other Parties to be joined into any arbitration between the Parties, thereby creating a multi-party arbitration. While this may be feasible, multi-party arbitration clauses require skilful drafting, and usually need to be prepared on a case-by-case basis. No satisfactory standard form of multi-party arbitration clause for international use has yet been developed.

如果倾向采用**联合国国际贸易法委员会**(UNCITRAL)(或**国际商会**以外的其他组织)的**仲裁规则**，在**专用条件**中可能需要指定一个提名仲裁员或执行仲裁的机构，除非在**仲裁规则**中已指明该机构(并规定了其任务)。在指定某一机构前，还需要确保该机构愿意承担提名和执行仲裁的任务。

对国际招标的大型项目，**仲裁地点**最好选在**雇主**或**承包商**所在国以外的国家。该国应有现代的、开放的仲裁法，并已批准了双边或多边公约(如1958年纽约承认及执行外国仲裁裁决公约)或两者都被批准。这样有利于仲裁裁决在**双方**所在国执行。

在某些情况下，可能认为请**其他方**加入**双方**间的任何仲裁，形成一个多方仲裁比较好。尽管这可能是可行的，但多边仲裁条款需要起草技巧，且需要根据逐个案情而定。目前还没有编制出令人满意的、国际通用的多边仲裁条款的标准格式。

Annexes FORMS OF SECURITY

Acceptable form(s) of security should be included in the tender documents: for Annex A and/or B, in the Instructions to Tenderers; and for Annexes C to G, annexed to the Particular Conditions. The following example forms, which (except for Annex A) incorporate Uniform Rules published by the International Chamber of Commerce (the "ICC", which is based at 38 Cours Albert 1er, 75008 Paris, France), may have to be amended to comply with the applicable law. Although the ICC publishes guides to these Uniform Rules, legal advice should be taken before the securities are written. Note that the guaranteed amounts should be quoted in all the currencies, as specified in the Contract, in which the guarantor pays the beneficiary.

附件　担保函格式

招标文件中应包括认可的担保函格式：**附件 A 和(或)B** 附于**投标人须知**；**附件 C 至 G** 附于**专用条件**。下列范例格式(**附件 A** 除外)体现**国际商会**("ICC"，总部设在法国巴黎75008，38 Cours Albert1er,）公布的**统一规则**，应用时可能需要修改，以符合适用的法律。虽然**国际商会**出版了对这些**统一规则**的指南，在起草担保函前还应听取法律咨询建议。还应注意，保证金额应按**合同**中规定的，担保人向受益人支付的，所有币种分别列出。

Annex A EXAMPLE FORM OF PARENT COMPANY GUARANTEE

[*See page 156, and the comments on Sub-Clause 1.14*]

Brief description of Contract ....

Name and address of Employer ....

.... (together with successors and assigns).

We have been informed that .... (hereinafter called the "Contractor") is submitting an offer for such Contract in response to your invitation, and that the conditions of your invitation require his offer to be supported by a parent company guarantee.

In consideration of you, the Employer, awarding the Contract to the Contractor, we (*name of parent company*) .... irrevocably and unconditionally guarantee to you, as a primary obligation, the due performance of all the Contractor's obligations and liabilities under the Contract, including the Contractor's compliance with all its terms and conditions according to their true intent and meaning.

If the Contractor fails to so perform his obligations and liabilities and comply with the Contract, we will indemnify the Employer against and from all damages, losses and expenses (including legal fees and expenses) which arise from any such failure for which the Contractor is liable to the Employer under the Contract.

This guarantee shall come into full force and effect when the Contract comes into full force and effect. If the Contract does not come into full force and effect within a year of the date of this guarantee, or if you demonstrate that you do not intend to enter into the Contract with the Contractor, this guarantee shall be void and ineffective. This guarantee shall continue in full force and effect until all the Contractor's obligations and liabilities under the Contract have been discharged, when this guarantee shall expire and shall be returned to us, and our liability hereunder shall be discharged absolutely.

This guarantee shall apply and be supplemental to the Contract as amended or varied by the Employer and the Contractor from time to time. We hereby authorise them to agree any such amendment or variation, the due performance of which and compliance with which by the Contractor are likewise guaranteed hereunder. Our obligations and liabilities under this guarantee shall not be discharged by any allowance of time or other indulgence whatsoever by the Employer to the Contractor, or by any variation or suspension of the works to be executed under the Contract, or by any amendments to the Contract or to the constitution of the Contractor or the Employer, or by any other matters, whether with or without our knowledge or consent.

This guarantee shall be governed by the law of the same country (or other jurisdiction) as that which governs the Contract and any dispute under this guarantee shall be finally settled under the Rules of Arbitration of the International Chamber of Commerce by one or more arbitrators appointed in accordance with such Rules. We confirm that the benefit of this guarantee may be assigned subject only to the provisions for assignment of the Contract.

Date .... Signature(s) ....

附件 A　母公司保函范例格式

[见第 157 页,及第 1.14 款解释]

合同简述……………………………………………………………………

雇主名称和地址……………………………………………………………

……………………………………………………………（连同继承人和受让人）

我方已获知，……………………（以下称“**承包商**”）正响应你方邀请对上述**合同**提交报价，你方邀请条件要求报价要有一份母公司保函支持。

考虑到你方，**雇主**，将向**承包商**授予**合同**，我方(母公司名称)……………………不可撤销和无条件地，作为一项首要义务向你方保证，**承包商**根据**合同**规定的所有应履行的义务和责任，包括**承包商**按照其真实意图和含义遵守所有**合同**条款和条件。

如果**承包商**未能如上履行其义务和责任，未能遵守合同，我方将保障**雇主**免受因承包商根据**合同**应对**雇主**负责的任何该类违约造成的所有损害赔偿费、损失和开支(包括法律费用和开支)。

本保函将在**合同**全面实施和生效时，全面实施和生效。如果在本保函日期一年内，**合同**没有全面实施和生效，或如果你方表明不想与**承包商**签订**合同**，本保函将作废和无效。本保函将持续全面实施和有效，直到**承包商**根据**合同**规定的义务和责任全部解除为止，届时本保函应期满，应退还我方，我方在其下的责任应完全解除。

当**雇主**和**承包商**有时对**合同**进行修改或变更时，本保函仍适用并作为**合同**的补充。我方在此授权他们商定任何此类修正或变更，对**承包商**应履行和应遵守的修正或变更在此同样予以保证。我方根据本保函应负的义务和责任，不应因**雇主**对**承包商**做出的任何时限允许或其他宽让，或根据**合同**要实施的工程的任何变更或暂停，或对**合同**、**承包商**或**雇主**的组成的任何修改，或任何其他事项而解除，不论这些事项是否经我方知晓或同意。

本保函应由管辖**合同**的同一国家(或其他司法管辖区)的法律管辖。关于本保函的任何争端，应根据**国际商会仲裁规则**，由按该**规则**任命的一位或几位仲裁员最终解决。我方确认，本保函的权益仅可按照**合同**转让的条款进行转让。

日期……………………　　签字……………………………………

Annex B EXAMPLE FORM OF TENDER SECURITY

[*See page 156*]

Brief description of Contract ....

Name and address of Beneficiary ....

.... (whom the tender documents define as the Employer)

We have been informed that .... (hereinafter called the "Principal") is submitting an offer for such Contract in response to your invitation, and that the conditions of your invitation (the "conditions of invitation", which are set out in a document entitled Instructions to Tenderers) require his offer to be supported by a tender security.

At the request of the Principal, we (*name of bank*) .... hereby irrevocably undertake to pay you, the Beneficiary/Employer, any sum or sums not exceeding in total the amount of .... (say: ....) upon receipt by us of your demand in writing and your written statement (in the demand) stating that:

(a) the Principal has, without your agreement, withdrawn his offer after the latest time specified for its submission and before the expiry of its period of validity, or

(b) the Principal has refused to accept the correction of errors in his offer in accordance with such conditions of invitation, or

(c) you entered into the Contract with the Principal and he has failed to deliver a performance security complying with sub-clause 4.2 of the conditions of the Contract.

Any demand for payment must contain your signature(s) which must be authenticated by your bankers or by a notary public. The authenticated demand and statement must be received by us at this office on or before (*the date 35 days after the expiry of the validity of the Letter of Tender*) ...., when this guarantee shall expire and shall be returned to us.

This guarantee is subject to the Uniform Rules for Demand Guarantees, published as number 458 by the International Chamber of Commerce, except as stated above.

Date .... Signature(s) ....

附件 B　投标保函范例格式

[见第 157 页]

合同简述 ……

受益人名称和地址 ……

…… (招标文件中称为**雇主**)

我方已获知，…… (以下称**委托人**)正响应你方邀请，对上述**合同**提交一份报价，你方邀请条件(在题为**投标人须知**的文件中规定的"邀请条件")要求投标人报价要有一份投标保函支持。

应委托人请求，我方(银行名称) …… 在此不可撤销地承诺，在我方收到你方的书面要求和关于(在要求中的)下列情况的书面说明后，向你方，**受益人/雇主**，支付总额不超过 …… (即 ……)的任何一笔或几笔款额：

(a) **委托人**未经你方同意，在规定的提交报价的最终时间后和其有效期限期满前，已撤回其报价；

(b) **委托人**已拒绝接受对其按照上述邀请条件所做报价中的错误的改正；

(c) 你方与**委托人**签订了**合同**，但**委托人**未能遵照**合同**条件第 4.2 款提交**履约担保函**。

任何支付的要求，都必须有经你方银行或公证人确证的你方签字。经确证的要求和说明必须在(投标函有效期期满后 35 天的日期) …… 或其以前，由我方在本办公地点收到，届时本保函应期满，应退还我方。

本保函除上述要求外，应遵守**国际商会**以 458 号文公布的**即付保证统一规则**的规定。

日期 ……　　　　签字 ……

Annex C EXAMPLE FORM OF PERFORMANCE SECURITY - DEMAND GUARANTEE

[*See comments on Sub-Clause 4.2*]

Brief description of Contract ....

Name and address of Beneficiary ....

.... (whom the Contract defines as the Employer)

We have been informed that .... (hereinafter called the "Principal") is your contractor under such Contract, which requires him to obtain a performance security.

At the request of the Principal, we (*name of bank*) .... hereby irrevocably undertake to pay you, the Beneficiary/Employer, any sum or sums not exceeding in total the amount of .... (the "guaranteed amount", say: ....) upon receipt by us of your demand in writing and your written statement stating:

(a) that the Principal is in breach of his obligation(s) under the Contract, and

(a) the respect in which the Principal is in breach.

[Following the receipt by us of an authenticated copy of the taking-over certificate for the whole of the works under clause 10 of the conditions of the Contract, such guaranteed amount shall be reduced by .... % and we shall promptly notify you that we have received such certificate and have reduced the guaranteed amount accordingly.] [(1)]

Any demand for payment must contain your [minister's/directors'] [(1)] signature(s) which must be authenticated by your bankers or by a notary public. The authenticated demand and statement must be received by us at this office on or before (*the date 70 days after the expected expiry of the Defects Notification Period for the Works*) .... (the "expiry date"), when this guarantee shall expire and shall be returned to us.

We have been informed that the Beneficiary may require the Principal to extend this guarantee if the performance certificate under the Contract has not been issued by the date 28 days prior to such expiry date. We undertake to pay you such guaranteed amount upon receipt by us, within such period of 28 days, of your demand in writing and your written statement that the performance certificate has not been issued, for reasons attributable to the Principal, and that this guarantee has not been extended.

This guarantee shall be governed by the laws of .... and shall be subject to the Uniform Rules for Demand Guarantees, published as number 458 by the International Chamber of Commerce, except as stated above.

Date .... Signature(s) ....

(1) *When writing the tender documents, the writer should ascertain whether to include the optional text, shown in parentheses* [ ]

附件 C　履约担保函 – 即付保函范例格式

[见第 4.2 款解释]

合同简述……………………………………

受益人名称和地址……………………………………

……………………………………(合同中称为**雇主**)

我方已获知，……………………(以下称为**委托人**)是你方根据上述**合同**的**承包商**，**合同**要求其取得一份履约担保函。

应**委托人**请求，我方(银行名称)……………………在此不可撤销地承诺，在我方收到你方的书面要求和关于以下情况的书面说明后，向你方，**受益人/雇主**，支付全部总额不超过……(“保证金额”,即：……)的任何一笔或几笔款额：

(a)　**委托人**违反**合同**规定的义务；

(b)　**委托人**违反的方面。

[在我方收到经确证的根据**合同**条件第 10 条规定颁发的整个工程接收证书的抄件后,此项保证金额应减少……%,我方将立即通知你方,我方已收到该证书并已相应减少了保证金额。][1]

任何付款的要求都必须有经你方银行或公证人确证的你方[部长/局长](1)的签字。经确证的要求和说明必须在(预定**工程缺陷通知期限**期满后 70 天的日期)……………(“期满日期”)或其以前，由我方在本办公地点收到，届时本保函应期满，应退还我方。

我方已获知，如果到上述期满日期 28 天前，还没有颁发根据**合同**规定的履约证书，**受益人**可要求**委托人**延长此保函。我方承诺，将在该 28 天期限内，根据我方收到的你方书面要求,及未颁发履约证书是由于**委托人**应负责的原因造成的、以及本保函尚未延长的书面说明,向你方支付该项保证金额。

本保函除上述要求外，应受……………………法律管辖，并应遵守**国际商会**以 458 号文公布的**即付保函统一规则**的规定。

日期……………………　　　　签字……………………

(1) 起草人在起草招标文件时，应确定是否要包括方括号[　]中的备选文字。

Annex D EXAMPLE FORM OF PERFORMANCE SECURITY - SURETY BOND

[*See comments on Sub-Clause 4.2*]

Brief description of Contract ....

Name and address of Beneficiary ....

.... (together with successors and assigns, all as defined in the Contract as the Employer)

By this Bond, (*name and address of contractor*) .... (who is the contractor under such Contract) as Principal and (*name and address of guarantor*) .... as Guarantor are irrevocably held and firmly bound to the Beneficiary in the total amount of .... (the "Bond Amount", say: ....) for the due performance of all such Principal's obligations and liabilities under the Contract. [Such Bond Amount shall be reduced by .... % upon the issue of the taking-over certificate for the whole of the works under clause 10 of the conditions of the Contract.][1]

This Bond shall become effective on the Commencement Date defined in the Contract.

Upon Default by the Principal to perform any Contractual Obligation, or upon the occurrence of any of the events and circumstances listed in sub-clause 15.2 of the conditions of the Contract, the Guarantor shall satisfy and discharge the damages sustained by the Beneficiary due to such Default, event or circumstances,[2] However, the total liability of the Guarantor shall not exceed the Bond Amount.

The obligations and liabilities of the Guarantor shall not be discharged by any allowance of time or other indulgence whatsoever by the Beneficiary to the Principal, or by any variation or suspension of the works to be executed under the Contract, or by any amendments to the Contract or to the constitution of the Principal or the Beneficiary, or by any other matters, whether with or without the knowledge or consent of the Guarantor.

Any claim under this Bond must be received by the Guarantor on or before (*the date six months after the expected expiry of the Defects Notification Period for the Works*) .... (the "Expiry Date"), when this Bond shall expire and shall be returned to the Guarantor.

The benefit of this Bond may be assigned subject to the provisions for assignment of the Contract, and subject to the receipt by the Guarantor of evidence of full compliance with such provisions.

This Bond shall be governed by the law of the same country (or other jurisdiction) as that which governs the Contract. This Bond incorporates and shall be subject to the Uniform Rules for Contract Bonds, published as number 524 by the International Chamber of Commerce, and words used in this Bond shall bear the meanings set out in such Rules.

Wherefore this Bond has been issued by the Principal and the Guarantor on (*date*) ....

Signature(s) for and on behalf of the Principal ....

Signature(s) for and on behalf of the Guarantor ....

(1) *When writing the tender documents, the writer should ascertain whether to include the optional text, shown in parentheses* [ ]

(2) *Insert:* [and shall not be entitled to perform the Principal's obligations under the Contract.]
Or: [or at the option of the Guarantor (to be exercised in writing within 42 days of receiving the claim specifying such Default) perform the Principal's obligations under the Contract.]

附件 D　履约担保函 – 担保保证范例格式

［见第 4.2 款解释］

合同简述 ……………………………………

受益人名称和地址 ……………………………………

…………………………（连同其继承人和受让人，在合同中都称为**雇主**）

根据本**保证**，（承包商名称和地址）……………………（根据上述**合同**的承包商）作为**委托人**与（担保人名称和地址）……………… 作为**担保人**，对该**委托人**根据**合同**应履行的全部义务和责任，以总金额 ……………… （**"保证金额"**，即：……………… ），向**受益人**不可撤销地保持和坚定地担保。［上述**保证金额**在根据**合同**条件第 10 条颁发整个工程接收证书后，应减少 …… %］[1]

本**保证**自**合同**中规定的**开工日期**起生效。

在**委托人**履行任何**合同义务**中发生**违约**，或出现任何**合同**条件**第 15.2 款**所列举的事件或情况时，**担保人**应满足并偿清**受益人**因该项**违约**、事件或情况遭受的损害赔偿费，[2]但**担保人**的全部责任不应超过**保证金额**。

担保人的义务和责任不应因**受益人**对**委托人**做出的任何时限允许或其他宽让、或对根据**合同**要实施工程的任何变更或暂停、或对**合同**或**委托人**或**受益人**组成的任何修改、或任何其他事项而解除，不论是否经**担保人**知晓或同意。

根据本**保证书**提出的任何索赔必须由**担保人**在（预定**工程缺陷通知期限**期满后 6 个月的日期）…………（**"期满日期"**）或其以前收到，届时本**保证**应期满，应退回**担保人**。

本**保证**的权益可以依照**合同**转让的条款，以及**担保人**收到完全符合该项条款的证据，进行转让。

本**保证**应由管辖合同的同一国家（或其他司法管辖区）的法律管辖。本**保证**体现并应遵守**国际商会**以 524 号文公布的**合同保证统一规则**的规定，本**保证**使用的词语应具有该**规则**规定的含义。

本**保证**于 …… 年 …… 月 …… 日由**委托人**和**担保人**签署。

委托人代表签字：……………………………………

担保人代表签字：……………………………………

(1) 起草人起草招标文件时，应确定是否要包括方括号［］内的备选文字。

(2) 此处插入：［并不得履行**委托人**根据**合同**规定的义务。］
或：［或由**担保人**选择（要在收到提出该项违约索赔 42 天内以书面提出）履行**委托人**根据合同规定的义务。］

Annex E EXAMPLE FORM OF ADVANCE PAYMENT GUARANTEE

[*See comments on Sub-Clause 14.2*]

Brief description of Contract ....

Name and address of Beneficiary ....

.... (whom the Contract defines as the Employer).

We have been informed that .... (hereinafter called the "Principal") is your contractor under such Contract and wishes to receive an advance payment, for which the Contract requires him to obtain a guarantee.

At the request of the Principal, we (*name of bank*) .... hereby irrevocably undertake to pay you, the Beneficiary/Employer, any sum or sums not exceeding in total the amount of .... (the "guaranteed amount", say: ....) upon receipt by us of your demand in writing and your written statement stating:

(a) that the Principal has failed to repay the advance payment in accordance with the conditions of the Contract, and

(b) the amount which the Principal has failed to repay.

This guarantee shall become effective upon receipt [of the first instalment] of the advance payment by the Principal. Such guaranteed amount shall be reduced by the amounts of the advance payment repaid to you, as evidenced by your notices issued under sub-clause 14.6 of the conditions of the Contract. Following receipt (from the Principal) of a copy of each purported notice, we shall promptly notify you of the revised guaranteed amount accordingly.

Any demand for payment must contain your signature(s) which must be authenticated by your bankers or by a notary public. The authenticated demand and statement must be received by us at this office on or before (*the date 70 days after the expected expiry of the Time for Completion*) .... (the "expiry date"), when this guarantee shall expire and shall be returned to us.

We have been informed that the Beneficiary may require the Principal to extend this guarantee if the advance payment has not been repaid by the date 28 days prior to such expiry date. We undertake to pay you such guaranteed amount upon receipt by us, within such period of 28 days, of your demand in writing and your written statement that the advance payment has not been repaid and that this guarantee has not been extended.

This guarantee shall be governed by the laws of .... and shall be subject to the Uniform Rules for Demand Guarantees, published as number 458 by the International Chamber of Commerce, except as stated above.

Date .... Signature(s) ....

附件 E 预付款保函范例格式

［见第 14.2 款解释］

合同简述 ……………………

受益人名称和地址 ……………………

…………………… （合同中称为**雇主**）

我方已获知，…………………… （以下称为“**委托人**”）是你方根据上述**合同**的**承包商**，希望得到一笔预付款，为此，**合同**要求其取得一份保函。

应**委托人**请求，我方（*银行名称*）…………………… 在此不可撤销地承诺，在我方收到你方书面要求和关于以下情况的书面说明后，向你方，**受益人/雇主**，支付全部总额不超过 …………（“保证金额”，即：…………）的任何一笔或几笔款额：

(a) **委托人**未能按照**合同**条件付还预付款；

(b) **委托人**未能付还的款额。

本保函在**委托人**收到预付款［首次分付款］时开始生效。该保证金额应按你方根据**合同**条件第 14.6 款规定发出的通知中证明已向你方付还的款额，逐步减少。我方每次收到（自**委托人**处）据称是该通知的抄件后，将立即将相应修改的保证金额通知你方。

任何关于付款的要求都必须有经你方银行或公证人确证的你方签字。经确证的要求和说明必须在（*预定* ***竣工时间*** *期满后 70 天的日期*）（“期满日期”）…………………… 或其以前，由我方在本办公地点收到，届时本保函将期满，应退还我方。

我方已获知，如果到上述期满日期 28 天前，预付款还没有付还，**受益人**可以要求**委托人**延长本保函。我方承诺，根据我方在该 28 天期限内收到的你方的书面要求，以及关于预付款还没有付还、本保函还没有延期的书面说明，向你方支付该保证金额。

本保函除上述要求外，应受 ………… 的法律管辖，并应遵守**国际商会**以 458 号公布的**即付保函统一规则**的规定。

日期 ……………………　　　　签字 ……………………

Annex F EXAMPLE FORM OF RETENTION MONEY GUARANTEE

[*See comments on Sub-Clause 14.9*]

Brief description of Contract ....

Name and address of Beneficiary ....

.... (whom the Contract defines as the Employer)..

We have been informed that .... (hereinafter called the "Principal") is your contractor under such Contract and wishes to receive early payment of [part of] the retention money, for which the Contract requires him to obtain a guarantee.

At the request of the Principal, we (*name of bank*) .... hereby irrevocably undertake to pay you, the Beneficiary/Employer, any sum or sums not exceeding in total the amount of .... (the "guaranteed amount", say: ....) upon receipt by us of your demand in writing and your written statement stating:

(a) that the Principal has failed to carry out his obligation(s) to rectify certain defect(s) for which he is responsible under the Contract, and

(b) the nature of such defect(s).

At any time, our liability under this guarantee shall not exceed the total amount of retention money released to the Principal by you, as evidenced by your notices issued under sub-clause 14.6 of the conditions of the Contract with a copy being passed to us.

Any demand for payment must contain your signature(s) which must be authenticated by your bankers or by a notary public. The authenticated demand and statement must be received by us at this office on or before (*the date 70 days after the expected expiry of the Defects Notification Period for the Works*) .... (the "expiry date"), when this guarantee shall expire and shall be returned to us.

We have been informed that the Beneficiary may require the Principal to extend this guarantee if the performance certificate under the Contract has not been issued by the date 28 days prior to such expiry date. We undertake to pay you such guaranteed amount upon receipt by us, within such period of 28 days, of your demand in writing and your written statement that the performance certificate has not been issued, for reasons attributable to the Principal, and that this guarantee has not been extended.

This guarantee shall be governed by the laws of .... and shall be subject to the Uniform Rules for Demand Guarantees, published as number 458 by the International Chamber of Commerce, except as stated above.

Date .... Signature(s) ....

附件 F 保留金保函范例格式

[见第 14.9 款解释]

合同简述……

受益人名称和地址……

……(合同中称为**雇主**)

我方已获知，……(以下称为**委托人**)是你方根据上述**合同**的承包商，希望收到提前付给的[部分]保留金，对此，**合同**要求他取得一份保函。

应**委托人**请求，我方(银行名称)……在此不可撤销地承诺，在我方收到你方的书面要求和关于以下情况的书面说明后，向你方，**受益人/雇主**，支付总额不超过……(“保证金额”,即：……)的任何一笔或几笔款额：

(a) **委托人**未能履行根据**合同**规定他应负责的改正某些缺陷的义务；

(b) 此类缺陷的性质。

我方根据本保函的责任任何时候都不应超过，经你方根据**合同**条件第 14.6 款规定发出的通知，并给我方一份抄件证明的，你方放还给**委托人**的保留金的总额。

任何关于付款的要求都必须有经你方银行或公证人确证的你方签字。经确证的要求和说明必须在(预定**工程缺陷通知期限**期满后 70 天的日期)……(“期满日期”)或其以前，由我方在本办公地点收到，届时本保函将期满，应退还我方。

我方已获知，如果到该期满日期 28 天前还没有颁发**合同**规定的履约证书，**受益人**可以要求**委托人**延长本保函。我方承诺，根据我方在该 28 天期限内收到你方的书面要求和关于履约证书因**委托人**应负责的原因尚未颁发、以及保函尚未延长的书面说明，向你方支付该保证金额。

本保函除上述要求外，应受……法律管辖，并应遵守**国际商会**以 458 号文公布的**即付保函统一规则**的规定。

日期…… 签字……

Annex G EXAMPLE FORM OF PAYMENT GUARANTEE BY EMPLOYER

[*See page 184: Contractor Finance*]

Brief description of Contract ....

Name and address of Beneficiary ....

.... (whom the Contract defines as the Contractor).

We have been informed that .... (whom the Contract defines as the Employer and who is hereinafter called the "Principal") is required to obtain a bank guarantee.

At the request of the Principal, we (*name of bank*) .... hereby irrevocably undertake to pay you, the Beneficiary/Contractor, any sum or sums not exceeding in total the amount of .... (say: ....) upon receipt by us of your demand in writing and your written statement stating:

(a) that, in respect of a payment due under the Contract, the Principal has failed to make payment in full by the date fourteen days after the expiry of the period specified in the Contract as that within which such payment should have been made, and

(b) the amount(s) which the Principal has failed to pay.

Any demand for payment must be accompanied by a copy of [*list of documents evidencing entitlement to payment*] .... , in respect of which the Principal has failed to make payment in full.

Any demand for payment must contain your signature(s) which must be authenticated by your bankers or by a notary public. The authenticated demand and statement must be received by us at this office on or before (*the date six months after the expected expiry of the Defects Notification Period for the Works*) ...., when this guarantee shall expire and shall be returned to us.

This guarantee shall be governed by the laws of .... and shall be subject to the Uniform Rules for Demand Guarantees, published as number 458 by the International Chamber of Commerce, except as stated above.

Date .... Signature(s) ....

附件 G 雇主支付保函范例格式

[见第 185：页承包商融资]

合同简述……

受益人名称和地址……

……(**合同**中称为**承包商**)

我方已获知，________(**合同**中称为**雇主**,以下称为**委托人**)被要求取得银行保函。

应**委托人**请求，我方(银行名称)……在此不可撤销地承诺，在我方收到你方的书面要求和关于以下情况的书面说明后，向你方，**受益人/承包商**支付总额不超过……(即：……)的任何一笔或几笔款额：

(a) **委托人**对于根据**合同**应付的某笔款项，未能在**合同**规定的该笔款项应付清的期限期满后 14 天内，全部付清；

(b) **委托人**未能支付的款额。

任何关于付款的要求，都必须附一份关于**委托人**未能付清款项的[有权收款的证明文件清单]……的抄件。

任何关于付款的要求，都必须有经你方银行或公证人确证的你方签字。经确证的要求和说明必须在(预定**工程缺陷通知期限**期满后 6 个月的日期)……或其以前，由我方在本办公地点收到，届时本保函将期满，应退还我方。

本保函除上述要求外，应受……法律管辖，并应遵守**国际商会**以 458 号文公布的**即付保函统一规则**的规定。

日期……　　签字……

通用条件
GENERAL CONDITIONS

专用条件编写指南
GUIDANCE FOR THE PREPARATION OF PARTICULAR CONDITIONS

投标函、合同协议书和争端裁决协议书格式
FORMS OF LETTER OF TENDER，CONTRACT AGREEMENT AND DISPUTE ADJUDICATION AGREEMENT

设计采购施工（EPC）/交钥匙工程合同条件

Conditions of Contract for **EPC/Turnkey Projects**

投标函、合同协议书和争端裁决协议书格式

Forms of Letter of Tender，Contract Agreement and Dispute Adjudication Agreement

国 际 咨 询 工 程 师 联 合 会

FEDERATION INTERNATIONALE DES INGENIEURS-CONSEILS
INTERNATIONAL FEDERATION OF CONSULTING ENGINEERS
INTERNATIONALE VEREINIGUNG BERATENDER INGENIEURE
FEDERACION INTERNACIONAL DE INGENIEROS CONSOLTORES

GENERAL CONDITIONS

GUIDANCE

FORMS

LETTER OF TENDER

NAME OF CONTRACT:

TO:

We have examined the Conditions of Contract, Employer's Requirements and Addenda Nos .... for the above-named Works. We have examined, understood and checked these documents and have ascertained that they contain no errors or other defects. We accordingly offer to design, execute and complete the Works and remedy any defects therein, in conformity with such documents and our enclosed Tender (including this letter) for the prices set out in our Tender.

We accept your suggestions for the appointment of the DAB, as set out in ....

[*We have included our suggestions for the other Member of the DAB in part* .... *of our Tender, entitled List of Potential Members of the DAB.*]. *

We agree to abide by this Tender until .... and it shall remain binding upon us and may be accepted at any time before that date.

If this offer is accepted, we will provide the specified Performance Security, commence the Works as soon as is reasonably practicable after the Commencement Date, and complete the Works in accordance with the above-named documents within the Time for Completion. We guarantee that the Works will then conform with the Performance Guarantees included in this Tender.

We understand that you are not bound to accept the lowest or any tender you may receive.

Signature .... in the capacity of ....

duly authorised to sign tenders for and on behalf of ....

....

Address: ....

....

Date: ....

* If the Tenderer does not accept, this paragraph may be deleted and replaced by:

> We do not accept your suggestions for the appointment of the DAB. We have included our suggestions in our Tender, in the list of potential members of the DAB. If these suggestions are not acceptable to you, we propose that the DAB be jointly appointed in accordance with Sub-Clause 20.2 of the Conditions of Contract, [*after a Party gives notice of its intention to refer a dispute to the DAB*]

投标函

合同名称：

致：

我方已研究了对上述**工程**的**合同条件**、**雇主要求**和第______号（填文件编号）**补充文件**，我方已检查、了解和核对了这些文件，未发现它们有错误或其他缺陷。据此，我方愿以我方**投标书**中表明的价格，遵照上述文件及所附我方**投标书**(包括本投标函)，承担所述**工程**的设计、实施、竣工、以及其中任何缺陷的修补。

我方接受你方在______________中表明的关于任命争端裁决委员会（以下简称DAB）的建议。

[我方已在**投标书中**题为 DAB 备选成员名单部分,包括了 DAB 另一名人选的建议。]*

我方同意遵守本**投标书**，直至______________；在该日期前，本**投标书**对我方一直具有约束力，随时可接受中标。

倘若我方中标，我方将提供规定的**履约担保**；将在**开工日期**后，尽早开工，并在**竣工时间**内，按照上述各文件完成工程。我方保证**工程**将遵守本**投标书**中的**履约保证**。

我方理解你方没有必须接受你方可能收到的最低标或任何投标的义务。

签字______________________ 职务______________________

正式授权代表______________________________________

______________________________________签署投标书

地址______________________________________

____

日期______________

* 如果投标人不接受该建议，可删除本段，并以下文代替：

> 我方不接受你方关于任命DAB 的建议。我方已在**投标书**中的 DAB 备选名单中，提出了我方的建议。如果你方不能接受这些建议，我方建议，按照**合同条件第 20.2 款**的规定，[当一方提出将争端提交DAB 的意向的通知后]，共同任命DAB 。

CONTRACT AGREEMENT

This Agreement made the .... day of .... 19 ....

Between .... of .... (hereinafter called "the Employer") of the one part,
and .... of .... (hereinafter called "the Contractor") of the other part

Whereas the Employer desires that the Works known as .... should be executed by the Contractor, and has accepted a Tender by the Contractor for the execution and completion of these Works and the remedying of any defects therein,

The Employer and the Contractor agree as follows:

1. In this Agreement words and expressions shall have the same meanings as are respectively assigned to them in the Conditions of Contract hereinafter referred to.

2. The following documents shall be deemed to form and be read and construed as part of this Agreement:

   (a) The memoranda annexed hereto (which includes a breakdown of the Contract Price)
   (b) The Addenda nos ....
   (c) The Conditions of Contract
   (d) The Employer's Requirements, and
   (e) The Contractor's Tender.

3. In consideration of the payments to be made by the Employer to the Contractor as hereinafter mentioned, the Contractor hereby covenants with the Employer to design, execute and complete the Works and remedy any defects therein in conformity with the provisions of the Contract.

4. The Employer hereby covenants to pay the Contractor, in consideration of the design, execution and completion of the Works and the remedying of defects therein, the final Contract Price at the times and in the manner prescribed by the Contract.

[5. The Contract shall come into full force and effect on the date when the following conditions are satisfied:
[List of pre-conditions]
The Employer shall promptly confirm to the Contractor the date on which all these conditions have been satisfied. If any of these conditions has not been satisfied within .... days of the above-mentioned date on which this Agreement is made, this Agreement shall be void and ineffective and any securities issued in relation to the above Works shall be returned. *optional*]

[5. The Commencement Date shall be .... *optional*]

In Witness whereof the parties hereto have caused this Agreement to be executed the day and year first before written in accordance with their respective laws.

SIGNED by: ....

for and on behalf of the Employer in the presence of

Witness: ....
Name: ....
Address: ....
Date: ....

SIGNED by: ....

for and on behalf of the Contractor in the presence of

Witness: ....
Name: ....
Address: ....
Date: ....

合同协议书

本协议书于______年______月______日由__________的__________（以下简称“**雇主**”）为一方，与__________的__________（以下简称“**承包商**”）为另一方签订。

鉴于**雇主**愿将名称为________________________________的**工程**交由**承包商**实施，并已接受了**承包商**提交的关于承担这些**工程**的实施、竣工、及修补其中任何缺陷的**投标书**，

雇主和**承包商**达成协议如下：

1. 本**协议书**中的词语和措辞的含义，应与下文提到的**合同条件**中分别赋予它们的含义相同。

2. 下列文件应被视为本**协议书**的组成部分，并应作为其一部分阅读和解释：

   (a) 对此所附备忘录（包括**合同价格**的细目表）；
   (b) **补充文件**第____________号（填写各补充文件编号。译注）
   (c) **合同条件**；
   (d) **雇主要求**；
   (e) 承包商的**投标书**。

3. 鉴于**雇主**将按下文所述付给**承包商**各种款项，**承包商**特此与**雇主**签约，保证遵照**合同**的各项规定，承担上述**工程**的设计、实施、竣工及修补其任何缺陷。

4. 鉴于**承包商**将承担上述**工程**的设计、实施、竣工、及修补其任何缺陷，**雇主**特此立约，保证按**合同**规定的时间和方式，向**承包商**支付**合同价格**。

[5. 本合同应在下列条件得到满足的日期全面实施和生效：

[前提条件表]
雇主应立即向**承包商**确认这些条件全部得到满足的日期。如果在上述本**协议书**签订日期__________天内，其中任何条件还没有得到满足，本**协议书**应作废和无效，任何关于上述**工程**的担保应予退还。备选]

[5. **开工日期**应为__________备选]

本**协议书**由双方根据各自法律签字之日起生效，**特立此据**。

签字人签字：______________________　　签字人签字：______________________

在下列证人在场下代表**雇主**签字　　在下列证人在场下代表**承包商**签字

见证人：______________________　　见证人：______________________
姓　名：______________________　　姓　名：______________________
地　址：______________________　　地　址：______________________
日　期：______________________　　日　期：______________________

DISPUTE ADJUDICATION AGREEMENT

[for a one-person DAB]

Name and details of Contract ....
Name and address of Employer ....
Name and address of Contractor ....
Name and address of Member ....

Whereas the Employer and the Contractor have entered into the Contract and desire jointly to appoint the Member to act as sole adjudicator who is also called the "DAB" to adjudicate a dispute which has arisen in relation to .... *

The Employer, Contractor and Member jointly agree as follows:

1. The conditions of this Dispute Adjudication Agreement comprise the "General Conditions of Dispute Adjudication Agreement", which is appended to the General Conditions of the "Conditions of Contract for EPC/Turnkey Projects" First Edition 1999 published by the Fédération Internationale des Ingénieurs-Conseils (FIDIC), and the following provisions. In these provisions, which include amendments and additions to the General Conditions of Dispute Adjudication Agreement, words and expressions shall have the same meanings as are assigned to them in the General Conditions of Dispute Adjudication Agreement.

2. [*Details of amendments to the General Conditions of Dispute Adjudication Agreement, if any.]*

3. In accordance with Clause 6 of the General Conditions of Dispute Adjudication Agreement, the Member shall be paid a daily fee of .... per day.

4. In consideration of these fees and other payments to be made by the Employer and the Contractor in accordance with Clause 6 of the General Conditions of Dispute Adjudication Agreement, the Member undertakes to act as the DAB (as adjudicator) in accordance with this Dispute Adjudication Agreement.

5. The Employer and the Contractor jointly and severally undertake to pay the Member, in consideration of the carrying out of these services, in accordance with Clause 6 of the General Conditions of Dispute Adjudication Agreement.

6. This Dispute Adjudication Agreement shall be governed by the law of ....

SIGNED by:	SIGNED by:	SIGNED by: ....
for and on behalf of the Employer in the presence of	for and on behalf of the Contractor in the presence of	the Member in the presence of:
Witness:	Witness:	Witness ....
Name:	Name:	Name: ....
Address:	Address:	Address: ....
Date:	Date:	Date: ....

[A brief description or name of dispute to be added]*

争端裁决协议书

[用于一人 DAB]

合同名称和内容 ……………………………………………………………………
雇主名称和地址 ……………………………………………………………………
承包商名称和地址 ……………………………………………………………………
成员名称和地址 ……………………………………………………………………

鉴于雇主与**承包商**已签订**合同**，并希望共同聘请成员作为唯一裁决员，也称“**DAB**”，以对因……………………………………………………………………*引起的争端进行裁决。

雇主、承包商和成员共同达成协议如下：

1. 本**争端裁决协议书**条件由**国际咨询工程师联合会**(FIDIC)出版的《(**设计采购施工)EPC/交钥匙工程合同条件**》1999 年第一版所附的“**争端裁决协议书一般条件**”，及下列条款规定组成。这些规定，包括对**争端仲裁协议书一般条件**的修改和补充；其词语和措辞应与其在**争端裁决协议书一般条件**中赋予相同的含义。

2. [对**争端裁决协议书一般条件**修改的细节，如果**有**。]

3. 依照**争端裁决协议书一般条件**第 6 条，应向成员支付日酬金每日……………………。

4. 鉴于**雇主**和**承包商**将按照**争端裁决协议书一般条件**第 6 条的规定，支付这些酬金和其他付款，**成员**承诺，根据本**争端裁决协议书**担任 DAB（裁决员）的职务。

5. 鉴于提供这些服务**雇主**和**承包商**共同并各自承诺，按照**争端裁决协议书一般条件**第 6 条向**成员**付款。

6. 本**争端裁决协议书**应受……………………法律管辖。

签字人签字……………	签字人签字……………	签字人签字……………
在下列证人在场下代表**雇主**签字	在下列证人在场下代表**承包商**签字	在下列证人在场下**成员**本人签字
见证人……………	见证人……………	见证人……………
姓　名……………	姓　名……………	姓　名……………
地　址……………	地　址……………	地　址……………
日　期……………	日　期……………	日　期……………

[*填列争端的简单描述或名称]

DISPUTE ADJUDICATION AGREEMENT

[for each member of a three-person DAB

Name and details of Contract ....
Name and address of Employer ....
Name and address of Contractor ....
Name and address of Member ....

Whereas the Employer and the Contractor have entered into the Contract and desire jointly to appoint the Member to act as one of the three persons who are jointly called the "DAB" [*and desire the Member to act as chairman of the DAB*] to adjudicate a dispute which has arisen in relation to ....

The Employer, Contractor and Member jointly agree as follows:

1. The conditions of this Dispute Adjudication Agreement comprise the "General Conditions of Dispute Adjudication Agreement", which is appended to the General Conditions of the "Conditions of Contract for EPC/Turnkey Projects" First Edition 1999 published by the Fédération Internationale des Ingénieurs-Conseils (FIDIC), and the following provisions. In these provisions, which include amendments and additions to the General Conditions of Dispute Adjudication Agreement, words and expressions shall have the same meanings as are assigned to them in the General Conditions of Dispute Adjudication Agreement.

2. [*Details of amendments to the General Conditions of Dispute Adjudication Agreement, if any.*]

3. In accordance with Clause 6 of the General Conditions of Dispute Adjudication Agreement, the Member shall be paid a daily fee of .... per day.

4. In consideration of these fees and other payments to be made by the Employer and the Contractor in accordance with Clause 6 of the General Conditions of Dispute Adjudication Agreement, the Member undertakes to serve, as described in this Dispute Adjudication Agreement, as one of the three persons who are jointly to act as the DAB.

5. The Employer and the Contractor jointly and severally undertake to pay the Member, in consideration of the carrying out of these services, in accordance with Clause 6 of the General Conditions of Dispute Adjudication Agreement.

6. This Dispute Adjudication Agreement shall be governed by the law of ....

SIGNED by:	SIGNED by:	SIGNED by: ....
for and on behalf of the Employer in the presence of	for and on behalf of the Contractor in the presence of	the Member in the presence of
Witness:	Witness:	Witness ....
Name:	Name:	Name: ....
Address:	Address:	Address: ....
Date:	Date:	Date: ....

[**A brief description or name of dispute to be added.*]

争端裁决协议书

[用于三人 DAB 的每位成员]

合同名称和内容
雇主名称和地址
承包商名称和地址
成员名称和地址

鉴于雇主与承包商已签订合同，并希望共同聘请**成员**作为由三人共同称作的“**DAB**”的一员，[并希望**成员**担任 DAB 主席职务]，以对因 ______ *引起的争端进行裁决。

雇主、承包商和成员共同达成协议如下：

1. 本**争端裁决协议书**条件由**国际咨询工程师联合会**(FIDIC)出版的《(**设计采购施工**)EPC/**交钥匙工程合同条件**》1999 年第一版所附“**争端裁决协议书一般条件**”，及下列条款规定组成。这些规定，包括对**争端仲裁协议书一般条件**的修改和补充，其词语和措辞应与其在**争端裁决协议书一般条件**中赋予相同的含义。

2. [对**争端裁决协议书一般条件**修改的细节，如果**有**。]

3. 依照**争端裁决协议书一般条件**第 6 条，应向**成员**支付日酬金每日 ______。

4. 考虑到**雇主**和**承包商**将按照**争端裁决协议书一般条件**第 6 条的规定支付这些酬金和其他付款，**成员**承诺，按本**争端裁决协议书**所述，担任共同组成三人**DAB** 中的一名**成员**的职务。

5. 鉴于提供这些服务，**雇主**和**承包商**共同并各自承诺，按照**争端裁决协议书一般条件**第 6 条向**成员**付款。

6. 本**争端裁决协议书**应受 ______ 法律管辖。

签字人签字	签字人签字	签字人签字
在下列证人在场下 代表雇主签字	在下列证人在场下 代表承包商签字	在下列证人在场下 成员本人签字
见证人	见证人	见证人
姓　名	姓　名	姓　名
地　址	地　址	地　址
日　期	日　期	日　期

[*填列争端的简单描述或名称]